PENGUIN BOOKS

SMART MONEY MOVES

James Lowell is the editor of the award-winning *Fidelity Investor* and the chief portfolio strategist for Advisor Investment Management, a research and advisory firm specializing in mutual fund investing. Lowell is also president of the Fund Family Shareholders Association. A recognized authority on mutual fund and retirement-oriented investing, he advises on over $300 million in mutual fund–related investments for Boston-based advisory firms. The featured on-line investing columnist for the *Dow Jones Investment Advisor* magazine, and the featured mutual fund columnist for *P.O.V.* magazine, he is also the author of the comprehensive financial books *How to Survive in the Real World* (published by Penguin, 1996) and *Investing from Scratch* (Penguin, 1997).

Lowell has written and lectured extensively on investing and personal finance for national magazines, TV, radio, and the on-line media. Most recently, he was the editor-in-chief of *FundsNet Insight,* a leading national mutual fund newsletter. He is quoted on money issues in prominent media such as *Barrons, Bloomberg, CNBC, Fortune, TheStreet.com, The Wall Street Journal,* and *Your Money.*

He was the senior writer at Financial Planning Information, where he produced several major personal-financial-planning books for Jonathan Pond, including *The New Century Family Money Book, The ABCs of Money Management,* and *1001 Ways to Cut Your Expenses.* He was also the senior financial reporter for *Investment Vision* and *Worth* at Fidelity.

Lowell was educated at Vassar College (B.A.), and holds master's degrees from both Harvard University and Trinity College, Dublin. He is a published poet and a former lecturer in the Department of Philosophy and Religion at Northeastern University College in Boston. He lives near Boston with his wife and daughter. You can reach him through his Web site, Fidelityinvestor.com, or fundworksinc.@msn.com.

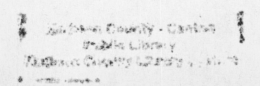

$MART MONEY MOVE$

Mutual Fund Investing from Scratch

JAMES LOWELL

PENGUIN BOOKS

PENGUIN BOOKS

Published by the Penguin Group
Penguin Putnam Inc., 375 Hudson Street,
New York, New York 10014, U.S.A.
Penguin Books Ltd, 27 Wrights Lane,
London W8 5TZ, England
Penguin Books Australia Ltd, Ringwood,
Victoria, Australia
Penguin Books Canada Ltd, 10 Alcorn Avenue,
Toronto, Ontario, Canada M4V 3B2
Penguin Books (N.Z.) Ltd, 182–190 Wairau Road,
Auckland 10, New Zealand

Penguin Books Ltd, Registered Offices:
Harmondsworth, Middlesex, England

Published in Penguin Books 2000

1   3   5   7   9   10   8   6   4   2

PUBLISHER'S NOTE

This publication is created to provide accurate and authoritative information
with regard to the subject matter covered. It is sold with the understanding
that the publisher is not engaged in rendering financial, accounting, or other
professional services. If financial advice or other expert assistance is
required, the services of a competent professional should be sought.

LIBRARY OF CONGRESS CATALOGING-IN-PUBLICATION DATA
Lowell, James, 1960–
Smart money moves / James Lowell.
p.   cm.
ISBN 0 14 02.8849 X
1. Mutual funds.   2. Investments.   I. Title.
HG4530.L64   2000
332.63'27 21—dc21   99—045741

Printed in the United States of America
Set in New Baskerville
Designed by Victoria Hartman

ACKNOWLEDGMENTS

S*mart Money Moves* represents far more than my own mutual fund investment experience and insights.

David Pittelli, uniquely talented when it comes to the comprehensive daily analyses we run on funds, helped ensure that this book is as accurate as it is useful.

Jane von Mehren, Penguin's associate publisher, made sure the book was both timely and on time.

Barbara Hill Bink, executive editor of Phillips Publishing, Inc.'s mutual fund investment advisory newsletters, including my *Fidelity Investor,* keeps me fund-focused seven days a week. Zeba Khan, managing editor for the *Fidelity Investor,* knows how to zero in on fund-related topics that many journalists overlook, including the difference between Equity Income and Equity Income II. Melissa Benson, and Don Carelton, my editorial assistants, ensured that this book remained on course. Dan Wiener, chairman of the Fund Family Shareholders Association (FFSA) and editor of the *Independent Advisor for Vanguard Investors,* has been a steadfast friend who has a rare quality: useful investment advice.

Many other professionals help shape my insights with their keen observations and regular input. My team in the Investment Management Division at Adviser Investment Management, and in particular Dan Silver and Cindy Mulica, help real-world clients live a life of relative peace and certain financial security through mutual fund investing.

Finally, my wife, Terri, knows the intensive labor and dogged time that goes into a comprehensive book that covers the world of funds. Her unfailing support is my strength and good fortune.

CONTENTS

INTRODUCTION

Mutual Fund Investing
Is a Smart Money Move

Not surprisingly, this book contains almost everything you'll need to know about mutual funds and investing in them. But that's just the beginning. The fact is that this book is designed to help you put into practice what you learn. In doing so, it will prove to be more than a valuable resource—it will prove to be a solid investment in its own right.

That said, you've heard all the braggart claims and bogus promises: from your best friend's friend who says he put his college loan money into Ebay (and who now claims he can buy the whole college) to the even more bogus promises of get-rich-quick schemes and scams by hucksters on late-night TV. At least your friend's friend may have made some money—even if putting all his eggs into a one-stock basket is about as smart as licking dry ice. But it's the latter camp, promising get-rich-quick schemes, that does us all more harm than good. Either these charlatans make it seem too easy or, like the boy who cried wolf, they make us all wary of any claims about becoming financially secure. True, in doing so they've done us a service (since it isn't possible unless you knock off a bank or a rich uncle who has you in his will). But they've also done us a disservice, since they make it hard to hear the truth in what I'm about to say. But I'm going to say it anyway—because it's true.

This book is dedicated to showing you how you can reasonably ensure that you will become a millionaire. You don't have to sell all your body parts, kidnap the investment banker next door, invent cold fusion, or inherit a fortune. You will have to invest time, energy, and your money. You will have to be persistent and patient.

In fact, although you will create your investment base and discipline in five years, the million-dollar payoff won't come until thirty or so years down the road—just when you'll need it most.

No matter if you have been or have just begun investing in funds: there are many smart money moves you can make to create and enhance the returns of what I like to call the $10,000 portfolio. This book will show you how. In fact, this book will help you see:

[ ]   The best funds in the fund forest
[ ]   The clear-cut differences between fund types
[ ]   What the main investment styles are and what impact they have on your funds
[ ]   Benefits of investing in mutual funds
[ ]   Drawbacks of investing in mutual funds
[ ]   What to look for in a prospectus
[ ]   What to look for in a manager
[ ]   The best resources for fund research
[ ]   Which stock funds suit you and your objectives best
[ ]   If you need to own a bond fund
[ ]   How to create your own portfolio
[ ]   How to buy and sell funds
[ ]   How to track your portfolio's performance
[ ]   How to create portfolios for most types of market conditions

Herein you'll find all the fund investment tools and skills you need to build a profitable portfolio of mutual funds for both your short-term and your longer-term goals. It shows you how you can find and build $10,000 in some pretty surprising places—from hidden resources which many of us overlook to obvious ones which require disciplining yourself. (You spent $19 on a new CD—"evildoer." You saved $19 to invest—"good thinking.") It even provides several model $10,000 portfolios that can help you take advantage of nearly every market environment you're likely to encounter in your lifetime.

In fact, creating your very own $10,000 portfolio over the next five years is the single best way to achieve financial independence down the road. That's a key destination which, once achieved, can lead you to shorter-term investment goals. The trouble is, if you don't have a goal in mind, such as saving and investing in a $10,000 portfolio, it's easy to get sidetracked and spend money as though it's going out of style. Believe me, you'll be living in some bargain-basement apartment for the rest of your life if you do.

The fact that it will take only 5 years to set yourself up for life should serve as incentive enough to get started. And the truth is that many of us are doing a significantly better job than our parents at saving for our retirement. But there's a larger truth: you and I can do a better job at saving for investing and at investing in the mutual funds where we are placing our financial fate. This book will help you ferret out funds that suck and find funds that will most likely shine.

Don't just take my word for it. Take a look at a picture, which in this case is worth 10,000 words. The chart shows you what $10,000 invested in the first mutual fund would be worth today. (For my mini-history of funds, see Chapter 28.)

MFS Mass Investors Trust A

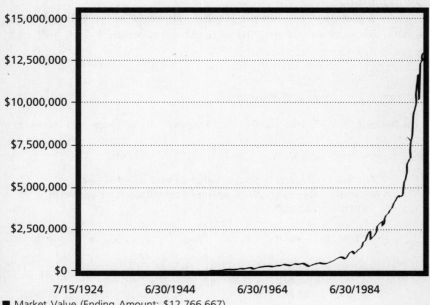

■ Market Value (Ending Amount: $12,766,667)
Copyright © 1993–1999 by CDA/Wiesenberger

Go back. Take a second look. *Count the zeroes.* You're not seeing double. You're reading it right. The sum of $10,000 invested in the first mutual fund (which, for people who like fund trivia, my grandfather was on the advisory board of) would be worth a staggering $13 million bucks today.

Thirteen million bucks is enough to get by on in your golden years. But, of course, the drawback to the rosy picture is that it took 75 years to grow that sum. By then, you think, "I'll barely be able to gum a key lime pie or climb three flights of stairs without strapping on an oxygen mask." But since I'm a great believer in investing wisely and well so that you can live well and wisely, the strategies employed in this book will reward you while there's still plenty of time to enjoy the fruits of your youthful labor.

Consider this. Suppose you opened an IRA at age 23 and deposited $2,000 in your account each year until you reached age 30. You would—assuming you invested your money in mutual funds earning 8 percent—accumulate as much as someone who waited until age 30 to open an IRA and who put $2,000 aside each year until reaching age 65! How can this be? It's the effect of compounding.

Here's another eye-opening table, showing what the following annual investment earning 10 percent compounded daily will yield years down the road.

Per Year	You Will Have In			
You Deposit	10 years	20 years	30 years	40 years
$2,000	$	$	$	$

Annual Returns 10%	Annual Deposit $2,000	Shows value at end of each year With annual contributions at year-end
Year	Value	
1	$2,000	
2	$4,200	
3	$6,620	
4	$9,282	
5	$12,210	
6	$15,431	
7	$18,974	
8	$22,872	
9	$27,159	
10	**$31,875**	
11	$37,062	

Annual Returns 10%	Annual Deposit $2,000	Shows value at end of each year With annual contributions at year-end
Year	Value	
12	$42,769	
13	$49,045	
14	$55,950	
15	$63,545	
16	$71,899	
17	$81,089	
18	$91,198	
19	$102,318	
20	**$114,550**	
21	$128,005	
22	$142,805	
23	$159,086	
24	$176,995	
25	$196,694	
26	$218,364	
27	$242,200	
28	$268,420	
29	$297,262	
30	**$328,988**	
31	$363,887	
32	$402,276	
33	$444,503	
34	$490,953	
35	$542,049	
36	$598,254	
37	$660,079	
38	$728,087	
39	$802,896	
40	**$885,185**	

Two thousand dollars a year? Sounds like a lot. But hold on. Let's take a look at how much your Starbucks coffee and non-brown-bag lunch cost you. Two thousand dollars? You got it. Break it down. You could invest $166 each month (which totals to $2,000 in 12 months). Think of it as a necessary bill that must be paid along with all your other bills—only this time, you are paying yourself! Or why not consider getting a second job, the proceeds of which you invest in an IRA? Better yet, if your company offers you an opportunity to invest in a 401(k) or 403(b) plan, take advantage of it. Either way, you give yourself a tax break while at the same time investing in your own future. Good deal.

Finding the money to fund your $10,000 portfolio may seem like an impossible dream. But it isn't. The key is to know where to look in your own life for some hidden resources. Chapter 1 will help you do just that.

PART I

LIFE
SMARTS

ONE

Funding Your Life

Welcome to funding your life—if you don't do it, who will? In a matter of minutes I'm going to lay out the basic financial road we all travel, and later, I'll provide you with a way to create a personalized investment portfolio to account for your short-term and long-term goals.

LIFE IS GOOD, BUT IT ISN'T CHEAP

While personal finance is a well traveled path (and one we may have traveled together in my book, *How to Survive in the Real World*), it's still the best place to begin in order to ensure that real-life roadblocks won't derail the best-laid mutual fund investment plans.

Most of us will encounter a similar series of roadblocks, no matter what we're currently doing or dreaming about becoming. Death is obviously there—but I'm putting Sartre 101 aside for now. I'm talking about some moneymaking do's and don'ts. The basics—from planning where you want to go to dealing with the bills at your door. For example, chances are good that you have to make student loan repayments while contemplating a car loan and, within the next 5 to 10 years, having to save for your first home purchase. Such decisions affect the way you'll want to save and invest your money today. They also determine the types of funds you'll want to invest in—as well as the amount of money you'll need to scrimp and save.

To "scrimp" sounds about as ugly as it can get. To "save" sounds about as good as it is. No matter how the terms may sound, however, scrimping and saving aren't as hard as we make them out to be—though it isn't as easy to scrimp and save as your parents and grandparents will have you believe. (Case in point: you could save over $1277.50 a year by drinking water instead of indulging that $3.50 a day Starbucks habit. Still want to live the high life? OK. Save $912.50 by making your own pot of coffee.)

Investing in your own future is especially important, since no one else will invest in it. Uncle Sam will probably be bankrupt by the time you reach out your hand to him. Your parents will be paying for longer lives and a more expensive retirement than they have probably prepared for. You may have triplets.

Choices, opportunities, pitfalls, and potential profits await us all—right from the outset of our independent lives. But most of us fail to do much more than struggle along from paycheck to paycheck.

QUICK TIP

Do:
- Balance your checkbook.
- Know where you stand in terms of debts and income.
- Get into a health plan and ask around for a good doctor. Get a dentist too.
- Start participating in your 401(k) plan at work.
- Get renter's insurance.
- Get into the habit of saving money.
- Pay cash instead of using credit.
- Pick a bank that's convenient and doesn't charge hefty fees.
- Save often.
- Invest more.

Don't:
- Don't buy life insurance unless you really need it.
- Don't rack up credit card debt.
- Don't buy too expensive a car.
- Don't live beyond your means.
- Don't invest all your savings.
- Don't bite your nails.

And many of us will find to our dismay that, faced with the impossibility of living solely on social security, the only thing "golden" about our later years will be the arches of our postretirement employer's corporate logo. I know. I know. It sounds as if I should be talking to someone who is twice your age. But the truth is that by that time, it's too late. The time to start planning and investing in your own future is now. To start, you'll need to hone your saving skills: find out where some hidden resources are.

This chapter will help you do that. It's a hands-on, do-it-yourself guide to getting more out of your own financial life today so that you can save up $10,000 in fewer years than it will take to pay off a car. It's easy once you get the hang of it. If you don't, you'll run the risk of being hanged by debt.

Figuring out where to start isn't as difficult as you think. The following real-life worksheet will help you do just that. Take a minute to fill it out.

Real-Life Roadmap

[ ] Moving out of your parents' home
[ ] Renting your first apartment
[ ] Buying a car
[ ] Repaying your student loans
[ ] Taking out a loan
[ ] Investing
[ ] Paying taxes
[ ] Record keeping
[ ] Budgeting
[ ] Spending
[ ] Bill paying
[ ] Saving
[ ] Insuring
[ ] Balancing your checkbook
[ ] Reconciling what you earn with what you owe
[ ] Living a life you can actually afford
[ ] Maintaining a good credit history
[ ] Setting aside some of what you earn so that you can reach your personal goals
[ ] Covering yourself and your assets from uninsured losses
[ ] Controlling your own financial destiny

DECISION MAKING MADE EASY

Whether you're single and embarking on a new career or thinking about getting married or thinking about changing your job, you'll face a host of decisions. Fortunately, you can also make a host of smart money moves—even before you begin to invest. The more smart money moves you make with regard to paying off your debt and buying the right amount of insurance, the more savings you'll have left to invest. That, my friend, is the only way to achieve true financial independence and success.

Financial planning, the portal through which all our lives must pass, doesn't just mean filling out paperwork in a bank or a human resources office. It means making strategic decisions so you'll be protected from unexpected financial losses. (Health insurance is a must.) It means picking the right options for you, so you'll have peace of mind about important things like medical care and know that you're not spending more than you should. (Too little insurance is a costly mistake—but so is too much insurance.) And it means paying attention to how much you can set aside for saving and investing to make your life as good as it can be, both now and later.

BE HONEST WITH YOURSELF

You passed calculus. Maybe you even passed organic chem. (OK, so you majored in basket weaving. At least you can add and subtract.) I bet you've had your unbalanced checkbook on your desk for a few months and you're wondering if it really makes any difference whether you balance it or not. It does. In fact, it pays to do it. That's right—it pays to do it. Here's how. If you bounce checks, it will set you back by as much as $50 per bounced check. If you balance your checkbook, not only are you less likely to bounce a check, but you're also more likely to stay within your budget.

Did someone say "budget"? Yup. This is a key task that no one—not you, not me, not even your rich Uncle Damascus—can afford to overlook. Fortunately, it's a snap. Use the following budget planner to get yourself up to snuff on your current financial condition. (Quick tip: Have a box of Kleenex handy. It's not going to be pretty.)

YOUR BUDGET

Monthly Income:
Monthly take-home pay: $_____
Other income $_____

Total Monthly Income: $_____

Fixed Monthly Expenses:
[ ]   Rent $_____
[ ]   Food $_____
[ ]   Utilities $_____
[ ]   Car loan $_____
[ ]   Student loan $_____
[ ]   Bank loan $_____
[ ]   5% of pay to your savings account $_____
                              Subtotal: $_____

Other Fixed Expenses:
[ ]   Health insurance $_____
[ ]   Car insurance $_____
[ ]   Renter's insurance $_____

Total Monthly Expenses: $_____

Total Monthly Income: −$_____

Income for Irregular Expenses: =$_____

Irregular monthly expenses:
[ ]   Emergency fund
[ ]   Gas
[ ]   Telephone
[ ]   Laundry
[ ]   Clothing
[ ]   Car maintenance
[ ]   Medical/dental
[ ]   Goals $_____
[ ]   Tuition for continuing education $_____
[ ]   Club membership dues $_____

MOVING ON

Sure, there's rent to pay. Student loans, in many cases. Car payments, perhaps, or a car that needs work. Old friends to see and new ones to make. A new boss to please and a bank account that could use some help. Use the following Net Worth Statement to

YOUR NET WORTH

What You Have

Take-home (after-tax) pay	$_____
Checking/savings accounts	$_____
Certificate of deposits	$_____
Investments	$_____
Loans owed to you	$_____
Cash in your pocket	$_____
Other (birthday checks, etc.)	$_____

Total of what you have $_____

What you owe

Rent	$_____
Car loan	$_____
Education loans	$_____
Credit card	$_____
Store charge cards	$_____
Furniture loans	$_____
Money you owe (to a friend, etc.)	$_____
Other outstanding debt	$_____

Total of what you owe $_____

What you have	$_____
What you owe	−$_____
Your net worth	=$_____

help you calculate exactly where you stand (financially speaking) so that you can determine the best route to take to where you want to go. (Quick tip: Get another box of Kleenex.)

IT'S A PUZZLING LIFE

This is an exciting time of life, no question about it. But it's also a time that can be puzzling—full of questions, mistakes, and lessons. This is your chance to make a few good decisions that will give you a leg up over peers who zig and zag their way through their early working years, living from check to check without a plan to follow or goals to achieve. I know it sounds about as thrilling as having to go back to gym class for one last lap—but, believe me, it's the best way to sprint ahead with your own life.

In fact, now, right now, is a great time to break old habits that may have plagued you as a student (like running up credit card bills), and to start new ones that will stand you in good stead as you move up in the world, like saving even a small part of every paycheck. As in most things, planning can help. So can taking advantage of some hidden resources which, once discovered and put to use, can actually save you money—keep more money in your pocket—so you can invest more of it for a better future.

WORK IS YOUR LIFE

You're young. Happening. Employed. The paycheck is cool. But everyone (from your new best friend in cubicle number 9 to your manager and your mom) is talking about the great benefits your company offers. You hear the term, see the book, and roll your eyes. What's the benefit of benefits?

You might be surprised to find that work provides more than the obvious ways to be rewarded. Your paycheck and 401(k) plan are just the beginning. And while this may be the first time you've ever had to figure out things like a budget, your net worth, or even what health insurance plan to join and whether to consider vision benefits or long-term disability, your place of work is a hidden resource for making informed, cost-efficient moves that can leave you with more cash to invest at the end of every week.

So, droll as it may sound, it pays to pay attention to your human resources people. They know more than you'll ever need to know about the best ways to squeeze out some dollars from plans that would otherwise eat you up. Seize the opportunity to study and really understand what's being offered to you at work. Don't just do what the guy sitting next to you does. And don't blow off the decisions simply because they're confusing or new. Make sure you get everything that's coming to you.

One of the added advantages of benefits offered at work is that your portion of the cost for these programs is deducted from your paycheck. In some cases, your contribution comes out before taxes, saving you money. And in all cases, it's a convenience that helps you with your financial planning.

COVERING YOUR BENEFIT BASES

You may be surprised and find that you enjoy this process once you dig into it. Planning your benefits and finances is all about getting what you want. Make solid choices now, and you'll feel better in your head and in your wallet.

Of course, you'll have to think about what you have. Let's step back and think about how to get the most out of what's being offered to you at work. If someone offered you $100 in exchange for work you did, would you take only $75 and tell him or her to keep the rest? Hard to imagine. Certainly, you'd take the $100 as fair payment for your time and labor. Selecting your benefits is no different. It's part of your pay package.

Here are some key benefits for you to consider:

[ ]   Health insurance
[ ]   Dental insurance
[ ]   Vision insurance
[ ]   Life insurance
[ ]   Disability insurance
[ ]   Pension benefits
[ ]   401(k)

BENEFITS OF BETTER PLANNING

Health Insurance. Health insurance is crucial. Even if you're so healthy you've never missed a day of work with so much as a sniffle, health insurance is a big deal. If you had to pay for it on your own, it would be very expensive. When you are part of a group, coverage costs less. And chances are, your employer is paying a big chunk of the premiums.

Ask around, if the cost hasn't already been broken out for you. If you're a single person, the cost of insuring you is probably north of $1,500 a year. If you're like most workers, your contribution to that is anywhere from half, or $750, to 10 percent, or $150. Only the most generous companies foot the entire bill. Not only do most firms want to share the high costs of medical care; the thinking is that people place a greater value on things they pay for than things they get free.

Granted, if you're shelling out $150 a year and you never have to go to a doctor, health insurance may seem like a waste of money to you. But you should look at health coverage—and any kind of insurance, for that matter—as risk that's spread out over time. There's a good chance you'll need medical care over a 10-year period. You may well need care worth more than the $1,500 ($150

× 10 years) you'll pay in contributions to the plan (assuming your rate stays the same over a decade). Indeed, just a few days in a hospital could exceed $1,500. One doctor's visit typically costs more than $100.

Health insurance isn't just for people who get sick. It's for everybody. You never know when you might twist your knee snowboarding or get in the way of an angry dog with sharp teeth. You could catch a bad bug and need prescription drugs, or you could find that you need to see an eye specialist or a dermatologist. Bottom line: you can't afford *not* to have health insurance.

It's tough to put a price tag on your health and safety. For instance, a gym membership might seem too pricey to you at $400 a year. But what if staying in shape is very important to you and you live in a neighborhood where it's not safe to run alone at night? It may be worth the gym membership to keep yourself safe and in shape. Weigh questions like this as part of your plan.

The next order of business is to pick a health plan. There's a difference between traditional indemnity plans and managed health care plans, like HMOs. Many employers offer a choice. Compare the prices and your needs.

You've probably heard about the rising costs of medical care. The jump in costs was out of control in the 1980s, before managed care became the mainstream. Now medical costs are rising at a slower pace, but the inflation is still significant. You should expect your health care premiums and contributions to rise periodically, perhaps every couple of years.

If you pick an indemnity plan, perhaps because you already have

---

QUICK TIP

Many young professionals don't have a doctor. They're usually very healthy and may be straight out of school. If this is you, an HMO may be a great choice. You can pick from a long list of doctors and hospitals and establish a relationship with a doctor. Then if you do get sick, you'll have someone to call.

HMOs typically have only small out-of-pocket costs, like a $10 copayment when you see a doctor or fill a prescription. And a company's HMO, or some other managed care option, is often the least expensive choice on the health benefits menu.

QUICK TIP

If you do choose an indemnity plan, and you expect to have major out-of-pocket medical expenses in the coming year, consider a **flexible spending account,** if your employer offers the option. These accounts let you set aside money on a pretax basis to pay eligible medical expenses not covered under your plan.

---

a favorite doctor who's not on the HMO's list, remember to budget for the out-of-pocket costs that can accompany such a plan. Indemnity plans tend to come with deductibles and coinsurance, or bills you have to pay a percentage of. Be sure you can afford the maximum you might have to shell out per year if you were to get sick or have an accident.

Dental Insurance. You'll want to think about dental insurance in the same way as health insurance. Don't look at dental coverage as a luxury; look at it as a necessity. Let's boil it down to vanity, if we must. Most dental plans cover two cleanings a year, often at no cost to you at all. Those cleanings help keep you looking good, and they keep your teeth healthier. By preventing cavities and other dental problems, you can stave off big-ticket bills and unpleasant procedures at the same time.

Once again, saving a couple of hundred bucks on a filling means more money in your pocket.

Life Insurance. Your company may offer a set amount of term life insurance at no cost to you—often an amount equal to your base salary. With any luck, you won't need this benefit anytime soon. But you should still assign a beneficiary you'd want to have the money in the event you were to die. The same goes for **accidental death and dismemberment insurance** (wow, what a horrifying name)—take what the company offers you free. It could prove useful if you were to lose a limb in the paper shredder or lose your sight staring into your PC screen.

You may have the option to buy additional life insurance. Don't waste your money. You don't need it—yet. If no one is depending

on you and your salary, your money is probably better spent elsewhere. Invest it.

Disability Insurance. This is a different story. Most employers pay
for short-term disability, which would cover part of your pay in the
event of a sickness or an accident. But you should give some thought
to what you'd do in the case of an illness or accident that kept you
out of work for a long period of time—say six months or longer.

How would you pay your rent? How would you pay for heat,
lights, and the phone? How would you pay for HBO—which you'll
definitely die without if you're bedridden for a few months? Most
young professionals forgo disability insurance, but I'd consider it.
Some employers pay for long-term disability. If yours does, sign up
and know it's there for you if you need it.

If it's offered on your benefits menu but you have to pay for it,
either partly or entirely, it's still worth thinking about. Look at the
cost of the coverage and your likelihood of injury, based on your
work and lifestyle. People can't predict whether they'll be in a car
accident, of course, or whether a casual game of football will land
them in a leg cast. But the risks of injury are different for construction workers, for example, and computer programmers.

Most important, look at your savings—and your ability to pay for
your basic needs if you were to be out of work for many months.
It's generally a good idea to have enough cash in the bank to cover
at least 3 months' worth of expenses. Very cautious people try to
put 6 months' worth of cash away. And those are emergency funds—
not savings to be tapped for luxuries like vacations.

If you're confident that you've got enough money to tide you
over in a health emergency, you may decide to take a pass on long-
term disability for now. But remember to think about this benefit
again in the future, if your circumstances change. Should you buy
a house or get married, you may want to reconsider.

BENEFITS OF INVESTING

Now that you've decided on the best use of benefits that are designed to protect your health and your wallet, it's time to think
about saving and investing through your work-sponsored plans. Making smart money moves at this juncture can help you launch yourself on a path toward greater wealth and well-being.

If your company offers a defined-benefit pension plan, or a retirement savings plan that is funded entirely by your employer, sign up by all means. You'll need to find out how long it takes to be "vested" in the plan—that is, how long you need to work for the company to reap benefits in retirement. This will factor into your other retirement planning.

Here's why: if you have to work for the company for at least 10 years before you earn benefits, there's a good chance you'll never qualify. Most workers change jobs as many as seven times over the course of their lives. Perhaps your career plan has you moving to a new firm within 5 to 7 years.

You should sign up for the plan in any case, because you never know for sure how long you'll stay with a company. Be mindful of the vesting schedule, because you just might hang on for a seventh year, for example, instead of leaving in your sixth year, if it meant locking in substantial retirement money for later.

Traditional pensions are becoming rarer all the time. But it's likely that your employer offers a 401(k) plan. (For details on investing in a 401(k) and other tax-advantage plans, including IRAs and Roth IRAs, turn to Chapters 21 and 22.) These are contributory plans, meaning that much of the money you set aside and invest in them is your own. On your instructions, the money comes straight out of your paycheck—before state and federal income taxes. How much you save is entirely up to you.

This is one of the most significant financial decisions you can make in your life.

QUICK TIP

Understanding your company's retirement plans could be a factor in your career planning. Even if you decide to leave a company when you're just shy of meeting a vesting hurdle, you need to know how much money you're walking away from. You should take that into consideration when negotiating compensation with your new employer.

Time is important when it comes to saving and investing. Years logged on the job—and retirement benefits accrued—are valuable.

It may be tempting to put off making 401(k) contributions until you're older, or until you have more money. You figure you have plenty of time.

Think again.

Start setting something aside as soon as you can. Remember the power of compounding, which we discussed earlier. Even small amounts saved now can turn into big money four decades from now. If you're 25 and you invest just $179 a month—or about $6 a day—for 40 years, you'd have $1 million at age 65, assuming a 10 percent average annual gain over that time. If you wait until you're 35 to start putting money away, you'll need $481 a month—or $16 a day—to reach the same goal.

There's nothing better than seeing how much your money will grow when you start young. Forty years is a lot more than 30 years when it comes to investing. But 30 years will be enough to net you more than you're likely to need—as long as you heed the font of fund investing info this book provides.

TWO

Funding Your Retirement

The objective of anyone in control of his or her financial faculties is to retire in a style that is comfortable, safe, and secure. I'm not talking penthouse apartments from Cancún to the Riviera. Instead, I'm talking about something that you can realistically attain. Can you do it? You can. But you'll have to get cracking. After all, when we retire we seek to never have to work again. This can mean having to live for 25 years or more off what we earned in our lifetime. That's a long time to have to go without a paycheck and still meet all the bills. That's a long, long time.

Fortunately, creating your $10,000 portfolio today can ensure that you surpass even your current dreams of financial freedom for tomorrow. The key to unlocking a secure financial future? Don't spend more than you make. Do invest more than you save. Don't put your hard-earned money into losing propositions. Do invest in a portfolio of funds that will help your money grow, and grow, and grow.

LIFE IN THE FAST LANE

A car is an example of a bad investment. It's been said that you lose about 5 percent of your investment when you drive the car off the lot. That's not the half of it. Fortunately, this book will show you how to avoid making investment mistakes. But to put a losing investment into better perspective, let's take a look at that car. Today you can afford it. But what kind of toll will today's car take on your financial well-being down the road? No doubt you've been told time and again that matching your retirement objectives with the mutual funds you invest in is an important first step in your overall retirement-oriented fund selection process. In fact, it's crucial. Here's why: the majority of those nearing retirement age today are finding they are falling shy of the mark. Way shy. Simple steps taken today can help ensure that you won't become one of them. Or you could just ignore the following table, and call your portfolio the *Titanic*.

KNOW YOUR OBJECTIVE

Your retirement objective should be the realistic, realizable financial endpoint of your plan. It's the destination of your most important investment journey—and your $10,000 portfolio. Once you have set your objective, you must go shopping for funds whose management styles mesh with what you're trying to achieve—be it aggressive growth of capital or conservative preservation of income. But be careful out there. Many funds still have misleading names that don't reflect their objectives. Be sure you know what you're buying.

FOURSCORE AND SEVEN YEARS

When you are setting your retirement objective, the most important consideration is how much time you have until you plan to retire, not how much money you would like to make. This may seem to fly in the face of what most savers and investors think: that making more money is the only answer to a better financial future. You want to make as much money as possible? No kidding. But that answer won't help you to invest wisely and well for your financial future. So for the moment forget about how much you want, and concentrate on figuring out what your time horizon is. Depending on your age now and when it is that you hope to hang up your hat, your time horizon could be as close as twenty-five years or as distant as forty.

Remember that you will not need the money you earmark for your retirement all at once. If you are age 25, and 35 years from your planned retirement, the average time period before spending your savings is not 35 years, because you aren't going to suddenly spend everything the day you retire. More likely, you'll want the money to

DIMINISHING RETURN OF BUYING A CAR

In this example, total cash outlay for the car is: $44,425
The car is sold at the end of the period for: $10,455
Leaving a net profit/cost for: –$33,969

However, if that money had instead been invested in stocks at 10% annually, it would be worth: $57,464
Leaving a net profit/cost of: $13,040

Hence the opportunity cost of the car is the difference in net cost and net profit: $47,009

Loan Rate 8.0%	Annual Depreciation –16%	% Down 25%	Sales Tax Rate 5%	Inflation 3%	Miles/Yr 12000	$/Mile $0.12	Stock Mkt Returns 10%

Loan Principal $18,750	Year	Car Value	Payments	Sales Tax	Insurance	Fuel & Maintain	Cash Outlay	Invested Value
	Initial	25,000	6,250	1,250	1,000		8,500	8,500
	1	21,000	4,562		1,030	1,440	7,032	16,382
Loan Years	2	17,640	4,562		1,061	1,483	7,106	25,127
	3	14,818	4,562		1,093	1,528	7,183	34,822
5	4	12,447	4,562		1,126	1,574	7,261	45,565
	5	10,455	4,562		1,159	1,621	7,342	57,464

Annual Payment $4,562

29,061

	Car	Stocks
Total Outlay	44,425	44,425
Residual Value:	10,455	57,464
Net Profit/Loss	–33,969	13,040
Net Opportunity Cost:	47,009	

hold out for at least 25 more years, meaning that on average your savings will be spent 10 years after retirement, or 45 years from now.

With a time horizon of over 40 years, you should pursue long-term, growth-oriented stock funds. As the horizon gets closer, you'll gradually ease into less aggressive growth and income-type investments, until at a 5-year horizon, you should be invested in a roughly equal mix of growth (stock) and income (bond) investments. (Remember, this point won't be reached until sometime after your retirement.) But that's putting your retirement cart before your earning years' horse.

HOW MUCH IS ENOUGH?

The trickier factor in planning for your retirement *now* is estimating how much money you must save to meet your retirement objectives. Put it another way: Is the amount you are saving today enough to meet your objective of a secure financial future? To find out the numerical answer, you can click onto any number of Web calculators. (I like the ones found at fidelity.com and vanguard.com best.) But to put the numbers into a meaningful context, read on.

CALCULATING YOUR SUCCESS

For some investments, this is easy. You buy a treasury bill for $9,400; you know it will be worth $10,000 when it matures in a year. For other investments, it is much more difficult. You need to make assumptions about likely returns. For example, if your stock-invested portfolio grows by 7.2 percent a year in real (inflation-adjusted) terms, it will double every 10 years. This is a reasonable figure, but it does little good at clearing things up when you have a long series of additions to your savings, followed by a long series of withdrawals, as is likely to be the case with your retirement savings. But while mastery of Excel spreadsheets may be necessary to calculate your exact situation, the following table should prove helpful in retirement planning.

What portion of your income do you have to save in order to retire on 60 percent of your current pretax income (not counting social security and other pensions)? If you are 40 years from retirement, you need only save 3.7 percent of income. If 35 years, 5.7 percent, and so on:

Years	Percent to save
40	3.7%
35	5.7%
30	8.7%
25	13.6%
20	22.0%
15	37.4%

Assumptions: I have assumed an average 8 percent real (after inflation) return before retirement, and 5 percent real return after retirement (when you will be somewhat more conservatively invested). Such returns are reasonably conservative but cannot be guaranteed. These figures also assume that your income is growing at the inflation rate. (If it grows faster, then you will get somewhat more than 60 percent of your current real income to retire on.)

Most important, this table assumes that you can live as a retiree on 60 percent of your current real (inflation-adjusted) income. If, for example, you want to do a lot of traveling, you may actually want to spend *more* after retirement than you're making now. The above figures can simply be ramped up proportionally. (E.g., if you want to retire on 120 percent of your current real income, just double the above savings percentage figures.)

As you can see, an early start makes retirement savings much less painful. But even if you do start today, you should put at least 10 percent of your income into your 401(k) or another retirement account, if possible. You will probably never regret having too much tax-advantage savings, or getting the head start that may allow you either to retire early or to skip a few years while you are putting your children through college. Or catch a sunset before you're too old to see it. Or catch a wave before your own hair turns blue.

THREE

Funding Your $10,000 Portfolio

As you saw in Chapters 1 and 2, finding money to fund your $10,000 portfolio is one thing, but planning your $10,000 portfolio is another. Planning requires prior knowledge of many related fund investing steps: knowing where you stand (financially speaking); coming to terms with how the economy and securities markets work; coming to grips with risk; understanding and selecting the best types of funds for your $10,000 portfolio's long-term goal.

For starters, you'll need to determine:

1. What you can invest on a regular basis. Many of us feel as if we have little or nothing to invest. (This chapter shows you how to increase your savings and boost your fund investment dollars.)

2. Where you should invest. More of us, however, are beginning to invest in our future, through tax-advantage retirement plans like the 401(k). The benefits of doing this are unquestionable—as long as you view your 401(k), your IRA, or any other tax-advantage retirement investment as an active portfolio in its own right, not just a part of your overall investment portfolio and plan.

3. What you're investing for. If you're investing for your retirement, you can afford to be far more aggressive in terms of the types of investments you select for your portfolio. If, on the other hand, you're investing for a short-term goal like the down payment on a home, then you'll need to be far more conservative.

4. What rate of return you'll need to achieve your objectives. Certainly, you'll want to stay well ahead of inflation (recently about 3 percent). And for longer-term objectives, you'll probably need to find investments that deliver an average annual return of at least 8 to 10 percent. Where does history tell you to turn? For the most part, to stock funds, since only stocks have achieved such returns over the long run.

5. What allocation—what division of your money among stocks, bonds, and cash—will optimize your chances of success? If history can be repeated, concentrating your assets in stock funds is likely to be your best bet. But, as even a parrot can tell you, past performance is no guarantee of future success. Asset allocation decisions are critical to the overall performance of your portfolio—not simply as it stands today, but also going forward, since these decisions affect how your portfolio will fare in tough and robust markets and economic cycles.

Asset allocation begins with your determination of which main categories of investments (stocks, bonds, and cash) you want to allocate your assets in. Determining the percentage of your investment for each category leads you to a decision about how you want to allocate your assets *within* that category. For example, if you're investing for retirement and it's more than 10 years down the road, then chances are you will be best served by concentrating your assets in stock mutual funds (and/or some individual stocks).

Once you have made up your mind about this step, you need to take another: determine within the investment category how much of your investments should be placed in higher- and lower-risk investments. From that standpoint, you can move into the realm of selecting the individual investments you want to include in your $10,000 portfolio.

INVESTING FOR THE LONG HAUL

People often ask what's the best fund to buy. Unfortunately, the right fund for another person may not be right for you—and rarely is one fund going to meet all your investment needs. It's up to you to determine what type of investor you are, in terms of tolerance of risk and investment objectives. Further, if you have complicated or multiple objectives, or if you need advice about estate planning or trusts, especially from a tax standpoint, you should consult one on one with an estate planner, an accountant, an attorney or some other professional who can get to know your particular needs. That said, the following model portfolios should help you find an appropriate benchmark for your current portfolio.

If you're building a retirement war chest, time is either on your side or weighing heavily against you. The younger you are, the more important it is to concentrate on categories that have the highest growth potential. There's one: stocks. With that in mind, consider the following:

Stock funds	80%
Bond funds	20%
Real estate	(Nope. You need to be sure you're saving for your down payment.)

QUICK TIP

I am not a great believer in investing in real estate other than your own home, at least until you own your home free and clear. At that point, real estate might be an option—though for growth investors it's rarely an attractive one relative to stocks and stock funds.

INVESTING IN STOCK AND BOND FUNDS

Once you have determined what percentage of your assets you want to invest in each category, you need to decide how you want to invest in each.

Investing in stock mutual funds makes the most sense for investors like you and me. To get the needed diversification from direct ownership of individual stocks, you'd need to own a bare minimum of 40 different stocks, while one fund can offer you 500-plus stocks in one basket. But owning one fund isn't the way to go—since it would bias your portfolio toward a single investment style and a single manager's focus, which in turn would no doubt favor some industries over others. How many funds are enough? You don't need 30—in fact, don't go overboard with the number of funds in your portfolio. Instead, concentrate on how and where each fund is invested. Five funds should be plenty.

Step 1. Determine which major stock fund categories you wish to invest in—as well as what percentage you want to invest in each category. This book will show you how.

First, you'll need to make a geographical decision: the percentage of domestic (U.S.) and foreign assets in your stock allocation. Foreign markets are often far more volatile than ours, especially for dollar-based investors (like you). With currency movements and frequently illiquid markets, some foreign stock markets will rocket twice as much in a given time period, while others will plummet twice as far as the U.S.—or further. But foreign markets don't always move in the same direction as the U.S., so over the long term, portfolios with an 80 percent stake in U.S. common stocks and a 20 percent stake in established foreign-market stocks (like the U.K. and Germany, as opposed to Thailand or Mexico) have outperformed portfolios consisting of all U.S. stocks, with little or no added risk. (Aggressive younger investors may put even more overseas, including in emerging markets, for greater long-term growth potential, albeit with more short-term volatility, or risk.)

The following allocation among major stock fund categories could potentially suit your longer-term objective.

U.S. growth	80%
International	20%

Step 2. Now, you need to decide how you want to allocate your investments in each stock fund subcategory (here defined by investment style and market capitalization, as well as country allocation).

Capital appreciation	20%
Large-cap growth	30%
Sector	10%
International	20%
High yield	20%

Step 3. Make sure your objectives mesh with your funds' objectives and risks. And don't make the mistake of assuming that a fund's name accurately reflects its current management style—scrutinize that prospectus. All too often these days, funds are being managed to meet objectives that have precious little to do with the names they bear.

Step 4. Find out the fund managers' investment styles and performance records. Investment styles tend to divide themselves into two camps: value and growth. Once you know the investment style and the average market capitalization of the companies the fund invests in, you can compare its performance against an appropriate market index. For example, if the fund invests in large-cap companies, an index like Russell 1000 Growth Versus Value Index provides a good performance benchmark. You will also want to know about each fund's industry concentration, as well as each manager's ability to deliver solid results. And while past performance is no guarantee of future results (sorry, metaphysics man), average annualized 1-, 3-, and 5-year returns will help you get a sense of how the manager has done and might continue to do. Be sure to compare the returns of each fund with those of other similarly invested funds. What if the manager is new to the fund you're thinking of buying? Find out what his or her record was at a previous fund.

Step 5. Determine what types of industries and stocks each fund typically invests in. This may take a lot of research—but not a lot of time. In fact, you can call and ask the prospective funds you're thinking of buying (or the ones you own) for this information. True, the info may be a bit stale—3 months old or so—but it's still relevant. Or you can research past issues of the numerous personal finance magazines. Chances are, your fund and manager have been profiled in one or another.

Step 6. Establish how the funds in your current (or potential) portfolio correlate with each other. One of the most common mistakes fund investors make is thinking that owning many funds automatically guarantees diversification. Two funds that own similar stocks will tend to move up and down together, and they provide little more diversification than either fund held alone. How can you tell if the funds you currently (or potentially) own are more or less likely to behave similarly? All the above steps (i.e., in choosing funds by objective) will come into play in a general way when it comes to distinguishing between funds' potential performances.

Step 7. Don't chase hot funds. Last year's best-performing fund is seldom this year's darling. Better to buy a fund you believe will perform reasonably well over two or more years than to try and buy one that has only recently rocketed skyward.

Step 8. Don't buy a fund simply because your friend says to. Just because your friend likes a fund doesn't mean it's a good one. And just because your friend may in fact own a good fund doesn't mean it's the best one for you. This is *your* financial life we're talking about.

Step 9. Don't buy more than one fund for each role in your portfolio. Why own two of the same thing when one will do? (OK, if we're talking beer, then two of the same thing makes sense. But when we're talking about investing, this isn't the case.)

Step 10. Do buy more than one fund for your portfolio. Rarely can one fund serve all your investment needs. In fact, I can't think of one fund that does.

Step 11. Learn as much as you can about what mutual funds are and what they can do for you. Chapter 4 will help you accomplish this in less time than it takes to learn to grill a hot dog.

PART II

STREET SMARTS

FOUR

Become a Market Maven

I know you're champing at the bit, trying to get to the chapter that tells you how to invest your money wisely and well. But understanding the actual and virtual marketplaces that trade the stuff our funds are made of (stocks, bonds, cash, etc.) is one ingredient for fund investors—arguably more important than it is for individual stock and bond investors, since investing in funds nets us the whole marketplace as opposed to small pieces of it. Moreover, having at least a rudimentary understanding of where your money manager is putting your money every day will help you better comprehend the reasons for his or her own moves. It will also help you see just how smart those moves are.

To begin with, it's good to get a sense of where your money goes to work. The following market snapshot will help you picture where your money is.

New York Stock Exchange (NYSE). Wall Street—11 Wall Street, to be exact—is where you'll find our oldest, most venerable, and largest exchange. Launched in 1817 under a buttonwood tree on Wall Street, so called because of a wall erected to defend New Yorkers from northerly attacks, the New York Stock Exchange grew to its current size and shape virtually unrivaled by smaller, more regional exchanges, with one exception, the New York Curb Exchange (begun in 1842). That exchange grew alongside the NYSE and is known today by the name it took in 1953, the American Stock Exchange. Companies on the NYSE are among the bigger companies; on the Street, the term for these is "large-caps," meaning companies with large capitalization (typically in excess of $3 billion).

American Stock Exchange (AMEX). Known as the market for mid-cap companies, the AMEX is often referred to as NYSE's little brother. It's based in New York (on Trinity Street, as opposed to Wall Street).

National Association of Securities Dealers Automated Quotation System (NASDAQ). The NASDAQ celebrated its twenty-fifth anniversary in 1996, having grown from a tiny 100-stock over-the-counter service in 1971 to its current 5,500-plus universe of stocks ranging from mega-Microsoft to micro-companies struggling to stay aloft. As a result, NASDAQ is known as the market for small-caps; but in fact, as NASDAQ has itself grown from puny to gigantic, so have many of the companies that list there, including Intel and MCI.

Commodity Exchanges. These are the exchanges where contracts on everything from coffee to pork bellies abound—real stuff we all like to consume, especially pork bellies (yum). Exchanges are defined by the type of instruments their contracts are based on. For example, the Chicago Board of Options Exchange (CBOE) is the main market for auctioning puts and calls on NYSE stocks, S&P 100 and S&P 500 futures, and treasury bonds. The New York Cotton Exchange (NYCE) is dedicated to trading futures in cotton and orange juice.

International Markets. These markets offer investors a chance for some thrills—and spills. Not all foreign markets are created alike, however. Some, like the London Stock Exchange, are as secure as the Tower in that city; others, like the Italian market, resemble the frangible dunes of Cape Cod.

Emerging Markets. If foreign markets can sometimes throw investors for a loop, emerging markets are like a roller coaster ride on a Möbius strip—infinitely volatile. While there are ways to minimize the risk of investing in these countries (for example, investing in a well diversified emerging markets fund—or, better yet, investing in a well diversified international fund that includes emerging-market securities in its portfolios), no strategy can shield the investor from the volatility inherent in these markets. Are the rewards worth the risk? Well, in any given period, some emerging-markets funds deliver eye-popping returns. Some just poke your eye out.

FIVE

Become a Performance Maven

Getting to know the marketplace is a far more complex task than learning a handful of trading places. The next step on our fund investment learning curve is to get to know the basic standards by which you and I can measure a fund's performance. A few years back, you might have thought that the term "benchmark" referred to sitting on a freshly painted bench. Today, the term has become synonymous with the S&P 500 Index, the standard by which many investors measure their portfolio's overall performance. This isn't an adequate standard, however. In fact, there are several other indices that you and I can use to measure funds' and fund managers' performance more accurately—whether it's an active manager of a large-cap growth fund or a "passive" manager of an index fund (see Chapter 9).

True, the science of measuring market performance is mathematically based. But this doesn't mean that an index is a "pure" measure. In fact, there's a lot of room for judgment in terms of what gets included in an index—and what gets left out. The following indices are the ones I most commonly use to measure a particular fund's performance as well as to measure a group's relative standing.

U.S. STOCK MARKET INDICES

Dow Jones 30 Industrial Average (DJIA). This is the most commonly seen measure of the U.S. stock market. Since 1896 (when Charles Dow introduced this index), the Dow has pretty accurately reflected the movement and mood of the overall market. In fact, even when it is compared with the broader indices that its critics propose as replacements, the Dow withstands the test of time. For example, when compared with the S&P 500 (a market-cap-weighted index which does reflect the market better and serves as the benchmark against which many money managers and fund managers gauge their performance), the Dow usually shows little divergence. The DJIA index, then, continues to serve as an adequate measure of the U.S. market. It's worth paying attention to—if only because everyone else is paying attention to it—but not exclusively. The DJIA is best used in conjunction with other indices that better reflect their particular markets.

What are the Dow's drawbacks as a measure of the U.S. market? First, it's invested in only 30 rather arbitrarily chosen stocks, so the level is itself somewhat arbitrary. (Thirty stocks were a lot to add up when you had to use a pencil but aren't many when you have computers to do it.) Second, the Dow's stocks are basically all large-cap "industrials," a term broadly defined to mean companies producing goods and services other than transportation or utilities. (Dow Jones also has long-standing Transportation and Utilities indices.) Third, the Dow is not market-cap-weighted but rather share-price-weighted, meaning stocks with higher-priced shares are weighted more heavily. That's a pretty arbitrary way of doing things; it means, for one thing, that after a stock splits (where, for example, the number of shares doubles while the share price is cut in half, so that there is no real effect on investors), a company's shares have only half as much representation in the index. Fourth, while the index does take splits and mergers into account (after the index's 30 stock prices are added up, they are divided by that which would be 30 but is now actually much lower—below 1—because it is reduced after stock splits and is also altered whenever one stock is replaced by another in the index), the Dow values you see in the news don't reflect stock dividends. The Dow thus is not a total-return index. (On the other hand, most indices, including the S&P 500, have this same flaw, and nowadays stock dividends are usually pretty trivial anyway, not much over 1 percent annually. When you see an index "return" figure in the newspaper, it usually leaves out the dividends.)

Standard & Poor's Large-Cap 500 (S&P 500). Charles Dow created the first standard to measure the markets, and it was the only commonly accepted measure until 1928, when Standard & Poor's created a market-weighted index based on 90 stocks. Twenty-two years later, the S&P 90 had become what it is today—the S&P 500. Perhaps the benchmark most broadly used to gauge successes and failures versus the overall market, the S&P 500 is a tough performance standard to live up to. This index consists of approximately (not exactly) the 500 largest companies in the United States (in terms of total stock market value), including industrials, utilities, and financial companies. These 500 companies represent almost 80 percent of total stock market value in the United States, but of course the index doesn't tell you anything about how small-cap or mid-cap companies are doing.

While the Dow gets more coverage in the daily press, the S&P 500 is, for market professionals, by far the most important index of U.S. stocks. That's because index funds tracking the S&P 500 are by the far the most popular type of fund in that category (over $600 billion is explicitly indexed to the S&P 500, and the portfolios of many actively managed large-cap funds come close to replicating the index as well) and because this broader large-cap index is the most common performance yardstick for stock portfolios.

One drawback of investing in S&P 500 index funds is that they are all forced to buy the same companies on the last day of the year, just as these companies are being added to the index. Generally, such companies have already seen a lot of market gains during the year (moving them from the mid-cap to the large-cap range of stocks), and their prices are generally further inflated at year-end precisely because everyone knows that all the index investors will have to buy them. The most famous recent example is America Online (AOL), whose stock was up 368 percent for 1998 through December 18, and up a whopping 615 percent by the close of December 31. (It was down a bit in January of 1999 but then saw modest gains.) Investors in many actively managed funds (and investors in index funds holding mid-caps) benefited from AOL's predictable bid-up, at the expense of investors in S&P 500 funds. Of course, with returns close to 28.6 percent in 1998, S&P 500 indexers weren't exactly crying into their beer. (In fact, they beat most other investors hands-down despite paying too much for AOL.) But if they hadn't been so narrowly obsessed with exactly matching the index, they could have made more money, at very little risk, by buying AOL stock a couple weeks before year-end.

MARKET-CAP WEIGHTING

A company's total stock market capitalization (its "market cap") is the total value of all its shares of common stock, or its share price multiplied by the total number of shares outstanding. As far as the free market is concerned, that's what the company is worth. The S&P 500 (like most market indices other than the Dow) is market-cap-weighted. This means that the largest companies, like Microsoft, exert more influence on the index (as on the stock market as a whole) than do the not-so-large companies, like The Gap. Why not weigh all the companies equally? You'd have three problems: (1) you wouldn't really be reflecting the action of the stock market; (2) you'd have to rebalance the index's stock weightings frequently, ideally every day; and (3) you'd have a ridiculous system whereby after a corporate merger, the new company's stock would count only half as much as the two companies' premerger stocks. With a market-weighting system, by contrast, no rebalancings are needed except to compensate for share offerings, buybacks, and mergers. (If a stock rises, it takes up a larger portion of the index, but it also takes up a larger portion of your index or indexed portfolio, so no rebalancing is needed.) In the long run, this is much less arbitrary than weighting the companies on the basis of their per-share market prices.

Standard & Poor's Mid-Cap 400 (S&P 400). Just as its sibling S&P 500 index is used to represent the large-cap market, the S&P 400 index is used to help investors gauge the performance of mid-sized companies. It is composed of companies ranking from five-hundredth largest to nine-hundredth largest in the United States. What happens if a company's stock goes up so much that it no longer qualifies? As mentioned above, this happened to AOL in late 1998. Since the S&P 400 index is rebalanced only at year-end, the stock remained on, and dominated, the index until then, when AOL was moved up to the S&P 500 index. (Like almost all market indices except the Dow, the S&P indices are market-weighted, meaning that big companies are weighted more heavily, and this heavier weighting happens automatically as a stock goes up in value.)

Standard & Poor's Small-Cap 600 (S&P 600). This index is used to measure the performance of small companies. The S&P 600 consists basically of companies ranked between nine-hundredth and fifteen-hundredth largest in the United States. While there's nothing wrong with this index, it is not encountered as commonly as the Russell 2000 small-cap index (below), primarily because the Russell has been around for a decade longer than the S&P 600 (which goes back only to 1994).

NASDAQ Composite. The NASDAQ Composite Index is an index of over 3,000 domestic OTC stocks. (OTC means traded over the counter.) At one time, NASDAQ's small companies would leave for the New York Stock Exchange or the American Stock Exchange as soon as they got big enough to be exchange-listed, but that's no longer always true, especially for technology companies. Since this index is market-cap-weighted, its performance is tightly tied to the leading technology companies that dominate it (like Microsoft and Intel). Thus this index has gained wider acceptance as a market indicator in all the media from newsprint to TV. But while it's a pretty good indicator of the tech sector, it's certainly not a pure tech index, and it can no longer be viewed as an exemplary small-company index.

QUICK TIP

Here's a fact that may save you some time hunting down quotes: while stocks traded on the New York Stock Exchange (NYSE) have 1- to 3-letter ticker symbols, OTC stocks have 4- or 5-letter symbols. On the American Stock Exchange (AMEX), most stocks have 3-letter symbols, but some have 2- or 4-letter symbols.

Russell 2000. This index has been used to measure small companies' performance since it was launched in 1984 (and Russell has back-calculated data from 1979 on). The Russell 2000 is made up of the smallest 2,000 companies in the Russell 3000 Index; that's basically the companies ranked between thousandth and three-thousandth largest in the United States. Russell 2000 companies represent approximately 10 percent of the U.S. market's total market capitalization.

Wilshire 5000. This is now actually more than 7,000 stocks, essentially all the publicly traded stocks in the United States. Wilshire Associates produces a lot of other indices, including large-, mid- and small-cap indices, and growth and value portions of the same, but the Wilshire 5000 is its one indispensable offering. Naturally, since the S&P 500 large-cap stocks constitute about 80 percent of the U.S. market (and thus of the market-cap-weighted Wilshire 5000 index), this index doesn't deviate all that radically from the large-cap index. Still, because it includes the whole market, it is often the best measure of comparison for a stock fund or portfolio that has no restraints on market-cap (i.e., that isn't limited to small-caps or, on the other hand, to large-caps).

Wilshire 4500. This too is actually about 7,000 stocks and includes all the stocks in the Wilshire 5000 that are not in the S&P 500. Therefore, it is made up of all the mid-cap and small-cap stocks in the United States, but naturally the mid-caps dominate it by virtue of their size (the index is market-weighted).

Barra Growth/Value Indices. Barra, in conjunction with Standard & Poor's, has "Growth" and "Value" subsets of the S&P 500, S&P 400, and S&P 600 indices. In each case, the broader index is divided into halves (equal in market weighting, not in number of stocks) based on price/book value ratios (P/B). High P/B stocks (those selling for many times the book value of the company's tangible assets) are put in the Growth group, and low P/B stocks (those that are cheap relative to assets) are put in the Value group. Growth and Value funds and managers can be more fairly compared with these index subsets than to the undivided S&P indices. Note that the Vanguard Index Value and Vanguard Index Growth funds also represent these Barra subsets of the S&P 500 large-cap index. (Note also that over the longest term, Value stocks have tended to beat Growth stocks, but Growth has been ahead for most of the past bull market.)

FOREIGN INDICES

While there are several sources of foreign market returns, Morgan Stanley is the gold standard in this area—with numerous country, regional, and global indices; with index values available both in local currencies and in the U.S. dollar; and with small-cap indices available for many markets. While there are many other foreign indices, especially single-country indices such as the Tokyo Nikkei 225 and the Frankfurt DAX, many of these are expressed only in their local currencies (i.e., they are not converted into dollar terms, which would be more "real" for U.S.-dollar investors) and most are more arbitrary and limited in scope than the Morgan Stanley indices. In other words, they're more like the Dow than they're like the S&P 500.

EAFE or MSCI EAFE Index. This is shorthand for the Morgan Stanley Capital International Europe, Australasia, and Far East index, the most meaningful and most popular broad measure of established foreign markets. This index includes the markets of Western Europe and Japan as well as some of the more advanced Asian and Pacific nations (e.g., Australia and Malaysia, but not Thailand). This index will help you benchmark your international funds' performance.

Europe. As Europe continues to unify economically and even politically, with the gradual introduction of the euro as currency, European investing and Europe-wide funds will probably continue to grow in popularity. I use the MSCI Europe index as the best measure of this area.

Japan. Japan has been in the doldrums since the end of 1993. But just as the years of great performance up to 1994 did not make this market a great buy in 1994, the years of lousy performance since then do not make it a bad buy now. With the benefit of hindsight, it is much more logical to move assets into Japan now than it was at the end of 1993 (when people were actually doing that in droves). This doesn't prove that moving to Japan is now a great move but does make it much more likely. Take a look at Morgan Stanley's Japan index and its Japan Small Company index.

Asia. Despite currency crises and subsequent tough markets from mid-1997 through 1998, Asia is still one of the world's most promising areas for explosive economic growth, and thus for superior long-term stock market performance. I use the MSCI AC Far East Free ex Japan index to keep track of this area. (This stands for Morgan

Stanley All-Country Far East excluding Japan; "Free" means including only free-floating shares, not closely held shares.)

SECTOR INDICES

The **Dow Jones 15 Utility** and **Dow Jones 20 Transportation** averages are the granddaddies of the sector indices. While there are many others, I generally use the Dow Jones U.S. Industry Groups to track these areas. These include 8 major industry (group) sectors and over 100 sectors in total. Dow Jones also tracks sectors in foreign markets.

BOND INDICES

Bond indices are much harder to come by and are rarely quoted in the media. The problem? Too many bonds in the market, most of which, apart from U.S. treasuries, rarely if ever trade. Usually bond market conditions are expressed only in terms of treasury yields and/or the price on the "bellwether" 30-year treasury bond (the "long bond"); but there are many total-return indices available from Wall Street's major bond houses, such as Salomon Brothers,

---

QUICK TIP

Most of these indices are on the Web. Here's a basic address book:

Morgan Stanley
www.ms.com

Russell
www.russell.com

Dow Jones
www.dowjones.com

Standard & Poor's
www.spglobal.com

S&P/Barra
www.barra.com

Wilshire Associates
www.wilshire.com

Lehman Brothers, Merrill Lynch, and J. P. Morgan. The only problem is that with so many bonds on the market (there are several times more bond offerings than publicly traded stocks), varying so much in terms of credit risk and average maturity, no index provides really useful information to all or even most bond investors.

Lehman Brothers has the most generally used indices for the performance of taxable and tax-free bonds in the United States. The Lehman Brothers Corporate Bond index includes all publicly issued, fixed-rate, nonconvertible, dollar-denominated, SEC-registered, investment-grade corporate debt. What this index does for corporate bonds, the Lehman Brothers Government Bond index does for U.S. treasuries and agency bonds. The Lehman Brothers Government/Corporate Bond combines the two. And the Lehman Brothers Muni Bond compares the performances of long-term, investment-grade, tax-exempt municipal bonds. Lehman also provides indices for high-yield (junk) bonds and mortgage bond funds.

SIX

Become an Industry Maven

You know the town. You know the streets. You step into the local café for a mug of coffee with *Baron's* or the *Wall Street Journal* under your arm. You walk up to the coffee bar. Ask for the mug—tall, plain. Pull up your stool and lay the paper down just like a miner from the old West with a prospector's chart. The absence of a six-shooter strapped to your side shows that prospecting for gold has become a lot tamer than it was in the past—but striking it rich hasn't become all that much easier.

Nowadays, every market is a blend of industries, making it hard to corral all the information you need to relate a fund's holdings to your sense of where the opportunities and dangers lie.

True, the managers of your funds are your hired guns in this new age and new economy. They've got the job of trying to outsmart the market and their peers every waking hour. But your managers aren't trying to chase down every possible investment. Instead, they tend to concentrate on a select group of stocks from a handful of industries within the overall marketplace.

Most good managers are "bottom-up" stock pickers: they check each company's fundamentals before investing. Other high-performing managers use a "top-down" method: these folks invest in what they think will be hot market sectors going forward. No matter which camp your manager falls into—and you should determine this for each and every fund you own—every manager concentrates on several main industries (described below) and multiple sectors.

INDUSTRY REVIEW

When it comes to mutual funds, understanding market industries and the subsectors of these industries can help you gauge an individual fund's strength or weakness—and can also help you put your portfolio's strength or weakness into perspective.

In fact, industry concentration may be the closest you can come to current weightings in any given fund you own. As a result, knowing where the fund is concentrated will help you judge its performance in light of what you know about industries and subsectors relative to current market conditions. And it will also help you avoid owning two funds that are invested in the same way. Likewise, when scanning the globe for new investment opportunities, you'll be far better off knowing in advance what industries are out there to choose from—so that you can wed what you know about the economy (for example, its cyclical nature) with your buying and selling strategies.

Industry analysis may sound difficult to wrap your mind around but, thanks to the many user-friendly resources at your peck and call (peck, in terms of using on-line services), it's become much easier to note top- and bottom-performing industries and sectors as well as top- and bottom-performing stocks and funds. Often the twain meet. To begin with, you'll need to get to know each major industry. From there, you can begin to unpack its constituent sectors and the companies making up each sector. Let's take a look at the following main industries.

Basic Materials. Basic materials are the raw materials that manufacturers use to produce their goods. Aluminum, chemicals, paper and forest products, and steel (commonly referred to as "deep cyclicals") are prime examples. Companies that harvest and produce such raw materials tend to have their peak earnings in the later stages of an economic recovery, when increased demand for manufactured goods (from cars to homes) begins to outstrip the supply of raw materials (aluminum and lumber), resulting in price increases that go straight to the company's bottom line.

Cyclicals. Housing and auto manufacturers top the list of cyclical industries. Sensitive to economic cycles, this group tends to rise quickly in economic upturns and to slide back just as quickly during downturns. The success of each sector relies on the consumer's willingness and ability to purchase the goods—which, naturally, slows during tough times and increases during better times.

Energy. This industry includes oil, natural gas, and energy services (oil exploration and pipeline suppliers). This is a commodity-based industry, meaning that supply and demand fundamentals have a direct impact on it and on the companies in it. Typically, growing emerging markets (which account for more than 25 percent of the world's economy) and economic recoveries in established markets are good news for this industry. In fact, emerging markets provide an increasingly positive picture, in terms of their demand for plants and their need to fuel them, as well as their increasing ability to buy cars. Both plants and cars are likely to be less energy-efficient, which means greater consumption and hence a stronger demand for oil.

Finance. Banks and savings and loans, financial services (broker-ages), and insurance companies (life and property/casualty) make up the financial industry. While nature can wreak havoc on prop-erty/casualty insurers, it can also benefit banks that are called upon to lend money to rebuild after a natural disaster. As a whole, this industry is sensitive to interest rates. Rising rates are typically nega-tive, while falling rates tend to be positive. Why? Higher rates can dry up loan demand, while lower rates tend to encourage greater borrowing and increase demand for loans. As a result, times of economic growth tend to bode well for banks and brokerages through increased loan and investment demand.

Health Care. This industry includes companies that design, manu-facture, or sell products or services used in health care (from hospi-tals to elder care), as well as companies involved in medical delivery and pharmaceutical manufacturing (from prescription drugs to over-the-counter cures). This industry is susceptible to politics (in the form of federally instituted price controls), as well as commer-cial and consumer demand.

Media and Leisure. This conglomeration includes everything from TV broadcasting, newspapers, and advertising to restaurants, casinos, hotels, and cruise lines. What do these two very different areas have in common? They exist primarily to help people spend their free time. (Also, each is too small to warrant its own category.) While people don't give up watching TV during a recession, ad revenues do decline, hurting media companies across the board. Leisure is also sensitive to changes in people's discretionary income.

Noncyclicals. Also referred to as consumer staples, this industry includes food, drugs, and insurance—the three staples for surviving in the real world. Name-brand products have come on far stronger than brand X products (although this wasn't the case in the early 1990s) and are likely to remain constants in the universe as more sales go overseas and more consumers want the best products. But loyalty aside, the companies in this sector tend to produce basics we all need and would find it hard to do without.

Retailers and Wholesalers. This is another smallish category. These firms include major discount chains such as Wal-Mart, as well as department stores, specialty retailers, and "category killers" such as Toys R Us. For the last several years, many retailers have been hurt by a major slump in apparel purchases. (Apparently, everyone bought all the clothes he or she needed in the 1980s, and with companies going casual, there's even less need for expensive replacements.)

Utilities. These companies move electricity, natural gas, or data (e.g., phone messages) into homes and businesses. Because they tend to be stodgier, low-growth, high-dividend stocks, they are generally most suited for more conservative equity-income investors. Because of their high, stable dividends, they are often held as bond substitutes, and they move closely with the prices of long-term bonds. This makes utilities the most interest-rate-sensitive sector. However, some telecommunications companies do have higher growth potential, and some of the newer areas (e.g., cellular) are often categorized with the technology stocks (see below).

Technology. From semiconductor manufacturers to software producers to telecommunications, this industry is likely to be a long-term success. All the sectors should prove to be excellent performers, benefiting from strong growth in our own economy as well as in emerging economies. Multimedia is the way this world is heading.

Expect short-term volatility, but we're long-term investors who can stand volatility—and we're smart enough to know that technology isn't just here to stay; it's here to rule.

SUBSECTORS

You'll need to unpack an industry into its constituent sectors. For example, with finance, you can examine each sector—banks, brokerages, and insurance—in order to scrutinize the performance prospects of the industry, the sector, and individual companies. From there, you can ferret out those funds that are most committed to particular companies and sectors within one industry. And you can then measure a company's or fund's past and potential performance against a pool of its peers, as well as against an adequate market benchmark.

The following table is an accurate mosaic of the types of industries that most publicly traded companies participate in. Why is knowing this important? For one thing, it's interesting just to see how multifaceted our markets are. For another, especially when it comes to mutual funds, sector concentration may be the closest you can come to current weightings in any given fund.

Dow Jones Industry Groups

Basic Materials
Aluminum
Other nonferrous metals
Chemicals
Forest products
Mining, diversified
Paper products
Precious metals
Steel

Consumer, Cyclical
Advertising
Airlines
Apparel
Auto manufacturers
Auto parts and equipment

Casinos
Home construction
Home furnishings
Lodging
Media
Recreation products
Restaurants
Retailers, apparel
Retailers, broadline
Retailers, drug-based
Retailers, specialty

Consumer, Noncyclical
Beverages, distillers, and
   brewers
Beverages, soft drinks

Consumer services
Cosmetics and personal care
Food
Food retailers and wholesalers
Health care providers
Household products
Medical supplies
Pharmaceuticals
Tobacco

Energy
Coal
Oil drilling
Oil integrated—majors
Oil—secondary
Other oilfield equipment and
  services
Pipelines

Financial
Banks, all
Diversified financial services
Insurance, all
Real estate
Savings and loan associations
Securities brokers

Independent
Conglomerates
Overseas trading companies
Plantations

Industrial
Air freight couriers

Building materials
Containers and packaging
Electric components and
  equipment
Factory equipment
Heavy construction
Heavy machinery
Industrial, diversified
Marine transportation
Pollution control and waste
  management
Other industrial and
  commercial services
Railroads
Transportation equipment
Trucking

Technology
Aerospace and defense
Communications technology
Computers
Diversified technology
Industrial technology
Medical tech/biotechnology
Office equipment
Semiconductors
Software

Utilities
Electrical utilities
Gas utilities
Telephone utilities
Water utilities

Once you've grasped the basic industries and their subsectors, you can begin to view every fund you own through the lens of where it's weighted. You can also begin to revise your portfolio in light of where you think the best market opportunities are.

SEVEN

Become a Stock Maven

Part II is immersing us in a different world, Stock World: from the marketplaces where everything is traded to the indices that relate performance to the sectors that are prospected for performance to the actual stocks that determine a fund's performance. It's the last item that this chapter is going to put into place.

"I don't invest in stocks. I invest in funds." I don't know how often I've heard that, but I've heard it often enough to know that it's a common misconception. The general risks of investing in mutual funds are determined by what those funds invest in. So, beyond the risk of poor management or being in the wrong region or the wrong investment style side, the stocks and bonds in which your fund is investing hold the key to its success (and the success of your $10,000 portfolio), and to the underlying risks. Since most of us concentrate our assets in stock funds (and rightly so), it's not an exaggeration to say that stocks are the financial fuel for a portfolio's engine.

The trouble is that many investors don't know much about what makes their fund engine tick. After all, most investors aren't professional money managers—they want a trouble-free ride, not daily maintenance. But coming to grips with the nuts and bolts of your fund's financial engine is a smart money move. It's the only move which will let you rest assured that you know what you're buying and what's driving your overall portfolio's performance.

My mini-guide will help bring you up to speed on the types of stocks your funds are most likely to invest in. Once you familiarize yourself with them, you'll be better able to check out each and every fund you own.

QUICK TIP

Your fund's prospectus lists the allocations (stocks, bonds, cash), markets, sectors, and stocks that it invests in. See Chapter 10 for details on reading your fund's prospectus.

STOCK RISKS

The underlying risk of investing in mutual funds is the stocks the funds are investing in. Fortunately, the underlying risks of stocks are straightforward—and they hold as true for you as they do for the managers of your funds: (1) a decline in the stock's price (you buy a stock at $10 and it drops to $3); (2) elimination or reduction of dividend income; (3) a decline in price *and* dividends. If you bought a stock at $10, a loss occurs when you sell it for $9.99 or less. Selling may still make sense—or it may not. In fact, since most stocks fluctuate in price, it may be best to hold tight and ride out the downward curve if you have reason to believe that there will be an upside. Doing so may enable you to see the stock price jump back from $3 to $14—or, as happened with IBM, sell it at $117, buy it back at $60, and rise again beyond $100.

COMMON STOCK

What exactly is a stock? A common stock represents ownership of a (small) share in a company. Think of a share as one vine in a vineyard—either a very large IBM vineyard, wherein your one plant amounts to a tiny portion of the harvest, or a small Netscape vineyard, wherein the one plant is a somewhat larger part of the whole. Depending on how well the vineyard grows its vines and prepares the harvest, and how many grape plants you own, you will either be able to live off the harvest or have to look elsewhere for sustenance (unless you want to live off raisins). Note that you could do well in the large vineyard or in the small one (at either place, one vine makes about the same amount of wine), but the large vineyard may rebound better from bad weather while the small vineyard may have more room for expansion in good conditions.

FOUR MAIN DIVISIONS OF STOCK

Consider the following main divisions and types of stocks as the most common apples in the barrel—and realize that in each type there are likely to be more than a few rotten individual stocks. The good news? Knowing what to look for and diversifying will help ensure that one rotten apple doesn't ruin your overall portfolio.

1: Growth Stocks. Growth stocks give investors an opportunity to invest in companies that promise to increase their stock's market value through earnings growth. These companies tend to be smaller companies, or in rapidly growing industries, or both. (But they could, like Wal-Mart, be large players expanding market share in a mature industry.) Because investors expect their earnings to grow, growth stocks tend to be expensive relative to their current earnings. Growth stocks typically rise in value more than other stocks, but they are also far more volatile and subject to greater declines in price. Growth stocks should be the choice of your generation: they're more exciting, they can be more rewarding over the long term, they are less likely to get you caught in the web of trying to time a specific economic cycle, and you can afford the greater risk for the potentially greater reward.

2: Value Stocks. Basically the opposite of a growth stock, a value stock is a share that is cheap relative to earnings or assets. Value stocks tend to be stodgier players in slower-growing, mature, defensive, or cyclical areas. One caveat: a value stock is sometimes in the eye of the beholder. Almost all fund managers claim that they are seeking "undervalued" stocks or that even their highest-flying holdings are cheap relative to (predicted) future earnings. After all, no self-respecting fund manager would admit that he or she made a habit of paying more for stocks than they were really worth!

3: Cyclical Stocks. Cyclical stocks are stocks in companies whose earnings fluctuate more than average with business cycles. Examples of cyclical industries are housing, automobiles, paper, and steel. Correct timing is the key to investing successfully in cyclical stocks. Get the cycle wrong, and you will know what it feels like to land on your head without a helmet. Crash! As with growth versus value, the cyclicality of stocks is a continuum. Some stocks are in the middle and might be considered cyclical by some investors but not by others.

4: Income Stocks. Income stocks are those that pay substantial or above-average dividends. Income stocks are most often value stocks, stocks of companies that are typically in more stable, mature industries. Stability enables these companies to provide steady dividends, which are a source of income for many retirees or—more relevantly from your vantage point—a source of reinvestment capital. (See below for more on the benefits and strategies of reinvesting dividends.) Examples of income stock industries would be utilities, telecommunications, and energy—but even many pharmaceutical companies (not exactly a stodgy industry) fall into this camp.

STOCK TYPES

Blue Chips. Blue chips are traditionally thought of as the highest-quality of all common stocks. Blue chips are typically larger, solidly performing, dividend-yielding companies, which can fall into any of the four categories above. Examples of blue chips are Coca Cola, General Electric, and IBM. I say "traditionally," because these giants can fall as mightily as the small. Like other stocks, a blue chip can be characterized as a growth, value, or cyclical stock (or somewhere in between).

Large-Cap Stocks. These generally have a market capitalization exceeding $5 billion. Typically, you'll know the best of breed in this category by name—and you'll have many of their products on your shelves and in your garage. Not all large-cap stocks are created equal. The trick is to invest in a manager who knows how to ferret out the best of the bunch at any given time in the market cycle.

Mid-Cap Stocks. These (and mid-cap funds) are an excellent group for long-term investors like you and me. Typically ranging in capitalization from $1 billion to $5 billion, the companies exhibit actual earnings and real market share. If they do both at once, they're an excellent hold. If they have one or the other ingredient, they make attractive buyout candidates. Either way, this group provides fodder for long-lived growth.

Small-Cap Stocks. These range from $500 million to $1 billion, or at least that definition is the basic consensus. With scant (if any) earnings, small (if any) market share, many of these stocks trade on a wing and a prayer. Nevertheless, some stocks in this group provide explosive opportunities. (The Internet stocks are the prime example.) The trouble is that the whole group is among the most volatile and least predictable class of assets. While many experts suggest that younger investors should overload on these puppies, I think that even 20 percent can be an overdose. In fact, I prefer the mid-cap group for more reliable and less volatile long-term growth.

Micro-Cap Stocks. These trade below the $500 million radar screen. They're tough to track, and even tougher to predict. They can skyrocket to the moon or explode in your hand. Even the best active micro-cap fund managers have had a hard time delivering consistently good returns (i.e., better than a simple large-cap index fund). A small stake can make sense—but be prepared to be left with nothing but the sizzle.

Initial Public Offerings (IPOs). These are new issues of new companies' stocks. Such companies issue stock in order to generate capital to expand their business (or to buy out company founders and venture capitalists, or both). Bottom line: be forewarned. One of the reasons why IPOs come so highly recommended is that the investment bankers who back their launching, as well as the brokerages who have come in line, need to sell their inventory of shares in the IPO (just as much as the IPO needs to sell more of whatever it makes in order to sustain itself as a viable company). A flashy new stock is often a flash in the pan. Nevertheless, every stock was, at one time, an IPO. As a result, you needn't avoid IPOs on principle the way you should avoid penny stocks. Instead, concentrate on the individual promise of the company and its long-range potential. It certainly helps if you are familiar with the company's products or know someone who is. That's a great grassroots approach to starting your investigation. But it can also lead you to become over-enthusiastic, since you might feel that the product is so good it can't help doing well. (If that always held true, then Apple Computer would probably be doing better than Microsoft and Intel.)

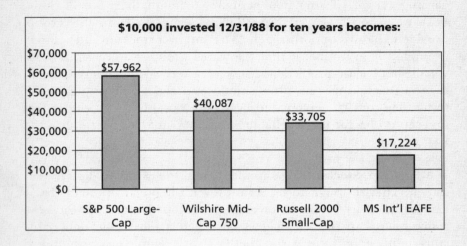

S&P 500 L	Wilshire M	Russell 2000	MS Int'l EAFE
$57,962	$40,087	$33,705	$17,224

$10,000 invested 12/31/88 for ten years becomes:

	S&P 500 Large-Cap	Wilshire Mid-Cap 750	Russell 2000 Small-Cap	MS Int'l EAFE
	$57,962	$40,087	$33,705	$17,224

Foreign Stocks. Many foreign stock markets have outperformed the U.S. stock market over the long term—and many haven't. As the economy goes global, foreign stocks will probably provide choice investment opportunities. The difficulty will be in selecting the right stocks in the right country at the right time—and knowing how best to invest in them. Since a country or a company may be foreign to our language and to our usual frame of reference for investigating stocks, you'll be up against difficulties that you would not normally face when investing in the United States. Nevertheless, taking advantage of stocks in a foreign country such as France, Great Britain, Japan, or Germany can make sense. After all, these countries have well established stock markets, and information abounds about them and their companies. But when it comes to hot emerging markets such as Hong Kong and Taiwan, you may experience information deprivation. In that case, be fearful.

Obviously, you can go many layers deeper into the stock market mine. My *Investing from Scratch* (Penguin, 1997) can help you do just that. But for now, this is all you really need to know about stocks in order to propel yourself from a naïve to an informed fund investor.

EIGHT

Become a Risk Maven

Fund investment risks come in many shapes and sizes—from what markets the fund manager concentrates his or her (really, our) assets in to what types of sectors and stocks the fund holds. But there are ways to ensure that you will understand the probable levels of risk and grasp some actual strategies for using risk to your advantage as an investor. Here goes.

We often wonder, "Is now a good time to get into the market?" This question has both short- and long-term aspects. In the near term, the concern is that we may be entering the market at an inopportune time. Essentially we're asking what the market will do over the next month, the next few months, or maybe the next year. Anyone who claims to have an answer should be treated with a strong dose of skepticism. The short-term answer is that we just don't know. We don't really have a good idea of what the market will do over any short time period, and I doubt those who say they do. (Of course, they may prove to have a technical edge that has helped them steer a better-than-average course. If so, I listen.) It's the nature of an auction market in equities, where stocks are worth whatever people are paying for them, that a fund's future performance (based on the prices of the underlying stocks it holds) is highly unpredictable in the short run.

But you don't have to leave the question as a total mystery. You can, for example, speak in terms of probabilities for most funds' returns.

For example, I can tell you with conviction that chances are good that a money market mutual fund will be up almost exactly as much as it was in the previous month, about 0.4 percent these days. A stock fund is much less predictable, however. On average, stock funds go up more than money markets, let's say 1 percent per month. But if the standard deviation of the fund's long-term monthly returns is typically 5 percent, the odds are about two-thirds that the fund's return next month will be within 5 percentage points of its 1 percent average, or between −4 percent and +6 percent. The odds are 95 percent that the fund's return will be within 2 standard deviations (10 percent) of its average, or between −9 percent and +11 percent. And in about 99 percent of all months, the fund's return should be within 3 standard deviations (15 percent) of its average 1 percent gain, or between −14 percent and +16 percent. (For definitions of standard deviations and risk, see the Glossary.)

Of course, every once in a while even these "limits" will be exceeded by a big move in the market. And as we all know, in an inefficient market surprises are the rule, not the exception. There are several ways in which we can go beyond the sort of simple probability assessments I made above. One way is to scrutinize fund management. Look to see who's in charge, what the manager owns and has owned in the past, and how well he or she has performed during both bear and bull markets. Also, watch the markets on a daily basis for signs of uncertainty or increasing strength sector by sector, market by market, and region by region. Easy enough, as long as you can read a paper or click into a solid investment website (see Chapter 26 for a host of these).

IS HALF A LOAF BETTER THAN NONE?

For most of the 1990s we had our investment cake and ate it too. But fat years can't last forever; that's why I continue to think it makes sense to diversify. It doesn't make sense to become Chicken Little and assume that the global market is going to fall on our heads. Instead, you should remember that most solid funds—no matter what market, region, or industry they invest in—take less than 3 years to recover from their worst losses. The key is to diversify so that if part of your portfolio suffers from a downturn in a particular area, the performance of your other investments will cushion the blow. When it comes to investing, half a loaf is typically better than none.

LOW-RISK STRATEGIES FOR HIGH-RISK TIMES

No matter what some experts would like you to believe, when it comes to investing you can't avoid risk altogether. Understanding investment risks, however, enables us to find ways to take advantage of them.

You may find this hard to believe, but sometimes it's difficult to stay on course when investing in funds, especially if markets become agitated. But the markets have never operated, and probably never will operate, dead calm (except when they're closed), so I advocate a strategy that is defensive in the near term and offensive over the long haul. You should look for low-risk, high-performance funds that can absorb the shock of a potential downturn but are nonetheless positioned to take advantage of the market's upside potential.

Look for risks in obvious and hidden places. The following checklist is a shorthand way to uncover—and avoid—many fund-related risks.

[ ] **Long-term performance.** Locate your fund's past performance to get a relative sense of how it has performed over time—in good and bad markets, economic environments, and industry cycles. Doing so will help you avoid funds that have performed consistently poorly (a risk not worth taking) and, hopefully, find some better performers that, over time, have provided a market-beating return.

[ ] **Near-term performance.** Some funds may have a spectacular record for a few months, one year, or maybe even a bit longer. But unless they've been consistently spectacular over 3 or more years, chances are they took big risks to shoot ahead and will soon run out of rocket fuel.

[ ] **Economic, market, and industry factors.** Keep abreast of developments in the economy, as well as in particular markets and industries, that could affect the funds you own. You should also be aware of fund-specific events like changes in investment objectives (see below) or fund management. These developments could affect the risks associated with particular funds in your portfolio.

[ ] **Portfolio objective.** Your objectives change—except for your long-term objective of a financially secure retirement—and your time frame for achieving them also changes: an intermediate-term objective becomes a short-term objective

when you have less than 3 years to go. You may have injected
a degree of risk into your overall investment plan that did
not exist when you initially assembled your portfolio. And
"life events" like marriage, divorce, the birth of a child, the
loss of a job, or an employment change for the better may
all affect your objectives and the means available for reaching them.

[ ]   **Fund risk.** Each fund in your portfolio has a degree of risk
that combines with the other securities or funds in the portfolio to create an average risk for your overall mix. You want
to be sure that this risk remains in line with your tolerance
and ability to manage it.

DETERMINING MARKET RISK

The best measure of risk is volatility. Volatility is the *standard deviation,* or uncertainty, of a fund's return. Not only is this a cool phrase
to let slip at some hip salsa bar. It's a key ingredient to getting the
recipe right for a well diversified $10,000 portfolio. Basically, a fund
that goes up about the same each month (i.e., a money market)
has very low risk, while a fund whose performance is more erratic
is said to be more "risky." To calculate a fund's volatility, I take its
monthly performances over the past 36 months and calculate the
standard deviation for this series of numbers. (See Glossary for the
formula—or just click into Morningstar.net for the answer.)

An example is the **Vanguard Index 500** fund. It's easy to guess
that its risk measure would be very close to 1.00, the same as the
S&P 500 Index, which it is designed to track. (For this *not* to be
true, there would have to be serious errors on the part of the fund's
management.) A more extreme case is **Fidelity Aggressive Growth,**
which concentrates its assets in highly volatile stocks of younger,
more speculative companies and industries and has among the highest risk scores for the Growth fund group (1.64 times the volatility
of the overall market). My analysis and common sense dictate that
this fund is, in fact, a risky investment. Conversely, **Fidelity Puritan,**
which invests in both stocks and bonds, has a risk measure of 0.71,
nearly 30 percent less volatile than the market.

These relative volatility numbers are similar in scale to *beta,* a
more commonly used measure of risk. Beta is similar to relative
volatility in that the S&P 500 has a beta of 1.00, and betas greater

than 1.00 indicate greater risk. But beta looks only at the portion of the risk that is due to the movement of the market as a whole. So a fund that invests its assets only in gold, which is a very risky fund but whose moves up or down do not generally follow the market, has a very high relative volatility but a low beta. Thus beta can give a very poor picture of risk for sector funds. And while most diversified funds have a beta only slightly lower than their relative volatility, you need to have the clearest possible picture of risk for every single fund: total risk, not just the market-related risk of beta. (Relative volatility is always at least as high as beta.)

RISK REDUX

As the table below shows, you can see just how volatile your fund may be by tracking what I call its **maximum cumulative loss** (MCL)—the largest total loss a long-term investor in the fund could have experienced to date. **Months to loss** indicates how long it took for the fund to accumulate its loss. **Month of trough** tells you when the fund's biggest drop ended. **Months to recovery** shows how long it took for the fund to regain its loss, effectively breaking even. The greater the maximum cumulative loss and the shorter the months to loss, the more volatile the fund. When you compare MCLs among funds, make sure you also weigh long-term returns and consider the funds' dates of inception. (And remember that in the investment business, it is generally, though by no means always, true that greater risks yield greater returns.)

Vanguard Index 500

Maximum cumulative loss:	−29.8%
Months to loss:	3
Month of trough:	Nov. 1987
Months to recovery:	18

Fidelity Magellan

Maximum cumulative loss:	−33.1%
Months to loss:	3
Month of trough:	Nov. 1987
Months to recovery:	17

NO RISK, NO GAIN

Finally, I think that as a *long-term* investor you should be more concerned with expected long-term returns than with a fund's "risk," which is really a short-term factor.

YOU CAN REDUCE INVESTMENT RISK

When we invest in one fund, we're really investing in two risk opportunities. The first risk opportunity is **market potential,** or performance. The second risk is **peer out-performance**—a standard by which you can begin to see a manager's relative strength or weakness.

More precisely, market potential is a fund's potential for good performance given the current and future conditions of the markets it's invested in. The number of holdings and portfolio turnover tell me whether or not the manager buys with conviction—and the fund's performance tells me if that conviction pays off. For a given fund, the percentage of assets that are locked into the top 10 holdings indicates to me the level of volatility and profit potential. Since these "top ten" typically account for one-quarter to one-third of a fund's assets, each stock on the list carries the potential to significantly affect the total portfolio's performance. The portfolio's average P/E, beta, and alpha tell you at a glance the relative market risk you can expect. The portfolio's sector weightings are integral to wedding the top-down and bottom-up research.

Each fund is a piece in a portfolio's mosaic, so keep your eye on asset allocation, particularly on the cash levels in each fund, in order to see the overall exposure that a given portfolio has to stocks, bonds, cash, and foreign issues.

Fees and tax efficiency, while not the driving force behind my recommendations, are clearly considerations that play a role in my analysis of every fund.

Tracking a manager's long-term and shorter-term relative performances tells you the extent to which his or her choices have tended to help (or hurt) the fund's performance. Here you should focus on a manager's record relative to closely correlated market benchmarks: these provide a more useful performance gauge than simple returns, or even returns relative to "the market" (usually the S&P 500 index), or returns relative to other mutual funds.

Among diversified equity funds, management is the most important determinant of performance. But with the narrowly drawn sector funds, a manager's performance record is less important than the fund's investment objective. I don't pick or avoid a sector fund on the basis of management, because in this case management factors are outweighed by market-related issues. And for bond funds, management is virtually a nonissue, except for those investing in junk bonds.

INCREASING DEFENSIVE SECTORS REDUCES RISK

Surprisingly, some sector funds can reduce risk and enhance returns. While sector funds make up only a moderate portion of many of your portfolios, they can play an essential role in your investment plan. Sector funds (see Chapter 9) concentrate their assets in one industry.

In selecting a sector fund, you should focus on top-down analyses of the global marketplace, wedded to sector fund fundamentals such as actual holdings, average P/E of the portfolio, manager, and your portfolio objectives. Sector funds that I think offer the best returns relative to long-term risk are energy, food, agriculture, pharmaceuticals, and utilities. Slightly higher-risk sector funds that you might consider in constructing a complete portfolio for near-term (i.e., under 12 months) defensively oriented gains include technology and telecommunications. Both moves are contrarian with respect to the normal use of select funds—typically employed by high-risk managers looking for fast money. Our low-risk strategy actually takes advantage of a hidden strength in select funds: sector funds can be used to reduce the risk of a portfolio as much as they can be used to increase its profit potential.

CONTROLLING CORRELATION REDUCES RISK

A fund correlation matrix (see page 98) shows how closely funds' returns correlate with one another. Simply put, for any two funds, there is a number, R^2, which shows what percentage of one fund's performance can be explained by the other fund. (A fund's R^2 compared with itself is 100 percent.) Why is understanding your funds' correlation important? It will help you ensure that your own portfolio is well diversified. How? If you hold only two growth funds that have a high correlation, your overall portfolio isn't as diversified as it should be. On the other hand, if you own two growth funds with a very low correlation, you've achieved added diversification (in terms of, for example, different capitalization and industry emphasis).

Why is reducing your portfolio's correlation to the market important? Because this is a market of selective, not general opportunities. Besides, there is no need to own all the risks of every market. Instead, concentrate on a handful of potential rewards.

INCREASING DEFENSIVE ALLOCATIONS

I prefer cash and ultrashort U.S. treasury bond funds as the best way to create an allocation for short-term needs with virtually no risks involving credit or interest rates. I continue to like bond funds more than bonds, since bond funds provide the ability to trade and participate in an expertly managed, low-cost pool of bonds at relatively low cost.

While junk bonds are riskier than investment-grade bonds (see page 139 for details), they aren't all that risky when seen as substitutes for stock funds. A good junk bond fund may be hard to find—but once found, it can reduce the risk of your portfolio. In fact, a junk bond fund can be a better way to enhance yield and hedge against stock market risk than real estate investment trusts (REITs).

Junk bonds have potential returns and risks close to those found in the stock market. But junk bonds are only partially correlated with the stock market, so they can diversify a portfolio that's otherwise mostly in stocks. And at times, junk will look particularly attractive relative to stocks and to high-quality bonds—when this is the case, you may load up on it and do quite well with a well-diversified portfolio of junk bonds.

Since you really can't build your own junk bond portfolio with less than $250,000, you're better off investing in a junk bond mutual fund. Even if you have the money to invest in junk bonds on your own, you will be hard-pressed to find an adviser who is excellent at choosing bonds, provides low-cost services—in terms of both transactions and annual fees—and is willing to keep turnover in your portfolio quite low, which in this case means under 20 percent per year. The junk bond marketplace is an arena where mutual funds provide the only practical way for the average individual investor to get involved.

PATIENCE IS MORE THAN A VIRTUE

Finally, remember that patience is more than a virtue; it's an essential ingredient in any recipe for long-term investment success. You and I are not compulsive buyers of one hot fund or another. Instead, we buy our funds with conviction, understanding how each fund plays its role on the stage of our portfolio. For those of us who are truly long-term investors, the current market climate is one in which opportunities always exist.

NINE

Become a Fund Maven

You know it. I know it. My 6-year-old niece knows it. Chances are your dog knows it. Mutual funds are by far the most popular form of investing today. And that's not surprising, given the fact that their many benefits and their low cost relative to investing directly in stocks and bonds far outweigh any downside. In fact, I think they're the single best avenue for investing, for both our short-term and our longer-term goals. True, in addition to the many positive features that funds offer most investors, there are some pitfalls you'll need to avoid—not the least of which is the common mistake of thinking that mutual funds are guaranteed to deliver positive results. (They're not.) But that, in part, is what *Smart Money Moves* is about: helping you minimize mistakes and maximize the rewards of investing in mutual funds.

Now that we've covered some essential smart money moves (i.e., finding the cold cash to invest as well as learning about the various ways you can invest), it's time to turn our full attention to the wonderful world of funds.

What exactly is a mutual fund? A **mutual fund** is a professionally managed, diversified portfolio of stocks, bonds, money market instruments, or other securities. Each fund is made up of many investors' money, pooled by the fund manager or managers to purchase these securities. "Pooling" the money gives you the potential benefits of a larger and more diversified portfolio than your own money alone could purchase. You'll still need to know what is in the pool, however, because it's all too easy to get in over your head before you realize you can't swim. Mutual funds don't magically protect you from the market's turbulence. The value of your fund shares still depends on the value of the stocks and/or bonds owned by the fund. And the value of the stocks and/or bonds the fund holds still depends on the market risks they are subject to (See Part II—Street Smarts for details on checking under the economy's, the markets', the industries', and your funds' hood.)

TOO MUCH OF A GOOD THING

Mutual funds used to represent an easy way for investors, large and small, to avoid the complications of picking a large portfolio of stocks and/or bonds. A decade ago there were fewer than 500 mutual funds and 5,000 stocks trading on the various exchanges. The number of stocks trading today is over 11,000, and the number of mutual funds has grown twentyfold. This chapter will help you learn how to sort through this superabundance of choices—as well as introduce you to a new, user-friendly way to buy mutual funds. But first, let's take a look at why funds should play such a significant role in your portfolio.

FUNDS CAN BE MORE OR LESS RISKY

Funds, like the stocks they hold, haven't exactly delivered a smooth ride and aren't likely to deliver one—but it's clearly been a very rewarding ride for those who've sat in their seats for the entire journey. And though you'll hear me say this time and again, it's worth reiterating now: investing today for the long term is the best way to ensure financial freedom for years to come. The sooner you begin, the better. A day late is a dollar short.

FUND PERFORMANCE

Of course, we want to know how our funds will perform today and tomorrow. And chances are that everybody you know who has ever invested in a fund has found a range of synonyms for "I'm a fund-picking genius"—as least for a day. In fact, in this sense investing is like fishing: exaggeration rules. It's unlike fishing, however, in that rarely do you hear people talking about "the fund that got away." Instead, you're more likely to feel that you failed to catch the brilliant fund your friend is ranting and raving about. Perfor-

	Vanguard	Fidelity Magellan	T. Rowe	Fidelity Overseas
1990	−3.32	−4.51	−20.47	−6.60
1991	30.22	41.03	38.60	8.61
1992	7.42	7.01	13.91	−11.46
1993	9.89	24.66	18.40	40.05
1994	1.18	−1.81	0.08	1.27
1995	37.45	36.82	33.84	9.06
1996	22.86	11.69	21.05	13.10
1997	33.21	26.59	28.80	10.92
1998	28.62	33.63	−3.46	12.84
1999	6.42	6.80	−1.49	2.47

	Vanguard	Fidelity Magellan	T. Rowe	Fidelity Overseas
1989	10,000	10,000	10,000	10,000
1990	9,668	9,549	7,953	9,340
1991	12,590	13,467	11,023	10,144
1992	13,524	14,411	12,556	8,982
1993	14,861	17,965	14,866	12,579
1994	15,037	17,640	14,878	12,739
1995	20,668	24,134	19,913	13,893
1996	25,393	26,956	24,105	15,713
1997	33,826	34,123	31,047	17,428
1998	43,506	45,599	29,973	19,666
1999	46,299	48,700	29,526	20,152

Stock funds in the 1990s

$10,000 invested at the end of 1989

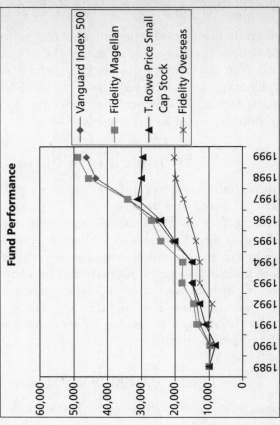

Fund Performance

- Vanguard Index 500
- Fidelity Magellan
- T. Rowe Price Small Cap Stock
- Fidelity Overseas

mance is attractive, but it can be deceptive as well. Right from the start, you need to know two performance terms inside and out: NAV and total return.

Net Asset Value (NAV). A fund's net asset value is determined by adding all the fund's holdings (its assets in securities and cash) and dividing this sum by the number of shares outstanding. For a no-load fund, the NAV is the share price you see listed in a newspaper—and the price per share you would pay (to buy) or receive (if you sold).

Total Return. A fund's total return is the sum of the change in share value—capital gain or loss—during a given time period, plus whatever income the share may have earned during that period. For example, if you purchased a share of Flyhigh Capital Appreciation Fund 12 months ago at $10 and it is now worth $11, and it also paid dividend income of $1, your total return is $2, which breaks down into $1 of capital gains and $1 of dividend income. Expressed as a percentage, that would be a 20 percent total return for the past 12 months.

Got it? Good. Let's move on.

ADVANTAGES OF A MUTUAL FUND

Selecting the best mutual funds to invest in has become quantitatively and qualitatively more difficult. And, while *Smart Money Moves* helps you sort out most of what you need to know about investing in funds, it's important to note that the advantages of investing in mutual funds remain the same today as when the funds were first introduced in the early 1940s. (See Chapter 28 for a mini-history of funds.)

Advantage 1. You can begin investing with a small amount of money. Some funds have investment minimums as low as $500 or even $100. True, most fund families have been upping the minimum required to $1,000 or more, and some require minimum investments ranging from $1,000 to $1 million. But there's a secret way around most fund minimums—and it works to your advantage. If you're buying funds through tax-advantage retirement accounts like IRAs and Keoghs, they generally have lower minimum investment thresholds, sometimes even under $500.

Advantage 2. Mutual funds are the quickest route to diversification. Even with a small initial investment (see above), purchasing shares in a mutual fund instantly gives you the sort of diversification only the biggest direct stock investors enjoy. Fund managers strive to build diversified portfolios not only to achieve the best performance but also because it's the law. SEC regulations set strict limits on how much of a fund's portfolio can be invested in any one stock and how much of any one company's stock a fund can own. This ensures diversification and prevents holding companies with controlling interests in other corporations from masquerading as mutual funds.

Advantage 3. Mutual funds are a convenient financial product to use. I know that makes them sound about as appealing as toilet paper—but the fact is that they're simple and, to my mind, a necessary vehicle to get us where we want to go. Features like 24-hour-a-day toll-free telephone account access and fund company websites— both of which allow you to trade shares from your phone or keyboard—mutual fund networks, automatic investment plans, and fund companies' involvement with 401(k) plans make investing in mutual funds a breeze. Of course, convenience can have its drawbacks: it's so easy to buy and sell shares that you must steel yourself against the impulse to make sell or buy decisions based on short-term market fluctuations.

Advantage 4. It's easy to get the information you want. Compared with other types of investments, mutual funds' performance is easy to track. Not only do the business pages of major newspapers quote fund shares like stocks, but you can also use any number of online services to follow your fund's performance. And websites as well as the financial press are chock-full of reporting on mutual funds: interviews with managers, in-depth analyses of particular funds and fund families, and quarterly and year-end reviews of each fund category's best and worst performers appear by the carload in daily, weekly, and monthly publications. The problem, of course, is information overload.

QUICK TIP

If you have invested in a fund that is very new, very small, or both, you may have trouble finding its price in the business pages. Funds must have either 1,000 shareholders or $25 million in assets to be included on NASDAQ's news media list, and some papers may not quote all the funds that NASDAQ provides through this service.

Advantage 5. Most mutual funds are managed by seasoned professionals. (Most are ruled by the market; some rule the market.) In theory, at least, when you buy fund shares you are getting the services of the sort of investment adviser only wealthy individuals can afford. And because fund performance is tracked so obsessively by the financial press, managers are under tremendous pressure these days to construct thoroughbred portfolios. If a fund goes through a protracted period of bad performance relative to its competitors, chances are good the manager will be handed a not-so-golden parachute.

In today's hyperventilating marketplace, keeping track of who is managing which fund has become about as difficult as following the career of a successful professional ballplayer. A high-performing manager can become a hot commodity pursued by rival investment companies. So when you are assessing a fund's performance, find out who its current and previous managers are. If a fund with a great 10-year performance record spent the last 12 months in the doghouse and it turns out that a veteran manager departed around the time when performance started to tank, alarm bells should start going off. They should ring particularly loudly if a comparison of recent annual reports shows that the new manager restructured the portfolio.

Advantage 6. There are funds designed to suit almost every investment strategy and every consumer's preferences. Are you convinced that the next administration is going to bring back the gold standard? You can buy a gold fund. Do you believe that only companies that prohibit their executives from wearing leather goods are behaving in a truly ethical manner? You can buy shares in a socially responsible fund. Beyond such extreme examples, there are funds tailored to meet almost every market and investment objective from speculative long-term growth to safe current income.

Advantage 7. The only investment more liquid than a mutual fund is a bank account. The spread of the notion of redemption on demand (from a cranky oddity to a defining feature) is a major theme in the development of the modern mutual fund. As noted above, you can place orders to buy and sell fund shares over the phone or via your computer 24 hours a day, although you should know that buy and sell orders are all batched together and executed only once daily.

DOWNSIDES OF A MUTUAL FUND

Downside 1. Mutual funds, like the securities in which they invest, can be risky. While today's American investors are probably considerably better educated and more market-savvy than any of their predecessors, there are still all too many shareholders who don't understand the risks inherent in their fund investments. Not all funds are sturdy houses for your savings: while some are built of bricks and mortar, others are woven from straw soaked in gasoline.

Downside 2. Mutual funds can charge ridiculously high fees. The day of the contractual plan may be well behind us (see the historical tour in Chapter 28) but fund companies still have plenty of ways to make consumers pay for the privilege of investing in their funds. Naturally, fund companies have to pay their managers (and let's face it, we do want them to hire the best brains money can buy) and have to cover their overhead and distribution costs, not to mention their profit margins. But there is a world of difference between funds with fair expense ratios and funds whose sales and management fees are so astronomical that they lead you to conclude you would be better off peddling their shares than investing in them.

Fund families run the gamut from hard-core no-load outfits like Vanguard to low-load lines like Fidelity to high-load funds like Evergreen that charge, in addition to management fees, loads to pay their salesmen and 12b-1 fees to cover their marketing expenses.

So before you open your checkbook, be sure to calculate and compare the expense ratios of the funds that catch your eye.

TYPES OF MUTUAL FUNDS

Mutual funds come in two distinct flavors: open-end and closed-end. Open-end funds are by far the more popular. They're the funds you find in the mutual fund section of your paper, and they number in the thousands. Closed-end funds (see page 73) are listed in the stock pages of your paper (and they are traded like a stock while acting like a bond); they number under 200.

There are many types of open-end funds to invest in, but the funds themselves invest in one or more of the following core investment categories. Of course, each core category itself is made up of dozens of investment vehicles. The three major fund categories are stock, bond, and money-market funds.

1: Stock Funds. A stock fund, also referred to as an equity fund, invests in individual stocks of large and/or medium and/or small companies, here and/or abroad. A stock fund is characterized by the kind of companies it invests in, and by its specific objective. Stock funds are the most appropriate place for you to invest your money and concentrate your investing dollars. As you get older, you'll want to shift more money to bond and money market funds because bonds typically show less short-term volatility than stocks. However, in your youth it's best to focus on investments that offer an opportunity for substantial growth. Stock funds are your answer. They should be the choice of the new generation—that's you.

There are several types of stock funds:

- **Aggressive growth funds** invest in new companies, new industries, and/or more speculative stocks in an attempt to achieve very high returns. Objective: maximizing capital gains.
- **Large-cap growth funds** invest in somewhat more established companies whose earnings are expected to increase steadily. You want to own these. Objective: an inflation-beating growth rate that steers clear of the risks associated with achieving occasional spectacular success.
- **Mid-cap funds** invest in middle-size companies that offer both demonstrated earnings and market share—two very attractive

qualities which, when coupled with growth potential, can make this range of funds very attractive. You want to own these. Objective: inflation-beating growth.

- **Small company funds** (commonly referred to as small-cap funds) invest in smaller companies whose earnings are expected to increase steadily. Objective: capitalizing on small companies' growth potential while focusing on earnings.
- **Growth and income (G&I) funds** tend to invest in more established companies whose stock tends to pay significant dividend income. These funds may also hold some assets in bonds. They vary in aggressiveness but tend to have less growth potential than the previous groups. G&I funds will no doubt come to serve a central, centering force in your overall investment portfolio. Objective: significant price increases combined with current income.
- **Equity income funds** generally invest about half their portfolio in dividend-paying stocks and the rest in convertible securities and bonds. Primary objective: current income. Secondary objective: long-term price increase. (These funds are not generally suitable for younger, more aggressive investors.)
- **Balanced funds** invest in common stock, preferred stock, and bonds. Again, these funds are not generally suitable for young, more aggressive investors. Objective: current income, growth, and lower risk than pure stock investing.

2: Bond Funds. A bond fund invests in bonds of companies or governments as varied as those the stock funds invest in. Bond funds tend to be more conservative when it comes to risk and growth. My suggestion: avoid bond funds altogether for the time being. Unless you're within 5 years of funding a child's college tuition or within 10 years of retiring, stick to stock funds. You'll want to invest in bond funds down the road—when you reach middle age. But even then, invest only a small portion (no more than 20 percent) of your money in bonds. You'll gradually increase the percentage of bonds as time goes on, but for now, you're young and stand to benefit most by investing in good stock funds.

Bond funds have limited potential for long-term gains and are generally more suited to retirees than to investors who haven't yet moved to a golf community. Nevertheless, as an informed investor you ought to know all your options—including bond funds.

Bond funds are often mistakenly thought of as a safe, sure-thing income-producing investment. Except for funds that invest solely in shorter-term government bonds, this simply isn't so. Bond funds have a significant degree of risk, particularly because rising interest rates will reduce the value of the instruments they invest in. A fund's duration reflects its sensitivity to interest rates—its *interest-rate risk*. This is an important factor to consider, given that different bond funds hold bonds of widely varying durations. For example, if interest rates were to rise by 1 percent, a fund with a duration of 10 years will (all other things being equal) fall 10 percent, while a fund with a duration of half a year would fall only 0.5 percent. (When interest rates decline, bond prices rise, and a fund with a 10-year duration would appreciate 10 percent in response to a 1 percent decline in rates.)

A reliable way to ferret out which speculative and/or conservative bonds might be in a given fund's portfolio is to note the letter ratings from Moody's and Standard & Poor's in tandem. These ratings are a reliable guide to the economic health of companies in a fund's portfolio. Only by examining both interest rate and credit risk in relation to how they affect a fund's performance in different market environments can you be assured that the bond fund you've selected matches your overall investment objective.

As with stock funds, there are several types of bond funds:

- **Short-term bond funds** invest in a mix of government and corporate bonds with maturities of 1 to 5 years. Basically, this is an investment in debt—and I'd rather have the cash. Objective: income with limited exposure to interest rate risk.
- **Intermediate-term bond funds** invest in a mix of government and corporate bonds with maturities of 5 to 10 years. Yawn. Objective: higher immediate income.
- **Long-term bond funds** invest in a mix of government and corporate bonds with maturities of 15 to 30 years. Snore. Objective: steady source of income.
- **High-yield bond funds** (a.k.a. **junk bond funds**) invest in bonds below investment-grade quality that offer potentially high profits at the expense of higher risk. Needless to say, these can be volatile. In the long term, however, they're an often overlooked but awesome ingredient for a portfolio like yours and mine. Objective: higher-than-average yield and solid returns.

- **Municipal bond funds** (better known as **munis**) invest in bonds of state and local governments. Objective: tax-free income. Note: Muni bond prices are hard to find. Muni bond fund prices are not.
- **Single-state bond funds** invest in bonds from only one state. Since interest earned from these funds is free of state (and often local) as well as federal income taxes, single-state funds often provide the highest tax-equivalent yields. Objective: double tax-free income.

3: International Funds. An essential subset of stock and bond funds is international and global stock and/or bond funds.

- **Global stock funds** invest in a combination of foreign and U.S. stocks. I prefer owning a U.S stock fund and an international fund rather than owning one fund that purports to rule two very different markets. Objective: to take advantage of both foreign and domestic investment opportunities, often hedging against currency risk.
- **International stock funds** invest only overseas, in the stocks of several countries or regions. A great way to participate in the new economy—which is going global. Objective: to take advantage of foreign stock market opportunities.
- **Emerging-market funds** invest in the wildest and woolliest places on earth—from Istanbul to Ixtapa, giving volatility a new name. These funds can make you feel like a sun god or like a sacrificial lamb on any given day. Objective: making a killing when blood is running in the streets.
- **Single-country funds** focus on one particular country's stocks and bonds. By far the most volatile of the bunch, single-country funds are generally best avoided unless, as in the case of Japan, the country is the largest market outside the United States with well established markets, industries, and accounting practices. You'll still have to do your research on such funds, however, since funds with the same single country can invest in different types of markets—as well as hedging or not hedging their bets against currency fluctuations. Objective: capital appreciation.
- **International bond funds** invest in foreign government or corporate bonds. I hate debt. I hate foreign debt even more than

most. I hate these funds most of all. Objective: income, diversification, and a hedge against a depreciating dollar.

4: Index Funds. As the other name for this category—**passively managed funds**—suggests, index funds are based on a premise that sets them apart from all the other products in the mutual fund universe. They eschew what many see as a prime attraction of mutual fund investing—access to the services of professional investment managers—in favor of replicating broad market indices like the Standard & Poor's 500 or the Wilshire 4500. An index fund manager's role is restricted to ensuring that the portfolio in his or her care does not stray from the index it is supposed to track, a task in which computers do most of the work. Objective: duplicating a broad section of the market in order to safeguard investors against below-market returns. (But this objective also eliminates the possibility of above-market returns.)

5: Money Market Funds. Money market funds, which invest in a variety of short-term interest-earning securities, are the investment world's equivalent of a bank's money market deposit account or savings account. They won't really make you money (after taxes and inflation), but they are a good place to store your short-term cash because they offer liquidity (easy access to your cash) and stability of principal (less risk). Objective: preservation of capital, liquidity, and as high an interest rate as can be achieved without sacrificing the first two objectives.

6: Real Estate Investment Trust (REIT) Funds. REIT funds invest in REITs—which are corporations that invest in real estate or mortgages and that trade on the NYSE. REIT funds aren't numerous. They are suitable for more conservative investors as a source of income.

7: Closed-End Funds. Unlike open-end funds, closed-end funds issue a fixed number of shares and trade just like a stock on the New York Stock Exchange (NYSE), American Stock Exchange (AMEX), or NASDAQ. Since they're traded like stock, you don't go through a mutual fund company to purchase or redeem shares in closed-end funds. Instead, you purchase them through your broker—and pay him or her a commission, usually at the same rate as for an individual stock.

Closed-end prices are set by supply and demand in the market. Often, closed-end funds trade at significant discounts or premiums to the actual value of their portfolio—with a closed-end fund you can often pay "too much" or, just as often, get a bargain. With an open-end fund, new shares are created whenever a new investor steps up to the plate—and you buy shares in an open-end fund directly from the fund company (or through a fund network, bank, or brokerage) at the NAV price (although often with some load or other fee charged). With a closed-end fund, the number of shares is limited, and unless you get in on the initial offering (more on that on page 75), you don't really buy closed-end shares from the fund company; you buy them from another investor who is selling.

8: Other Types of Funds. There are some funds that just don't fit comfortably into the categories above. Some, like sector funds, violate a central tenet of mutual fund investing—diversification—in order to give the investor an opportunity to focus on a particular industry. Others, like socially responsible funds, put social policy goals on the same plane as performance targets. While such specialized funds can offer the investor benefits and opportunities not found in more conventional funds, they can also bring higher risks.

- **Sector funds** invest in the stocks of a single industry, such as biotechnology, electronics, health care, utilities, and so on. If, for example, you think an industry is about to take off or rebound, then a sector fund may prove to be the best way to invest your money, as opposed to buying stocks in companies in the industry directly. Because of their focus on a single area or industry, sector funds behave more like individual stocks. Also as a result of this focus, sector funds often top the list of highest-performing mutual funds for a year. Unfortunately, the same funds that top one year's list are often found at the bottom of the next year's. Objective: Capitalizing on the success of one sector of the market.
- **Socially responsible funds** limit their investments to companies considered socially responsible. However, be sure that your conscience isn't your only guide, so that you research and screen

out poor-performing funds, too. Objective: achieving an adequate return without sacrificing the moral imperative.

There is no common definition of social responsibility. As a result, each fund's holdings will differ. Some, for example, will base their investments on companies to avoid (e.g., tobacco, alcohol, defense) while others will base their investments on companies to include (e.g., those that tend to promote women, or that provide health insurance for the partners of gay employees). Your biggest concern ought to be the performance of such funds, historically, versus "conscienceless" funds—after all, your money is used in a more focused manner when you actively support the charities you believe in through tax-deductible donations, as opposed to purchasing an investment product that supposedly does the work for you.

• **New funds.** While not a "proper" category, new funds are a phenomenon within the overall industry that you can't avoid— and so need to know about. Like IPOs (initial public offerings) in the stock world, new funds present investors with a dilemma: a new fund may offer a rewarding investment opportunity, but it has no track record on which it can be judged.

All funds were once new funds. But investing in new funds can be a risky business—unless, that is, you can afford the time to do research and identify those funds that offer real promise. Many investors view new funds from the largest fund families as their only source of new funds. Here, logic dictates that if a company has produced some of today's top-performing funds, its new progeny will do likewise come tomorrow. But the fact is that new funds from even the most successful families can wind up losing you money. In short, fund-family name-recognition isn't the best way to scan the fund horizon for the best possible investment opportunities in new funds.

PART III

FUND SMARTS

TEN

Your Fund's Prospectus

Once you get your major fund categories sorted out, you can begin the process of checking under the hood of each and every fund. A key tool: the prospectus. Before investing in any fund you'll need to get its prospectus. Trouble is, a prospectus is about as interesting as roadkill—and you may feel as though you've been hit by a truck after trying to read one. But you need to read it. Yes, you do. You just don't need to read all of it.

It's like being Mirandized: all fund families exhort investors to read the prospectus before investing in any fund. I'm not going to tell you not to read the prospectus (if I did, you would run the risk of not knowing what you were buying)—but I will tell you that most of the legalese contained within one prospectus (let alone five or more) is enough to kill anyone's idea of becoming a lawyer and an investor. While I don't think that reading the entire prospectus will actually be all that helpful, I do think you need to check into it for some basic details. The trick is to know where to look so that you can minimize the amount of time you'd otherwise waste.

THE MOST IMPORTANT INFORMATION
FOUND IN ANY PROSPECTUS

Every fund publishes a prospectus. The prospectus designates what type of fund it is (aggressive growth, balanced, etc.), details the specific objective of the fund and its past performance, states how the fund will be managed, and much more. To get your hands on a fund's prospectus, simply call the fund company and ask for it to be sent to you. (Or you can download the prospectus from a fund's website.) Once it arrives—and it will arrive quickly, since you're the fund's business—you may be a bit shell-shocked by the bombardment of information it contains. (For a thorough understanding of how to read a mutual fund prospectus, request a copy of *An Investor's Guide to Reading the Mutual Fund Prospectus* published by the Investment Company Institute, PO Box 66140, Washington, DC 20035-6140. This costs $0.40.)

QUICK TIP

When you ask for a fund's prospectus—which you must do for every fund you invest in—ask for the profile prospectus, too. This is a four-page fund profile that serves as crib notes for prospectus readers. It includes the fund's objective and investment strategies, the types of securities in which the fund will invest, any special investment practices, risk factors, expenses, and past performance.

1: Investment Objective. Although a fund's investment objective is only a paragraph or two long, it's the most important fact about any fund. The objective indicates what the fund manager's goals are, giving at least a broad outlook of what sorts of investments the fund will make. For example, does the fund seek growth from domestic stocks? Or from a particular subset of domestic stocks (e.g., small-cap versus large-cap, or high-growth versus high-dividend)? Or does it seek a stable share price from money market securities? You should weigh your personal objectives and goals against this fund objective. However, don't be fooled into thinking that an objective is all you need to know—or all there is to know—about how the manager is actually directing his or her fund.

2: Fund Fees. These are also featured in every prospectus. (For complete coverage of fund fees, see the Glossary.) It's important to keep fees as low as possible, or at least to avoid funds with above-average fees. The most common fees are loads, expense ratios, and redemption fees.

- **Loads.** A load is an up-front charge levied on your fund purchase. Loads come right out of your pocket. If a fund charges a 4 percent load, then you give up 4 percent up front, and the value of your account is always going to be 4 percent less than it would have been absent the load. If you're doing your own research and picking your own funds, you should stick to no-load funds or at least low-load funds (3 percent or less). If your broker is picking your funds, or you have bought into a contract plan, you may be paying loads of 8 percent or higher.
- **Expense ratios.** Even more important than whether or not a fund has a load is its overall expense ratio, which is the percentage the fund charges shareholders to cover management and marketing costs. Even if a fund has a decent past performance, it's likely to be handicapped looking forward if its expense ratio is high relative to funds with similar objectives. Since fund performance figures already take these expenses into account, don't double-count them by subtracting them from published returns. Note that the infamous 12b-1 fees (which are paid to brokers and other fund salespeople) are included in a fund's expense ratio; you should generally be more concerned with this total expense ratio than with its breakdown into 12b-1, management, administrative, and other expenses.
- **Redemption fees.** There's nothing particularly redeeming about these fees, which are also called back-end loads. Redemption fees come in two varieties: (1) those that are levied whenever you sell fund shares, no matter how long you have held them, and (2) those that are phased out after a certain period of time. The first kind is just as bad as a front-end load of the same size. But don't let it keep you from selling a bad or unsuitable fund; since you have to pay it some day, it makes no difference when you sell. The second kind is not a minus as long as you'll own the fund long enough to avoid it. It may even be a plus for you to the extent that it keeps other shareholders from selling out in a market decline. Moreover, unlike most other fees, many of these contingent redemption fees go to reimburse the fund (and remaining shareholders) for trading expenses and do not serve to enrich the fund's management or salespeople.

3: Investment methods and limitations. While these are tied to the fund's objectives, this section generally goes into greater detail about what the fund manager can and cannot do. For example, a growth fund, whose objective is to "seek growth from domestic stocks" may also be allowed to put up to 35 percent of assets into foreign securities and/or 35 percent into bonds, including junk bonds; or it may be able to invest defensively in money market securities without limit during times when the markets are "troubled"; or both.

One potential problem is that many funds give themselves the leeway to invest in almost anything (especially things like money market securities that are more conservative than the expected investments), whereas their shareholders reasonably expect to be invested in the securities implied by the fund's objective or its name. In general, most funds, "under normal conditions," must invest at least 65 percent of assets in the types of securities implied by their objective and name. For example, "Smith U.S. Growth Fund" will probably stick to no less than 65 percent in U.S. stocks, at least "under normal conditions."

4: How to Buy and Sell Shares and Other Services. Here the fund company tells you minimum investments and redemptions, what phone numbers to call for service, and how to transfer money by wire—information that you need to know, but it probably won't affect your decision making, although it can definitely affect your trading.

MORE NEED-TO-KNOW FUND INVESTING INFO

While the prospectus contains all the information the fund family is legally required to disclose before you make a purchase, it does not contain all the information you're likely to be interested in. The fund's annual or semiannual report contains the actual holdings (with a time lag, of course), and more performance information than the prospectus. Many funds also print in each report a brief interview with, or a letter from, the fund manager. There you can get the manager's strategies, his or her explanation for the fund's recent performance, and a recent outlook for the market. If you have strong opinions about how the market will be performing, this interview may affect your decision to buy or sell the fund. In any case, it's likely to be a lot more interesting than the prospectus.

Another way to get information can be to let your fingers do the walking. If you're connected to the web, go there. You can get it all—and then some. Most fund families are on-line (see Chapter 26 to learn how to find everything under the investment sun on-line). You can also pick up a phone. Customer service representatives at many fund groups have more recent information than can be found in the latest semiannual report, and they're happy to give it out. However, fund phone reps are generally pretty busy; you need to have specific questions for them to answer, and for legal reasons they're usually reluctant to give help that could be considered investment advice. (If you ask what aggressive growth funds they have, they'll have an answer; but if you ask what funds would be good for you, they won't, at least not until they've gotten you to say that you're looking for an aggressive growth fund). Also, while you won't be likely to encounter outright dishonesty from representatives, don't assume that they have the last word. At the very least, call twice and ask the same question or, better yet, if you're plugged into the Internet, click and click again.

ELEVEN

The Cost of Investing

In that prospectus you've just learned to read (see Chapter 10), you'll find out if you're investing in a load or no-load fund. I take a hard line and a one- or two-holds-barred approach to the subject of load versus no-load funds. And I want you to know this right from the start—since I am fully in favor of what many in the load fund industry consider the enemy, namely, no-load funds.

I've heard all the arguments. I've seen the numbers. I know the artful dodges and rhetorical knockouts that both load and no-load fund marketing departments can use. But, at the end of the day, there's really no contest. None. Nada. Zip. Doodly. Unless, that is, you're punch-drunk and come to the conclusion that you'd rather pay for something you could otherwise have free. Of course, if you like getting beaten up by punishing fees, then by all means step into the load fund ring. Personally, with the exception of sector funds, I'd rather go one round with George Foreman.

The day is not far off when George Foreman will probably stop doing muffler commercials and start hawking funds for a fund company. (We've already seen Don Knotts team up with Fidelity's former stock-picking guru, Peter Lynch.) After all, Foreman is affable, a world champion, and experienced at giving and taking punches in an arena where winning is predicated on outperforming one's opponent. In the months and years ahead, I think we'll start to see some fists fly in the fund industry.

Why? The lion's share of fund companies' assets resides in the coffers of load funds—funds that charge a fee for the privilege of doing business with them and assess such fees before they have a chance to prove you'll get your money's worth. Of course, the same thing can be said of both load and no-load companies in relation to their less obvious fees—expense ratios, 12b-1 fees, and more. So, to begin at the beginning of this knock-down-drag-out battle of the load and no-load Titans, you'll need to get up to speed on the many fees that can erode the overall rewards of your stated total return.

TO FEE OR NOT TO FEE

That's the question. There are many answers. First off, every fund charges a fee—the question is which funds assess low fees and show strong performance relative to their peer funds. Vanguard kicks the pants off most fund families in this regard. But that brings up another big debate: fund management styles, a topic we dive into in Chapter 12. For now, suffice it to say that few fund families offer solid no-load investing options. Which ones rule the roost? Typically, those with lower fees.

No matter what anyone tries to tell you, fees really make a difference—sometimes a big difference. True, a pure no-load fund with low expense fees won't guarantee you a better overall return, since a little glitch called stock selection dramatically affects the overall performance of a fund. However, all things being equal, if you invest $10,000 in a 4 percent load fund that turns in a 10 percent performance for the year, you earn the 10 percent, but not on $10,000. Instead, you earn 10 percent on $9,600. That's $400 short of what an investor in a no-load fund would earn. Over time, the impact of this can be considerable.

There's another twist that you need to be aware of. Just because a fund says it's no-load doesn't mean that there are no fees associated with it. There may be a redemption fee, and every fund charges management fees in one form or another. The trick is to find the funds whose fees are (far) more reasonable than others and whose performance is still solid relative to its objective, its peers, and your needs. To do this, you will need to do your homework—a task made easier by learning the following ways in which a mutual fund's fees can gouge your investment dollars.

Load. A load is an up-front sales commission charged to and deducted from your initial investment amount. (Load charges can be as high as 8.5 percent but are more commonly in the range of

3 percent to 4.5 percent.) There's little reason to purchase load funds when there are so many good no-load funds to choose from.

No-Load. No-load means no initial sales commission fee. No-load refers only to up-front sales commission charges. Many no-load funds have other fees (listed below). Nevertheless, no-load funds tend to be the best way to invest in mutual funds because more of your money is going to work for you.

Back-End load. Also known as "redemption fees," back-end load is a fee charged to the net asset value of your shares when you sell them. If you like having your hands tied behind your back, then you can either run for president or invest in back-end-load funds. Either your profit is cut or your loss is increased. No matter how you look at it, this load bites.

Deferred Load. (Contingent deferred sales fees.) On the surface, a deferred load seems as lousy as a back-end load. A deferred load is charged by some funds if and only if you redeem your shares before a specified time—typically a few years. While this may not be to your advantage if you're investing for the short term, the principle of discouraging investors from jumping into and out of the market on impulse is a good one.

Reinvestment Loads. Some fund companies dock your dividends, interest, and capital gains should you decide to reinvest them. Any fund that does this is discouraging a very wise investment choice— reinvesting dividends. Drop any of these funds from your list of possible investments.

12b-1 Fees. Some funds deduct from their overall assets the costs associated with advertising and marketing themselves. The charge associated with such deductions is called a 12b-1 fee, and it ranges as high as 1.25 percent. Some funds feed a portion of the fee to the broker who sold you the fund.

THE LOWDOWN ON LOAD FUNDS

The argument for load versus no-load funds typically runs this course: "Know nothing about investing? Do you live in fear of fund selection? You couldn't care less about the business of tracking performance and creating a portfolio, but you still want to invest wisely and well? Well, load funds may offer some advantages that you might find lacking in a no-load fund.'' And what are some of those advantages? "Low-cost advice" is often the response.

The problem is that advice is rarely disinterested—no broker, no matter how upstanding, is going to tell you that his or her fund line is full of overpriced underperformers and that you'd be better off buying directly from an outfit like Vanguard. Also, the advice is rarely as cheap as it sounds. When the sales fee gets skimmed off the top, instead of 100 percent of your investment dollar going to work for you, only 98 percent, 95 percent, or even, in the case of funds charging an 8 percent sales fee, 92 percent actually goes to purchase shares. Giving up a few percentage points may not seem like much, but the compounded value of those lost pennies can be quite substantial over the long term.

Without doubt, there are some load fund families that, when their low expense ratios are factored in, deliver a good product at a low price. The American fund family falls into this camp. There are also load funds that have delivered superior performance—superior enough to justify the loads they levy. Several Fidelity funds would meet this criterion, and you can also find some stellar examples in the John Hancock group. The problem is that load funds have to work overtime in the performance department to justify their sales fees, which means that when performance is off, they rapidly lose their attraction. Given the performance of some Fidelity load funds of late, for example, their current loads are unjustifiable (in my humble opinion).

Of course, don't let the fact that a fund is a no-load product blind you to a high expense ratio. Some of the no-load funds out there really sock it to investors when it comes to management, marketing, and administrative fees. Heartland Large Cap Value, for example, has a whopping 2.73 percent expense ratio, far exceeding the ratios of its peers. It's not a perfect world—you can find abuses on both sides of the load divide, so you have to be sure to look carefully.

BUY THE NUMBERS

The contrast between load and no-load performance can be more clearly seen in terms of the toll a load takes on your portfolio. The toll? Whatever the percentage you pay in load translates into the amount of money that doesn't go to work for you. However, you need to be discerning enough to realize that appearances can be deceiving. For one thing, investors choose individual funds, not fund categories.

Ask yourself, Do I feel lucky? Well, do you? If so, you might want to gamble that today's top-performing load fund might continue to beat out its closest no-load competitor and so justify its load—but if I were doing the answering, I'd say that there are so many no-load, lower-expense funds to choose from that if your adviser can't suggest some for you, it's time to switch advisers. Find a professional with a proven track record of solid no-load fund selection, or start reading that *Money Magazine* you've been subscribing to for the past few years. (Sector funds are an exception to my no-load rule: the only products available in this category all charge loads. Or log on and take a look at fund-related sites like SAGE on AOL. (For a complete fund investor's guide to the web, turn to Part IV.)

You've got a wealth of knowledge at your fingertips—all for less than the price of a ringside seat. But no matter what, before you select a fund, find out who's in charge and what the manager's investment style is. Enter Chapter 12.

TWELVE

Fundamental Differences

As you read a fund prospectus (Chapter 10 will help), you'll learn a lot about the fund's management. Among other things, it's the rule book that tells you what types of securities the fund can invest in. Even assuming that the fund is limited to investing in U.S. stocks, it may have still other restrictions or guidelines. It may be limited to large-, mid-, and/or small-cap stocks, or to growth and/or value stocks. It may also be limited to stocks paying high dividends, or to stocks not paying dividends at all. If it's a sector fund, it may be limited to stocks in one or a few related industries. Often, but not always, the fund will have the leeway to invest up to 35 percent of assets "outside the box"—securities that don't fit the stated rules.

Since the prospectus defines the universe of stocks from which the manager can choose, it also defines the benchmark against which the fund will be compared. For example, if the fund is limited to the large-cap U.S. stocks found in the S&P 500, then the S&P 500 will be the index to beat.

ACTIVE MANAGEMENT

Actively managed funds try to beat the market. The manager's job—and his or her career—will depend upon it. And while the fact is that the odds against beating the market are about 18 to 1, there are some active managers who stand head and shoulders above the herd. The key to investing in an actively managed fund is to buy the manager, not the fund.

INDEXING

Index funds are the complete opposite of active management—they try to match the returns of the index they're investing in. For example, an S&P Index 500 fund would try to match the returns of the S&P 500 Index. One virtually guaranteed way a fund manager can beat most of his or her peers is to "closet index" the fund; that is, just buy most or all of the stocks in the fund's particular investment universe, never make bets for or against any particular stock, and keep turnover to a minimum. Vanguard is the best-known purveyor of index funds (although many fund families offer them). Proponents of indexing take great glee in showing how many active funds have portfolios that essentially match the stock index investors are paying management to outperform. Bu there's a secret that index funds don't want you to know: there are many managers out there who have consistently surpassed the market-benched performance of index funds. Again, you just have to know where to look.

QUICK TIP

Check out Fidelity's universe of funds. In the rough-and-tumble world of investing, where only half of the managers can be above average, Fidelity's managers are on the whole much better than average. This is as true of Fidelity's domestic funds as of Fidelity's international fund managers. This is due to their collectively superior stock selection.

TECHNICAL CHARTING

Technical charting is the art of picking stocks on the basis of charts showing their price movements. It's easy; just find a stock whose price line looks like the outline of an upside-down man, and then buy as the line goes up by his left shoulder. But while technical charting may make marginally more sense than astrology, it doesn't have a much better record. Some market forecasters have gotten famous with a few correct market calls, but virtually all have sunk back into obscurity after making a few boneheaded ones. (Remember Joe Granville? If you weren't precociously following the market in 1982, you don't. And that's because he's been a perennial bear in the longest bull market in history.) Not many funds admit using technical charting, but it's more common than explicitly magical methods like astrology (Fidelity TechnoQuant Growth, for example, uses charting). Even a relatively successful chartist like Marty Zweig turns out to be the exception that proves the rule: he makes at least as much use of momentum and fundamental investing techniques as he does of technical techniques.

MOMENTUM INVESTING

Momentum investing is a seemingly simple method of picking stocks, arguably related to technical charting, though with less mumbo jumbo. (But a true trading system takes a world of experience to deliver.) Just buy what's been going up, and hope it continues to go up. Sometimes this works, sometimes it doesn't. When it works, that's called a "trend." When it doesn't, that's called a "whipsaw." If enough momentum investors chase the same hot stocks, the trend will continue for a while. Just be sure to be the first one to jump off the bandwagon. Needless to say, momentum investing tends to be pretty risky. (Suppose a lemming was the first to jump off?) Widely followed, it tends to increase the volatility of the market as a whole. It's a catch-22: do it at your peril; ignore it at your peril.

FUNDAMENTAL INVESTING

That leaves us with fundamental investing, which is part of an active manager's tool kit. It's my preferred approach, and I believe it's the only one where even a modest minority of skillful managers have passed the threshold of doubt between just being lucky and actually knowing how to beat the market.

What is fundamental investing? It means, simply, buying stocks because their underlying fundamentals (especially their earnings, sales, or assets) seem to be improving, or are high in relation to their price, or both. Of course, just about all market watchers consider fundamentals when picking stocks. So how does the fund manager gain an advantage over his or her competitors?

Tire-kicking. One approach is to get out of the office, go meet with company management, tour factories, and talk to suppliers and clients. The most famous exemplar of this method is Peter Lynch of Fidelity. In *One Up on Wall Street* and its two sequels he advocated going out to the mall to see which shops were busy and which products were selling well. (Lynch also told his readers to call up company presidents and ask how business was doing, obviously an option not available to the average individual investor.)

Of course, it's a lot of work and not much fun flying to places like Cleveland every week to see industrial pump designers and sleep in the local La Quinta Motor Inn. It's also hard to find important news about a major company before anyone else knows it. But sometimes company management will tell a visitor some particularly good or bad news that isn't yet public. With enough diligence, a tire-kicking fund manager can "beat the street," especially on smaller, less-noticed companies that don't have a lot of analysts following them. And that—not nostalgia for spring break—is why most successful fund groups send managers and industry analysts out on road trips.

Company Reports. Another source of stock data is news: annual reports and other corporate filings, conference phone calls, and industry analysts' estimates (which themselves depend on these other sources, on tire-kicking visits, or on both). This is a lot easier than visiting the companies, especially if you're wired to the Internet or, better yet, have a Bloomberg terminal in your office. Even retail investors can access most of this info, much of it free on the Internet. But while the average retail investor doesn't have access to analysts' conference calls, other fund managers certainly do, and one thing that's clear is that it's hard to make above-average returns with information available to everybody else.

So how does a fund manager make sense of the mountains of information available on the 500 or more stocks in his or her investment universe? It would seem to require superhuman abilities to sort through that much data on a regular basis. Naturally, that's where the computer comes in.

Quantitative Investing. Quantitative investing is a technique that uses the raw data-processing power of the computer to track various stock fundamentals and/or a stock's pricing history to identify promising investment opportunities. The most basic of "quant" techniques is the stock screen. For example, you might ask the computer to give you a list of stocks with P/Es under 20, a 10-year history of annual earnings growth of at least 10 percent, and a dividend over 2 percent. A more sophisticated (or at least more complicated) quant technique uses computers to analyze dozens of variables in order to extract a set of criteria for what constitutes a promising stock. A "neural network" computer is capable of this kind of learning.

Whatever the criteria used, once the computer spits out a list of possible "buys," the manager either winnows down the list using still more selection criteria or buys everything the computer recommends. In practice, few quant managers surrender all discretion to their silicon-powered colleagues.

So there you have it—fund management styles in a nutshell. No matter how many funds you encounter in your travels, the various management approaches you will find are sure to be some variation on the themes we've just explored. But understanding a fund's management style is only the first step on the road to choosing the right investment. Chapter 13 will show you what's next.

THIRTEEN

Finding the Right Funds for You

One you've mastered the art of reading a prospectus and understand how to compare funds on the basis of sales fees, expense ratios, and management styles, then you're ready to approach assembling your $10,000 portfolio. But selecting a group of funds that will keep you on track no matter how bumpy the market ride gets isn't as easy as buying and holding forever. First, you need to make sure that your investment vehicle is in working order; then you can map out a course that puts your investing know-how to the real-world test.

Be sure to ask yourself the following questions when taking stock of a potential mutual fund investment.

[ ]   What is the fund's objective? (Growth? Income? Some combination thereof? Does it match your objectives?)

[ ]   What is the minimum investment? (And can you meet it?) What loads and other fees are charged? (All else being equal, the lower the better.)

[ ]   How is the fund managed? (Does it differ radically from its stated objective, and how unusual are its investments relative to its peers?)

[ ]   How well has the fund performed to its peers and a comparable index? (While past performance, as they say, is no guarantee of future success, a fund with a long record of above-average performance must have been doing something right, and must generally be considered more promising than a fund with a long record of poor performance.)

[ ] How long has the fund been in existence? (If it's a new fund, then there is necessarily little record to go on. However, the fund manager, the fund group, or both may have a relevant performance record.)

[ ] Who is the fund manager, and how long has he or she been at the helm? (If the manager is a newcomer, then the fund's previous performance record is less significant, and you'd want to know whether the new manager ran a fund prior to this one, and how that fund did.)

[ ] How can you purchase and redeem shares? (In writing? By phone? On the net?) Is the fund convenient? Do you have enough money to get in? Does it offer the features you consider necessary?

FUND ANALYSIS

Stock funds can be parsed by their investment style (value versus growth); by their industry concentrations; and by their capitalization, the size of the companies the fund invests in—large-cap (over about $3 billion), mid-cap (between $3 and $1 billion), small-cap (under $1 billion), or micro-cap (under $500 million). Knowing each of these parts helps you picture the fund as a whole, as well as how one fund is likely to correlate with another. Remember, you don't get added diversification when you buy two funds that invest in the same things!

1: Investment Style. We have already talked about the main differences in management styles (see Chapter 9). Investment style is also a key ingredient in your overall success. Investment style can be divided into two camps: growth or value. (OK, three camps: growth, value, and blenders.) Value-style managers focus on stocks that are currently selling at low prices relative to their book value and/or earnings (price to book and price/earnings ratio). Value-style funds typically invest in mature, slower-growing stocks, like industrial equipment manufacturers and financial service companies. Growth-style managers, on the other hand, seek out rapidly growing businesses—even if the company's stock price is higher than the general market. That's why you'll find technology, health care, telecommunications, and other rapidly growing industries in growth-style funds.

Value-style funds typically tend to outperform growth funds in periods when the economy is recovering from a low point. (Economically sensitive stocks, like capital goods manufacturers, benefit as other companies expand capacity.) In a maturing economic recovery, growth funds tend to gain ground. Companies in these funds aren't hurt as much by an economic slowdown as are companies found in value funds.

The following chart shows you how the two camps have fared over the years.

Growth/Value

The S&P 500 Value Index has handily beaten the S&P 500 Growth Index over the long term. (For 1975 through May of 1999 S&P Value gained 5,173 percent while S&P Growth gained 3,791 percent.) However, 12-month relative returns have not always favored Value stocks, particularly for 1998.

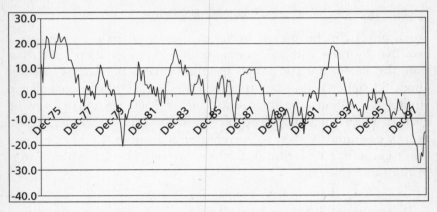

This graph shows 12-month returns for value minus 12-month returns for growth. Positive number means value led. Negative number means that growth led.

2: Industry Concentration. Investment style often determines the types of stocks a manager is most likely to own, as well as the fund's industry concentrations. (See Chapter 6 for my market industry breakdown.)

3: Capitalization. Many investors mistakenly think that value-style funds are inherently less risky than growth-style funds. You'll have to dig deeper to get at the real risk-related difference between these two investment styles—since a fund's average market capitalization often reveals more about its inherent volatility than its investment style reveals. In fact, if you took two value funds with similar industry concentrations, you might be surprised to find a wide divergence in terms of their volatility. One way to explain this is to look at each fund's holdings. Is one large-cap-oriented (focused on steady, reliable, liquid performers) while the other focuses on more volatile small-cap issues? Chances are the answer is yes. Similar investment style and industry weightings don't necessarily mean similar volatility.

4: Correlation. Your ability to put together a diversified portfolio depends on your ability to discern when funds that may seem to have different objectives have in fact had a similar performance history. Having $2,500 invested in each of two funds that are too much alike gives you little more diversification than putting the entire $5,000 in one fund. All you get is twice as much paperwork at tax time. The "correlation matrix" (on page 98) plots performance similarities, or the correlation, among a representative group of funds. (The table compares monthly total returns over the past 3 years.) If you find that you own two growth funds with a high correlation, chances are your portfolio's growth portion isn't as diversified as it could or should be. On the other hand, if you own two growth funds with a very low correlation, you've achieved added diversification.

INVESTING IN FUNDS

Once you're clear on what you want your mutual fund investments to accomplish, take the following steps.

Step 1: Determine How Much You Can Invest. Once you've determined what your investment objectives are, you'll need to figure out how much of your hard-earned money you can invest and are willing to invest.

Step 2: Figure the Percentages. Once you know why you're investing and how much money you can invest, you'll need to figure out how to divvy up your money among different types of funds. Why different types of funds? Because they will enable you to fit your investments to your goals and take advantage of the benefits

Correlation

	S&P 500	Russell 2000	Blue Chip Growth	Capital Appreciation	Contrafund	Destiny I	Destiny II	Disciplined Equity	Dividend Growth	Emerging Growth	Export & Multinational	Fifty
S&P 500	100	64	96	83	81	96	93	94	91	73	58	91
Russell 2000	64	100	63	81	72	60	58	73	74	75	76	76
Blue Chip Growth	96	63	100	85	87	94	94	92	89	80	62	89
Capital Appreciation	83	81	85	100	90	81	83	90	84	83	69	92
Contrafund	81	72	87	90	100	78	84	90	82	86	70	88
Destiny I	96	60	94	81	78	100	96	90	86	70	56	87
Destiny II	93	58	94	83	84	96	100	89	83	73	57	90
Disciplined Equity	94	73	92	90	90	90	89	100	90	80	65	93
Dividend Growth	91	74	89	84	82	86	83	90	100	79	70	88
Emerging Growth	73	75	80	83	86	70	73	80	79	100	80	79
Export & Multinational	58	76	62	69	70	56	57	65	70	80	100	65
Fifty	91	76	89	92	88	87	90	93	88	79	65	100
Growth Company	90	73	94	89	88	87	88	90	91	93	74	88
Large-Cap Stock	94	69	97	89	90	91	92	92	89	88	67	90
Low-Priced Stock	67	92	61	79	69	63	62	75	75	62	68	79
Magellan	94	68	96	89	92	91	93	95	88	79	62	93
Mid-Cap Stock	82	86	82	92	83	79	80	87	85	85	77	90
New Millennium	73	81	76	84	84	70	70	81	79	89	74	84
OTC Portfolio	74	76	81	84	85	72	74	79	84	92	80	79
Retirement Growth	89	71	92	87	85	85	85	88	91	86	68	87
Small-Cap Selector	60	93	59	77	71	56	57	72	72	70	78	74
Spartan Market Index	100	64	96	83	81	96	93	94	91	74	58	91
Stock Selector	92	76	90	90	91	87	88	98	89	80	69	94
Trend	74	87	76	91	84	71	73	82	78	81	75	87
Value	76	75	67	76	63	70	66	77	75	54	50	81

of diversification. Figuring out what percentages to place in which types of funds is asset allocation plain and simple.

Step 3: Select Your Funds. Select the funds you think will be best on the basis of prospectus, objective, and performance record as well as your own means, objectives, and goals.

Step 4: Know What Fees You Have to Pay. In fundsville, you don't necessarily get what you pay for—cost does not equal quality. Indeed, the highest-fee funds consistently turn up in the bottom of

Table

Growth Company	Large-Cap Stock	Low-Priced Stock	Magellan	Mid-Cap Stock	New Millennium	OTC Portfolio	Retirement Growth	Small-Cap Selector	Spartan Market Index	Stock Selector	Trend	Value	
90	94	67	94	82	73	74	89	60	100	92	74	76	S&P 500
73	69	92	68	86	81	76	71	93	64	76	87	75	Russell 2000
94	97	61	96	82	76	81	92	59	96	90	76	67	Blue Chip Growth
89	89	79	89	92	84	84	87	77	83	90	91	76	Capital Appreciation
88	90	69	92	83	84	85	85	71	81	91	84	63	Contrafund
87	91	63	91	79	70	72	85	56	96	87	71	70	Destiny I
88	92	62	93	80	70	74	85	57	93	88	73	66	Destiny II
90	92	75	95	87	81	79	88	72	94	98	82	77	Disciplined Equity
91	89	75	88	85	79	84	91	72	91	89	78	75	Dividend Growth
93	88	62	79	85	89	92	86	70	74	80	81	54	Emerging Growth
74	67	68	62	77	74	80	68	78	58	69	75	50	Export & Multinational
88	90	79	93	90	84	79	87	74	91	94	87	81	Fifty
100	97	67	91	88	86	92	95	68	90	89	83	66	Growth Company
97	100	66	95	87	82	86	92	63	94	90	82	67	Large-Cap Stock
67	66	100	69	82	72	66	68	91	66	79	87	84	Low-Priced Stock
91	95	69	100	85	80	81	91	65	94	93	81	74	Magellan
88	87	82	85	100	86	82	85	84	82	88	89	79	Mid-Cap Stock
86	82	72	80	86	100	87	81	75	73	82	83	67	New Millennium
92	86	66	81	82	87	100	90	71	74	79	82	57	OTC Portfolio
95	92	68	91	85	81	90	100	69	89	88	82	71	Retirement Growth
68	63	91	65	84	75	71	69	100	60	77	83	71	Small-Cap Selector
90	94	66	94	82	73	74	89	60	100	92	74	76	Spartan Market Index
89	90	79	93	88	82	79	88	77	92	100	86	77	Stock Selector
83	82	87	81	89	83	82	82	83	74	86	100	75	Trend
66	67	84	74	79	67	57	71	71	76	77	75	100	Value

performance rankings. Even though the few percentage points that fees shave off your investment dollar may be negligible, they really do make a difference.

Step 5: Consider a Fund Network. If you want the simplicity of one statement and one phone number but don't want to limit yourself to one fund family, consider fund networks, such as those at Charles Schwab, Fidelity, and Jack White. Each has hundreds of funds available without any transaction fees, and many hundreds more with modest fees.

Step 6: Open the Account. Open your account either by investing directly or through the fund company or by opening a brokerage account.

Step 7: Keep Accurate Records of How Much You've Invested, and Where. Establish some sort of straightforward record-keeping system for your investments, and file those statements as soon as they come in. (Don't stuff them in the kitchen drawer!)

Step 8: Keep Tabs on Your Funds' Performance. Think website. The next quickest way: a newspaper. Next: call your fund's 800 number and ask. But remember, the market is fickle. That's why keeping track of your funds' performance is a necessary, ongoing process. You may not buy this, but it's kind of fun looking at the financial pages in your newspaper and seeing how your funds are doing. It's even more fun to click into the web to keep track of the news that relates to the funds you own. Of course, if they aren't doing well the fun goes out of the picture pretty damn fast. But don't let a bad day or two cloud your judgment. For that matter, don't let a few lousy months or even a year do so. If you've selected a good fund and still believe in its basic ability to succeed over the long term, then stick with it. Making a move based on short-term market fluctuations will only increase the likelihood of an overall poor return on your investment.

Step 9: Keep Adding to Your Investment Portfolio. Plan on investing regularly. Plan, too, on increasing the amount you invest as you get older and your disposable income increases. (Chapter 27 details several ways to build an actual portfolio of mutual funds to suit your age, life style and objectives; and don't overlook Chapter 3, which details ways you can increase your savings and find more money to invest.)

PART IV

INVESTING SMARTS

FOURTEEN

Buying Your Funds

You've got the fund basics down. Now you need to know the mechanics of buying (i.e., investing) in them. Not surprisingly, buying mutual funds is easy. After all, it's in the fund company's best interest to ensure that your money can flow into its coffers as quickly and seamlessly as possible.

THE MECHANICS OF INVESTING IN A FUND

There are smart ways to regularly add to and protect your $10,000 portfolio. Here they are.

Automatic Investing. Automatic investing is a great way to begin investing and to stick with your $10,000 portfolio plan. (It's a way around most fund companies' minimum investment requirements.) You can have a set amount deducted from your bank savings, checking account, or money market fund and placed in an investment account with a mutual fund company or brokerage. The logistics of setting up an automatic investing account are easy. All you need is to request an automatic investment account from your brokerage or fund company. The rest is as easy as spelling your name.

Dollar-Cost Averaging. The prime directive of successful investing is to buy low and sell high. The aim of dollar-cost averaging is to do just that by investing a fixed sum of money at scheduled intervals. In this manner, you are automatically buying more shares when prices are low and fewer when prices are high. But don't look to dollar-cost averaging to guarantee a dramatic increase in the performance of your investments. Instead, look at it as the tortoise's strategy for winning the race.

Here's how dollar-cost averaging works:

Period	Amount Invested	Price	Number of Shares Purchased
1st	$260	$9	28.88
2nd	260	8	32.50
3rd	260	6	43.33
4th	260	8	32.50
5th	260	10	26.00
	$1,300		163.21

Total amount invested over 5 periods: $1,300
Number of shares purchased: 163.21
Average market price: $8.20
Average cost: $7.96

Like automatic investing, dollar-cost averaging is also a great way to discipline yourself to invest on a regular, scheduled basis. And the effect of both is basically the same. However, dollar-cost averaging is an investment method, whereas automatic investing is a method of withdrawal and deposit. The discipline of dollar-cost averaging helps you keep your cash flowing into investments, which, in turn, stand an excellent chance of providing you with a brighter financial future. There's no way to predict when to buy low, but dollar-cost averaging gives you your best overall shot at doing so. How? As the example above illustrates, investing on a regular basis can average out in your favor. Of course, if the stock is a dog that won't get up—or worse, one that keeps going down—then dollar-cost averaging won't help you.

Lump-Sum Investing. Is it better to invest your money in a lump sum or, given the market's recent heights, to invest that sum gradually in regular increments? The answer is that, historically, investing a lump sum right away is your best move—but this answer isn't always easy to swallow, because it naturally makes many investors nervous.

If you receive money in a substantial lump sum (e.g., you get an inheritance, or you were injured in an accident and your lawyer has made good on his ambulance-chasing TV promo), or you've been hoarding money in a savings account and are now ready to invest it, then you'll need an investment strategy to help you cope with short-term market uncertainty. You're in luck. There are two ways to proceed: invest it all at once or invest in increments over a short time frame.

The most aggressive form of investing your lump sum would be to **invest it all at once,** 100 percent in the market if your objective is growth. In fact, this is generally the best way to invest because it puts your money to work immediately—but psychologically it is also a difficult way for many investors to act.

Why? Let's say you inherited $10,000 from your grandmother and put it all in the stock market, only to watch the market immediately slip from the high point at which you invested. Watching your inheritance diminish isn't exactly what you had in mind when you invested the money—and many investors, especially those who are relatively inexperienced with the markets, panic and sell after a few down months. But, historically, this has been the wrong move to make. Investing a lump sum even at a market high puts you ahead of those who invested at the high and then sold out lower. The key is to stay invested.

If you think your tolerance for risk might be less than meets the eye, don't worry. **Investing your lump sum in scheduled increments** will still deliver the goods (and may even let you sleep better at night). The following incremental investing strategy is designed for the more cautious investor but nonetheless should help you remain steadfast to your goal of investing no matter what the short-term market moves. It suits your age and ability to reap the rewards from taking some additional risk in terms of potentially retreating from your entrance into the market.

Incremental investing is, in essence, a form of dollar-cost averaging (see page 103 for details). The following timetable should help you get into the market in a relatively painless way. As the timetable indicates, you go from 100 percent cash (invested in a money market mutual fund) to being fully (100 percent) invested. Within the first 12 months of this investment program, your stock exposure is increased from 0 percent to 100 percent.

Investment	*Within Next Period from 0% to Fully Invested*				
Category	*Now*	*3 Months*	*6 Months*	*9 Months*	*12 Months*
Stocks	0%	25%	50%	75%	100%
Cash	100	75	50	25	0
Total	100%	100%	100%	100%	100%

Value Averaging. This is another "automatic" investment method. The principal idea is to keep the value of your investment growing by a constant dollar amount. Rather than a set amount each month, you put in just enough to keep your investment on target. If the value of your shares goes up during the month, you put in less (or even take some out). If it goes down, you put in more.

However, even though your percentage return may be greater with value averaging than with dollar-cost averaging, total profits may be lower, because you invest fewer dollars. In short, since you put less money in as the share prices go up, you inhibit yourself from taking full advantage of a bull market. To be able to remain true to this method, you'll need cash in reserve for the months when your portfolio goes down. Since this reserve money won't be in the market, you'll need to include what happens to the backup money in order to calculate a meaningful total return.

Value averaging can outperform dollar-cost averaging in times of great market volatility when stock prices are bouncing around incoherently. When the market has a clear up or down trend, however, you're better off putting fixed amounts in at regular intervals.

THE MECHANICS OF BUYING A FUND

When it comes to buying mutual funds, you can simply click into or dial up the fund company and request an account application and the prospectuses for the funds you want (see Chapter 10 for my crib notes on how to read a fund prospectus). There are two great ways to purchase mutual funds, beyond those funds in your retirement plan: direct from the fund company or through a fund network. (There's also one lousy way—through a broker who will charge you for the privilege. Forget about it!) Let's look at the mechanics of buying shares in a fund.

Buying Direct. One option is to buy directly from a fund company. Once you have figured out the type of funds that are best for your portfolio, as well as the specific funds that interest you most, all you need do is contact the fund company by phone and request the prospectuses and applications of the funds that match your needs and interests. Appendix B will certainly speed up this process, but you can always dial up 800-555-1212 and ask for the fund company's toll-free number if one isn't listed in the back of this book.

You can also ask the investor representative to send you several fund prospectuses that relate to your investment interest and objectives. In addition, you can ask if the fund company has any pamphlets or brochures that explain mutual fund investing. Many companies do—and many of these brochures are well written and objective when it comes to discussing mechanics. You need to be sure, however, that such pamphlets aren't your only source of information about investing. (To become a fund maven, check out Part II.)

If you have web access, you'll find that just about every fund family has a website hot-wired to fulfill requests for prospectuses, annual reports, and investment guides. You'll simply need to fill in an electronic form or two; then let the fund company and the post office (or E-mail) do the rest.

As you fill out your application form, check to see whether the fund company gives you the option of establishing an automatic investment program. Such an arrangement enables your bank to wire a set amount of money from your account to the fund company for the purpose of buying additional fund shares (see page 103 above). Once your automatic investment program is up and running, you'll be magically transformed into a regular saver without having to do so much as sign a check.

Buying Through a Fund Network. It's easier to buy funds from several fund families today than it was just a few years ago, owing to the introduction of fund networks. Fund networks are basically supermarkets of funds, offering hundreds of funds from most fund families. While there are several fund networks that you can choose from, the three front-runners remain the three first-comers to this arena: Fidelity's FundsNetwork, Charles Schwab's Mutual Fund Marketplace and OneSource, and Jack White's Mutual Fund Network. While opening up a fund network account is a great idea for most fund investors—in particular for you, since the initial investment can be as low as $500 for an IRA account or $1,000 for a taxable account—there are differences between networks that you will need to know about in order to help you make the best selection for your specific needs and objectives.

Fund networks offer a menu from different fund families. This enables you to tailor-make your overall portfolio. Take a look at just some of the following fund families currently participating in the Fidelity, Schwab, or Jack White networks:

Ariel	Fidelity	Rainer
Artisan	Founders	Robertson Stephens
Babson	Gabelli	Royce
Baron	Guiness Flight	Rushmore
Benham	Heartland	Schafer
Berger	Hotchkis & Wiley	Skyline
Blanchard	IAI	SteinRoe
Bramwell	Janus	Strong
Bull & Bear	Kaufmann	United Services
Cappiello-Rushmore	Lexington	Vontobel
Cohen & Steers	Merger	Warburg Pincus
Crabbe Huson	Montgomery	Wasatch
Dreman	Neuberger & Berman	Wright Equifunds
Dreyfus	Oberweis	Yacktman
FAM	PBHG	

For a complete list of the specific mutual funds available through any of these networks, call the networks directly or visit them on-line for more details. As always, don't invest in a fund without reading the prospectus and comparing its cost and performance with the other funds in its peer group. And be sure to consider carefully whether or not it will be a good fit for your portfolio.

MORE ABOUT FUND NETWORKS

All for One? Is it advisable to invest in funds from different families? As with investing too much of your money in one fund, or in funds that are highly correlated, putting all your money in funds belonging to one family may not give your portfolio sufficient diversity. Though many fund companies will deny it, and though individual managers strive to maintain their independence, group-think can be a problem with funds under one roof. On the other hand, buying all your funds from one company does make life simpler when it comes to keeping track of your investments.

When it comes down to it, only two fund families are large and diverse enough to answer all the needs of the typical small investor: Fidelity and Vanguard. Except for these two behemoths, the fact is that many fund families striving to be full-service shops do not have the depth of expertise to offer top-notch products in all of the main categories. Some companies are strongest in equities, some have made a niche for themselves with bonds, and some have a better record abroad than at home. Participating in a fund network will enable you to select funds from families that have delivered superior results in the past, as well as enjoy access to lesser-known and newer funds.

NTF Funds. With the advent of the networks came a new fee category—the **no transaction fee (NTF) fund.** Basically, an NTF fund has no up-front transaction fee associated with your purchase. Funds charging loads are not NTF funds, although some load funds may waive their loads for fund networks.

This network snapshot will help you to picture how the networks compare with one another. While funds, fees, and minimums are subject to change, the following will also help you create your own network checklist before you sign up.

BROKERAGE ACCOUNTS

You don't need a brokerage account to invest. For example, you can invest in mutual funds by contacting the fund company directly. But if you're going to participate in two of the best innovations in the mutual fund industry in the last decade—tax-advantage retirement plans and mutual fund networks (more about this below)—you'll be better off with a brokerage account.

Types of Brokerages. There are three types of brokerages—**full-service, discount,** and **deep discount.** As with a gas station, it's in

A Supermarket Shopper's Guide

MUTUAL FUND supermarkets are listed alphabetically below. The guide includes information in a Yes or No format about whether the firm provides the cost basis of fund shares that you sold, whether its web site contains a database of mutual funds and whether the site contains tools to screen funds by criteria.

	Web Address (www. . .com)	Information Phone number (800)	Cost Basis of Fund shares sold	Fund Data available on-line	Fund Screening available on-line
Accutrade	accutrade	882-4887	N	Y	Y
American Century Brokerage FundChoice	americancentury	345-2071†	Y	N	N
Bidwell & Co. FundSource	bidwell	547-6337	Y	Y	N
Bull & Bear Securities	bullbear	262-5800	N	N	N
Bush Burns Securities	bushburns	821-4800	Y	Y	Y
Discover Brokerage Mutual Funds Center	discoverbrokerage	347-2683	N	Y	Y
DLJdirect	dljdirect	825-5723	Y	Y	Y
Dreyfus Lion Account	dreyfus	843-5466	N	Y	Y
E*Trade Mutual Fund Center	etrade	786-2575	Y	Y	Y
Fidelity FundsNetwork	fidelity	544-8666	Y	Y	Y
Freeman Welwood Fund Choice	freemanwelwood	729-7585	Y	Y	Y
Muriel Siebert & Co. FundExchange	siebertnet	872-0666	Y	Y	Y
National Discount Brokers Fund Vest	ndb	888-3999	Y	Y	Y
T. Rowe Price Asset Manager Account	troweprice	222-7002	Y	Y	Y
Quick & Reilly	quick-reilly	262-2688	Y	Y	Y
Charles Schwab Mutual Fund Marketplace	schwab	435-4000	Y	Y	N
Scudder Preferred Investment Plus	scudder	988-8316	Y	Y	N
Strong Prime Managers	strong-funds	368-1550	Y	Y	Y
Vanguard Brokerage Fund Access	vanguard	992-8327	*	Y	N
Waterhouse Fund Family Network	waterhouse	934-4410	N	Y	N
Jack White Mutual Fund Network	jackwhiteco	233-3411	N	Y	N
York Securities	yorktrade	221-3154	N	N	N

*Cost basis provided only for funds in the Vanguard family. †Area code 888 your favor to avoid full-service brokers, which cost you more money in fees and commissions every time you buy or sell (or even hold) a stock, bond, or mutual fund. You may like to pay more for the luxury of having someone fill your tank—but you get the same amount of gas in your tank for less money if you opt for self-service.

Discount brokers offer you an opportunity to service your account yourself, while at the same time providing you with many of the services that full-service brokers offer—from research to monthly account statements. Not only does opting for a discount broker make sense; it also gives you a more direct involvement with your money and your fund investments.

QUICK TIP

Brokerage fees. Large or small, brokerage firms all charge you a fee for just about any service they perform for you. That's why you need to know the fees you will be charged for every service that your brokerage (or mutual fund company) offers—and periodically review those fees, comparing them with what you were charged last year by your present firm and with what other firms are charging now for similar services. That's the only way you can rest assured that your firm's fees aren't outlandishly high.

Discount brokers are user-friendly, convenient, and reliable. But not all discount brokers are created equal. In fact, the difference between some discount brokers (in particular, between discount and deep-discount brokers) can be as significant as the difference between discount and full-service brokers. In fact, where a discount brokerage firm can save you in excess of 50 percent on commissions (the fees charged to your account for buying or selling), a deep discounter can save you as much as 90 percent on the same transaction, but there will be no service perks. And today, trading your account on-line can save you an additional 10 percent or more off regular full-service and discount brokerage commissions.

Best Discount Brokerages. The following brokerages are among the leading discounters for fund investors and offer you the convenience and cost advantage of on-line trading. Four of the largest discount brokerages, together with their toll-free numbers, are: Fidelity Broker Services, (800) 544-7272; Quick & Reilly, (800) 522-8712; T. Rowe Price Discount Brokerage, (800) 638-5660; Charles Schwab, (800) 648-5300; Jack White & Co., (800) 323-3263.

Comparing Costs. Firms, services, and charges for everything from placing a phone call to placing an order differ widely from one full-service broker to the next—and from one discounter to the next. As a result, you'll need to create your own comparison, using the following checklist as your guide:

[ ] How long has the firm been in existence?
[ ] Can you trade electronically?
[ ] Does it have an office in your area?
[ ] How many offices does it have?
[ ] What is the minimum commission charged?
[ ] Is there a dividend reinvestment plan you can participate in?
[ ] Does it offer IRA accounts?
[ ] What is the fee for opening, holding, and closing an IRA account?
[ ] Can you buy no-load, no-transaction-fee funds?

Opening Your Brokerage Account. Opening a brokerage account is mechanically as easy as opening a checking account at your local bank. (For that matter, many banks offer you the option of buying stocks, bonds, and even mutual funds—for a fee. But chances are the performance record of your bank's mutual funds isn't nearly as great as their marketing is designed to have you believe.)

As with a bank account, your brokerage account can be either a single account, in which only you are authorized to buy and sell investments, or a joint account, in which you and your significant other (or a family member or friend) both have authorization to make trades. Aside from the issue of whose name should be on the account, there are three other options to consider—whether you should open a cash account, a margin account, or a discretionary account:

1. **Cash accounts.** My recommendation—the best way to cover your investment bets is by paying for them up-front. This doesn't mean you have to show up at the investor center with

a suitcase full of twenties every time you want to buy stock. It simply means that you should have sufficient funds in your brokerage account to cover each trade as you make it. When you open a brokerage account, you can set up an associated money market account to hold your cash, or you can arrange to have funds transferred electronically from your bank account to your brokerage account as needed.

2. **Margin accounts.** In contrast to a cash account, a margin account enables you to buy shares in funds "on margin." Buying on margin is similar to taking out a loan to place a bet. Sound stupid? Well, some hotshots think they've got a sure thing— and they margin by as much as 50 percent of their brokerage account balance to place their bet. Don't do it. With a loan, you're charged interest on the margined amount (typically based on the prime rate plus 2 percent or more). What happens if the bet fails to materialize? The house wins, and it cashes in your remaining chips.

3. **Discretionary accounts.** What could be worse than you risking up to a 100 percent loss of your savings by investing on margin? Letting someone else do it for you! A discretionary account allows your broker to invest your money at his or her discretion without getting your authority for each trade. Wrong! Unless you have decided to hire a reputable money management firm, don't even consider this option.

Besides the question of what type of account best suits your needs, there are other questions requiring your attention. Will you be making annual lump-sum payments, monthly payments, or weekly payments into your account? How will your funds be allocated, when will they be disbursed, and at whose command?

Once you've figured out what type of brokerage and account is best for you, what amount you want to invest, and how you want to invest it, chances are you can do the rest of the work by simply clicking into the fund company's website (if you're buying directly or if the family also has a discount brokerage), or by picking up a phone and requesting the necessary paperwork.

TRACKING YOUR PURCHASES

Tracking your funds' performance is discussed in detail in Chapter 25. But you also need to keep accurate records of the transactions you make. After all, you're in the big leagues now. No one is going to watch out for your money—no one, that is, except you. You will need to keep tabs on your brokerage account much the way you do your bank account and loan statements. You should scrutinize every statement you receive from your broker to ensure the following:

[ ] Confirmation of all transactions (should be received within 24 hours, since you have a maximum of 5 days to settle the trade).
[ ] Authorization of all transactions.
[ ] Shares bought and sold at number and price agreed on.
[ ] No unauthorized trades.
[ ] In any discretionary accounts, no excessive trading (known as "churning," which is, basically, one way a broker can generate more commissions by trading your account often—too often).
[ ] What's in your account is what you expect to be there.

If there's any disagreement on one or more of the above, get a specific explanation from your broker. If you can't get satisfaction, try a higher level in the firm. Still no dice? You may have to contact the NASD (nasd.gov or at 800-289-9999) to get to the bottom of things. I hope not—since that means you'll be in arbitration hell while your friends will be snowboarding at Vail.

THE DECISION IS YOURS

Some fund companies more closely resemble full-service brokerage accounts, with fees to match or best even the most greedy brokerage. Others provide you with ways to get more of your money working for you from day one. Tough call.

FIFTEEN

Actively Managed Funds

Actively managed funds (touched on in Chapter 12) are driven by one shared investment credo: beat the market. Actively managed funds constitute the largest number of funds you can invest in—in fact, they constitute nearly 90 percent of the fund market—and they represent the antithesis of passively managed index funds (see Chapter 16). Trouble is, in the vast universe of actively managed funds, there are only a few star managers. The trick is knowing how to find them.

Among actively managed funds, management is the most important determinant of performance. (With the narrowly drawn sector funds, the managers' performance record is relatively less important than the funds' investment objective.)

With funds appropriately benchmarked, the next step in the analytical process is to show how a manager's record at each of his or her funds compares with the benchmarks. This enables me to graph the manager's relative long-term performance.

Unfortunately for us, however, most sources of advice focus solely on a fund's past performance relative to similar funds and one market index (typically the S&P 500 Index) to deliver a vague sense of its strength or weakness. Others pay lip service to "buying the manager, not the fund," but judge managers only by their fund's cover rather than by the manager's actual history of picking stocks. Both of these approaches are fundamentally misleading, since they focus on a fund's objective as opposed to a manager's actual skill at selecting stocks. They're easy to do, and they take much less time, thought, and due diligence. But it is possible to figure out how your existing (or potential) fund manager has fared relative to the market month in and month out since he or she began managing money, no matter in which fund or funds. And once this is done, not only does it give you an exclusive, comprehensive understanding of every manager you're investing in; it also provides a greater degree of certainty in terms of knowing how successful the manager is likely to be

To begin, it's important to grasp whether, how much, and how consistently each of our fund managers has beaten relevant market indices—and with how much risk. If you're considering a fund that's had the same manager for 5 to 10 years, it's usually a relatively simple matter of gauging the fund's (and thus the manager's) performance against competing funds with similar holdings and risk. But what if the manager has jumped around from fund to fund, as many managers do? How do you measure his or her performance? It's not as simple as it seems. But it's also not too tough.

YOU CAN RANK YOUR MANAGERS

For each fund manager, look at the performances of all his or her funds for the past 10 years, or since the start of his or her career. (If this sounds overwhelming, click into managerranking.com and they'll do it for you.) For each fund, obtain a close index equivalent (see Chapter 5 for help). A manager's record relative to close benchmarks is a more useful performance measure than simple returns, or even returns relative to "the market" (usually the S&P 500 Index), or returns relative to other mutual funds. Of course, one way a manager can beat (or lag behind) a particular benchmark is to make a bet outside of that index. If such bets pay off (or fail) then the manager deserves credit (or blame) for the resulting performance. Similarly, if a manager's individual stock picks beat (or lag behind) the benchmark average, he or she also deserves the credit (or blame) for that. But I don't want managers to get undue credit for a "good" performance if they're merely tracking a benchmark, or to be blamed for a "bad" performance if it's really the benchmark, and not the stock, which has been lagging. While a big "macro" bet—like loading up on a particular industry, asset class, or country—may explain much of a manager's outperformance or underperformance, it's also not as likely to be as indicative of future performance as is a record at picking large numbers of individual stocks. That's because a small number of big bets can help you or go against you almost as a matter of luck, whereas a record of doing well with hundreds of individual stock holdings strongly implies that you're good at picking individual stocks.

When analyzing a manager's performance, don't stop with just these raw measures. Look also at what sorts of risks the manager took, and why he or she beat or lagged behind the indices. Were the manager's funds more volatile than the market? Was the manager held back by large cash inflows? Was a lag due to a substantial "off-index" bet, and if so was that an appropriate action?

THE BEST MANAGERS

The best find is a manager who has beaten his or her benchmark without making large "macro" bets, especially bets outside the benchmark; whose outperformance has been relatively consistent; and whose funds have not shown significantly more volatility than their benchmarks.

As if "style" weren't fully covered in *Cosmo* and *GQ*, now investment magazines talk about it too. But what does the term mean? If a fund manager is guilty of "style drift," was he caught wearing a bell-bottomed leisure suit? And is a "style box" the source for advice on how to dress for success?

No. In the context of stock funds, "style" refers to the kind of companies the manager specializes in. There are many ways to categorize domestic stocks: most notably by sector, by market capitalization, and by valuations. While sectors are generally clearly divided, market cap is a continuum on which the market must be divided up rather arbitrarily into small- and large-cap groupings (or small-, mid-, and large-cap). Likewise, stocks may be measured and divided into two or three categories on a continuum of valuation measures. Where a fund sits on these two dimensions (market cap and valuation) defines its style.

MARKET CAP

You'll hear this term more often than your own name. A stock's total market capitalization is the total value of all its outstanding shares of stock—that is, the total number of shares multiplied by the share prices. A company's total number of shares doesn't change all that often. (A stock first goes public with an initial public offering, or IPO, and it can increase outstanding shares with a secondary offering or stock split, or decrease them with a share buyback.) But share price, and hence market cap, changes every day. Basically, a company's market cap is what the stock market says the company's worth.

Mid-caps are generally defined as those stocks with a total market cap between $1 billion and $5 billion. Naturally, then, small-caps are under $1 billion, and large-caps are over $5 billion. Of course, a definition like this would have to be adjusted over time to take into account inflation, stock market gains, and/or a growing economy. (In 1950 a $1 billion company was decidedly large-cap.)

Note that while some mid-cap funds define their investment universe as including any stocks within the capitalization range of the S&P 400, that actually gives them a lot of leeway to hold small- and large-cap stocks. The market-cap ranges of the major S&P indexes actually overlap quite a bit, in part because these indexes aren't rebalanced every time a stock goes up or down, and thus the S&P 400 mid-cap index is never exactly the five-hundredth to nine-hundredth largest U.S. stocks, although that's a useful approximation of the truth.

When looking at a fund's holdings, we aren't typically concerned with exactly how much is in every little stock, or every possible narrow market-cap range. What we do want to know is: Are the stocks in the fund primarily small-caps, mid-caps, or large-caps?

VALUATIONS

Although they're perhaps even more important than market-cap, stock market valuation terms are much less widely understood, so some definitions are in order. A **value stock** is stock in a company that is relatively cheap compared with its earnings or "book value" (mostly tangible assets). Value stocks tend to be stodgier players in slower-growing, defensive, or cyclical areas. In contrast, a **growth stock** is stock in a company that is relatively expensive compared with its current earnings or assets. (Note that the definition of "growth" in "growth stock" is narrower than the one typically meant when we refer to a "growth fund." For more on this, see Chapter 12's definitions of types of stock funds.)

Why would investors buy a fund that holds expensive growth

stock, or bid it up to such expensive levels? Because they expect the company to grow. To repeat, growth stocks tend to have a high price relative to current earnings, and to provide little if any dividend, because investors expect them to show above-average growth in earnings, or sales, or both. This belief is usually founded on a history of growing earnings or sales, or on the company's being in a promising, high-growth sector. In 1998, Internet stocks were the most extreme example of this type. Growth stocks also tend to have a high beta (or market risk), but they can offer long-term investors the potential for solid capital appreciation.

Note that almost all stock fund managers pay at least lip service to the concept of value. Just about any managers are likely to tell you that they're on the lookout for "bargains," for stocks that are "cheap" or "undervalued." It would be a rare manager indeed who claimed to favor stocks that are selling for more than they're worth, or companies whose value is sure to be headed for a decline. Even some aggressive growth players claim to be seeking "value-growth" or "growth at a reasonable price" (GARP). Likewise, even the most value-oriented fund managers prefer a stock that has at least some potential for growth.

SO WHAT IS VALUE INVESTING?

Value investing is based on the contrarian premise that the stock market is less efficient than people think. To the value investor, Wall Street is populated largely with herd-instinct types too busy running after the latest trend to notice unglamorous companies whose comparatively low share prices don't fairly reflect positives like good current profitability or bright future prospects.

In the long run, value stocks have tended to outperform growth stocks. All an underperforming company has to do is defy people's low expectations, while a growth stock has the more difficult task of meeting the sometimes stratospherically high expectations with which the market has burdened it. On the other hand, the danger with the value-investing approach is that what appears to be gold may indeed be dross. And even if that undervalued company remains a solid moneymaking enterprise, investors who are too thick-skulled to appreciate it today could be just as unperceptive tomorrow.

PRICE/EARNINGS RATIO (P/E)

Value stocks tend to be cheap relative to their earnings. (Trouble is, sometimes they stay cheap—or, worse, get cheaper.) The measure of this is a stock's **price/earnings (P/E) ratio:** its share price divided by its per-share profits. Usually, the profits are from the latest reported year (the past 4 quarters). This "trailing P/E" is found daily in most newspapers' stock tables. But industry analysts often write up a report expressing a stock's share price relative to what they estimate the company's profits will be in the present year, or even the upcoming calendar year. Such a prospective P/E number is always questionable, as it relies on predictions about the future; in contrast, trailing P/E is a pretty solid number. (Taking prospective P/Es to their absurd conclusion, all stocks should sell at about the same P/E if the earnings we're estimating are for a period about 5 years in the future.)

But back to the more reliable and objective trailing P/E. If the market is selling for 30 times trailing earnings, then those stocks with a P/E below 30 may be considered value stocks, and those with a P/E above 30 may be considered growth stocks. Which are the better buy? That depends. If a growth stock can meet or beat its expectations for growth, it can do very well; but if its earnings founder, it will probably do very poorly. By contrast, a value stock is less likely to make big moves up or down. That's because high hopes (which are what make a growth stock a growth stock) are more likely to be dashed than low expectations.

Of course, as any businessperson or accountant knows, earnings are a rather amorphous concept, and the same set of circumstances can often lead to widely varying stated earnings depending on accounting assumptions, depreciation and inventory methods, "special charges" and write-offs, how sales are booked, and how income is credited from contracts requiring a series of payments and/or services rendered over a period of time. While fraud occasionally enters into such discrepancies, there are plenty of legitimate decisions for an accountant to make that affect reported income. Some analysts factor out noncash factors such as depreciation and amortization to arrive at a figure known as "cash flow," which leads naturally to a ratio known as price/cash flow.

PRICE/BOOK VALUE RATIO (P/B)

Another way to evaluate a stock is to consider its **ratio of price to book value (P/B).** A company's book value is simply the total value of all its assets; one divides this by the number of shares outstanding to get per-share book value. An expensive (or growth) stock is one that is selling for a lot relative to its book value, which means that its P/B is above average. A value stock is one that is cheap compared with its book value, meaning that its P/B is below average.

Of course, book value, like earnings, is subject to interpretation. A company may value an asset at what was paid for it a half century ago, even though the asset may now be worth 100 times more. On the other hand, an asset may have depreciated in value far more than the books, and standard depreciation tables, would indicate, and thus be worth much less than its stated value. And finally, in a "knowledge society," a company's most valuable assets may be its employees, working relationships, and contracts, which may add little or nothing to corporate book value. (Microsoft, for example, is worth many times more than its office buildings and inventory.)

The S&P BARRA Growth and Value indexes are split from the S&P 500 using only P/B ratios, not P/Es. (And they split the S&P 500 into equal-sized halves, not thirds like some other sources of valuation categories.) For more information on these indices, see Chapter 7.

STYLE DRIFT

Style drift is a term applied to fund managers who invest in things they shouldn't invest in, that you wouldn't expect them to invest in, or at least that they never used to invest in. Suppose you buy a fund with "growth" in its name, only to learn that it's really a value fund. That revelation would hurt in 1998s growth-dominated market. Or say you buy a fund with "emerging" in its name, thinking it's going to invest in small- or mid-cap stocks; you may be annoyed if the fund suddenly switches into large-caps. Of course, in 1998 a switch to large-caps would provide a great boost to performance, and you might be happy anyway. But if you already have enough large-cap funds and you want to hold small-caps, you're more likely, under most market conditions, to be annoyed than pleased.

How to avoid this problem? The industry-standard "style box," supplied by Morningstar, Inc., tells you what a fund is actually holding, not what its prospectus or marketing material might lead you to think it's holding. In other words, you'll find out about any style drift.

Morningstar's style box (available free on its website) looks like the kind of grid on which you'd play a game of ticktacktoe, except that one of the nine squares is filled in with black ink. The filled-in square represents where the fund in question belongs. If it's in the top row, it's a large-cap fund; the middle row means it's a mid-cap fund; the bottom is for small-cap funds. The left-hand column is reserved for value funds, the middle column for funds with an average or 'blend" valuation, and the right-hand side for growth funds.

Note that by definition, a third of the stock market is composed of value stocks, a third is blend, and a third is growth. (Morningstar looks at both P/Es and P/Bs when calculating a fund's valuation style.) Market-cap, on the other hand, is inherently skewed, with about 80 percent of the U.S. stock market in large-cap stocks, even though less than 10 percent of the country's stocks are large-caps.

QUICK TIP

While the Morningstar style box is a useful tool, it does have limitations. First, it depends on the most recent reported fund holdings, which may be from the fund's last semiannual report, which could be up to 8 months old. (Fund groups can report holdings more often if they choose, but not all do.) Second, the style box rating describes the median holding (half the fund is in larger stocks than the median, half is in smaller stocks). If Morningstar reports a fund as a mid-cap, does that mean it holds only mid-caps, or that it also holds a lot of small-caps and large-caps, which balance out? Third, there are only three gradations for each dimension. That mid-cap fund could be leaning toward small-caps, or toward large-caps, and you wouldn't know it. And finally, funds experience "style drift," meaning that they change their holdings from one category to another without warning, and often in a way you wouldn't expect from the fund's name or objective.

Hence most stock funds are large-cap funds, even Wilshire 5000 Index funds, which have market weightings of all stocks, large-, mid-, and small-cap.

ARE THERE ANY VALUE STOCKS LEFT?

For most of stock market history before the huge bull market of the 1980s and 1990s, it was actually possible to buy many solid companies for less than their assets were worth. This was what Benjamin Graham generally advocated in his classic books on stock-picking, *Security Analysis* and *The Intelligent Investor.*

But at the start of 1999, the S&P 500 Index is selling for about 30 times trailing earnings and 6 times book value. And since virtually all stocks have P/Es above 13 (the historical postwar average P/E for the S&P 500) and P/Bs above 2, nowadays it is close to impossible to find a viable publicly traded corporation selling for less than its book value.

So by the measures that have worked for much of the past century, there are no value stocks. Can value investors buy stocks in such a climate, or should they stick to safer bonds and cash? The answer is clear: since a strict unchanging "value" orientation would have had you out of the market for most of the 1980s and all of the 1990s, languishing in bonds and cash while the stock market boomed, it's clear that you must approach value investing more flexibly. It's reasonable for a value investor to consider that up to half of the stock market will qualify as "value" at any given time. Perhaps, because of a lofty market or some other factor, long-term growth investors may want to lighten their stock market exposure somewhat, or move from growth stocks to value stocks; but moving entirely out of stocks is rarely appropriate for such an investor.

Selling all your stock funds isn't the answer because few if any people have shown an ability to benefit from such market-timing moves. For long-term growth, positions in stock funds will continue to be key. That said, growth sectors are more vulnerable to market corrections, and when the market looks especially pricey, most investors should consider stock funds that are likely to act in a more defensive manner when the market takes sudden downturns. This should entail a move to more value-oriented stock funds, those holding stocks that are relatively cheap in terms of P/E and P/B ratios. These moderate steps away from the riskiest areas of the stock market should fit most stock investors' long-term needs while providing an added level of comfort and safety.

CONTRARIAN INVESTING

A lot of managers claim to be contrarian investors (most notably, Fidelity's Contrafund and Contrafund II, Heartland's Small-Cap Contrarian, and Robertson Stephens's Contrarian.) This means buying "out-of-favor" stocks—stocks that are either cheap in terms of earnings or assets or stocks that have recently performed weakly (have gotten cheaper) compared with the rest of the market. The first category of contrarian investing is really the same thing as value investing. The second category, buying after declines, is also called bottom-feeding. (Note that bottom-feeding is the exact opposite of momentum investing, which is explained in Chapter 12). A third possibility is owning what other investors don't own, but this is impossible, if taken literally; after all, investors as a whole always have a "market weighting" in everything—they own all stocks and sectors in exact proportion to their representation in the market.

Like seeking "value," contrarian investing is one of those sensible-sounding strategies that almost everyone acknowledges, but few actually practice. Fidelity Contrafund's definition involves stocks whose "value is not fully recognized by the public." But of course, all active fund managers—value, growth, momentum, technical charting, you name it—can accurately say that they're seeking stocks whose "value is not fully recognized by the public." As it happens, Contrafund really hasn't fit any rigorous definition of contrarian investing in over a decade. That said, the fund has been a pretty good performer, and nothing succeeds like success (hence the sequel Contrafund II to replace sales of the closed $40+ billion Contrafund).

STYLE AND RETURNS

As most investors know, the large-cap S&P 500 Index, and large-cap growth stocks especially, have been doing quite well. What about the opposite kinds of stocks? They're the unloved, unwashed, dirty laundry of the mutual fund industry, which no respectable large-cap investor would think about buying. They're small-cap value funds—and in case you haven't heard, they've been taking it on the chin. In fact, small-cap stocks as a whole haven't beaten the large-cap S&P 500 since 1993. Most notably, in 1998, while the S&P 500 Index gained 28.6 percent, the S&P 600 small-caps were actually down 1.3 percent, and the S&P/BARRA Value half of this index declined 5.1 percent. So why consider this group worthy of your money? It's simple—these funds concentrate in an area that I think best suits most long-term investors, and chances are they can be had at a discount we're not likely to see for some time to come.

But don't just take my word for it. Ibbotson Associates, a Chicago-based research firm that tracks the historical performance of the stock market, finds that small-caps have earned annualized returns of 12.7 percent since 1926, versus 11 percent for the crowd-pleasing large-cap S&P 500 stocks. What's in a percent or two of compounding gains, you ask? Answer: $1 invested in your grandfather's favorite large-cap stocks 72 years ago is now worth $1,828; the same investment in small-cap stocks would provide nearly triple the cash: $5,520. So over the very long term, small-cap stocks, especially small-cap value stocks, have shown the best performance. But large-cap growth stocks have led the pack for most of the decade through 1998, and especially in 1998. So should we bet on a continuation of the long-term or the short-term trend?

I think you can be better served by avoiding today's highfliers and going bargain-basement shopping instead. At the very least, hold a diversified mix of large-, mid-, and small-cap stocks; don't assume that the S&P 500 is the place for all of your domestic stock assets. You'll find model diversified portfolios in Chapter 27 of this book.

WEBSITES

Morningstar
http://www.morningstar.net/

BARRA
http://www.barra.com

Ibbotson Associates
http://www.ibbotson.com/

SIXTEEN

Passively Managed Funds

Passively managed funds are more commonly referred to as "index fund investing." For the 10 years through 1998, some 91 percent of actively managed stock funds lagged the S&P 500, and 84 percent lagged the broader Wilshire 5000. Yeah, you say, but (unless you're Bill Gates) you can't buy the market. Well, actually you can. There are many low-cost no-load index funds out there tracking the S&P 500, the Wilshire 5000, and a host of other indices. These index funds generally track the returns for their index very closely, usually with a very slight lag due to their expense ratio of about 0.2 percent per year.

MARKET EFFICIENCY

The argument for indexing is largely premised on the axiom that the stock market, especially the U.S. large-cap stock market, is *efficient*. Efficiency here means that stock prices generally reflect what a stock is truly worth, and that stock prices respond so quickly to new information that no one can consistently outthink the market and achieve above-average returns. Note that even if this is perfectly true, some managers will still show better returns than others. Their success, so the argument goes, can be attributed to luck. Hence, a manager with a great record one year will be no more likely than any other manager to outperform the market in the following year.

While I don't believe that the efficient market theory is perfectly true, it is true that:

1. **Investors in general don't beat the market.** For every investor who beats the market averages, another must lag the market. (Actually, it is the dollar amounts, not the number of investors, that must balance out.) Looked at another way, investors will on average match the market as, taken together, they are the market. And in fact, they must, on average, slightly lag the market because of brokerage commissions and other expenses. Further, most real actively managed funds will further lag the market in the long run because they tend to hold 5 percent to 10 percent of assets in cash and equivalent income securities in order to meet redemptions.

2. **It is very hard to beat the market over the long run.** For any finite period of time, outperforming the market can be due to luck. Over a short time period (say, a year) outperformance is almost certainly due to luck. Over a long time period (say, 20 years), a large outperformance, while relatively more likely to be due to skill, might still be due to luck.

WHAT ABOUT PETER LYNCH?

In every discipline, a few outstanding individuals will emerge from the crowd. That goes for money management as well as for music. Despite having retired years ago, Peter Lynch is perhaps still the best-known fund manager in the country—and that's not because he's played straight man for Don Rickles and Lily Tomlin. Lynch ran the Fidelity Magellan fund for 13 years from 1977 to 1990, achieving an average annual return of 29.2 percent (versus 15.7 percent for the S&P 500 Index).

But even if efficient market theory is wrong, and Peter Lynch was skillful, not lucky (which I'll grant is true), there's still the question whether you can spot the next Peter Lynch before he's recognized as Peter Lynch. The odds are better than you might think—especially in light of Chapter 15's guide to ranking your own fund managers. Still, if you pick a young fund manager with a great record over the last 3 years, is that enough time to ensure that his or her performance wasn't due to luck, or to being in the right kind of fund at the right time? And if you wait for a great 20-year record, can you ensure that the manager is not slowing down, playing lots of golf, and anticipating a rich retirement, while letting the fund "run itself" to be run by interns from Wharton? Believe me, their performance will tell the tale.

Nevertheless, the index investing folks argue that the best way to take advantage of the stock market's long-term growth potential is to construct a portfolio that resembles the overall market as closely as possible, and the best way to achieve this goal is through an index fund. (If you think their theory is situated on higher moral ground than actively managed funds, consider the fact that index funds have to market their products to a competing audience.) A look at the following chart shows they have some truth in advertising.

Currently, funds that mirror the S&P 500 Index are the most common vehicle for achieving this "full investment" goal. The companies in the S&P 500 generally represent just under 80 percent of the entire value of publicly traded U.S. stocks, which is fairly complete market coverage. If you want to own literally every publicly traded U.S. stock, the Wilshire 5000 Index is your ticket to investment performance, and now there are Wilshire 5000 Index funds to provide you with a close approximation to this index.

There are some rebuttals to arguments regarding the long-term superiority of index funds. According to some industry advocates, one reason S&P 500 funds have done so well of late is that their rapid growth has driven up the share prices of the stocks making up the index. Given how long this has gone on, and how major a part of the U.S. market the index represents (80 percent), this argument isn't very compelling. But the fact that the S&P 500 has, for whatever reason, beaten smaller-caps for most of the past decade would to some extent reduce the meaningfulness of comparisons between active stock funds and S&P 500 returns. The Wilshire 5000 statistics do not rely on such a market-cap factor: for the 10 years through 1998, 84 percent of actively managed stock funds have lagged the Wilshire 5000.

EXPENSES AND TAXES

Wherever you stand in the debate over indexing, its advocates do have an indisputable claim to superiority in one area: cost. An index fund manager is basically a caretaker. All he or she needs to do is make sure that portfolio weightings do not stray from the index being tracked. Trades are made only to keep the portfolio in balance as stocks are added or removed from the index (generally once a year,

	Vanguard	Fidelity Magellan	PBHG Growth
1990	-3.32	-4.51	-9.72
1991	30.22	41.03	51.62
1992	7.42	7.01	28.39
1993	9.89	24.66	46.71
1994	1.18	-1.81	4.75
1995	37.45	36.82	50.35
1996	22.86	11.69	9.82
1997	33.21	26.59	-3.35
1998	28.62	33.63	0.59
1999	6.42	6.80	-5.01

	Vanguard	Fidelity Magellan	PBHG Growth
1989	10,000	10,000	10,000
1990	9,668	9,549	9,028
1991	12,590	13,467	13,688
1992	13,524	14,411	17,574
1993	14,861	17,965	25,783
1994	15,037	17,640	27,008
1995	20,668	24,134	40,607
1996	25,393	26,956	44,594
1997	33,826	34,123	43,100
1998	43,506	45,599	43,355
1999	46,299	48,700	41,182

Stock funds in the 1990s

$10,000 invested at the end of 1989

Vanguard Index 500 versus Best
Fidelity Active versus PBGH Growth

Legend: Vanguard Index 500 — Fidelity Magellan — PBGH Growth although sometimes a change is due to a corporate merger or spin-off), and when new money comes in or redemptions are made.

The index fund sponsor doesn't need to pay a bunch of analysts to search for good buys. With comparatively low brokers' commissions and research costs to cover, index funds can charge much lower management fees than their actively managed counterparts. How much lower? The expense ratio for a good no-load larger-cap index fund will be around 0.2 percent, versus about 1 percent (and often much more) for an actively managed stock fund. And these incremental differences in fund expenses can make a big difference when compounded over the long run. (But they're already factored into the return statistics comparing funds with indices.)

The greatest cost advantage of index funds comes into play when we take a look at taxes. When a fund manager makes trades resulting in capital gains, the law requires that these realized gains (minus any realized capital losses) be passed on to shareholders. This is the dreaded capital gains distribution, and you will be taxed on it even if you automatically reinvest those distributions in the fund. But since an index fund makes only the bare minimum of trades required to keep the portfolio in balance and meet redemptions, it tends to make much smaller capital gains distributions, if any. This is especially true of total market and large-cap indices that are market-weighted (e.g., S&P 500 Index funds) and thus have little need to sell positions as part of rebalancing or some other change in index composition. (A small- or mid-cap index fund must sell a stock if it has had a big enough run-up to move up to the large-cap indices; and a Dow index fund has to sell shares after a stock split, because that index is share-weighted, not market-cap-weighted.)

Because most gains in an index fund are not distributed, leaving only small stock dividend distributions, index funds have some of the tax-deferral advantages of holding your fund in an IRA, or of buy-and-hold investing in individual stocks. But unlike IRAs, index funds don't limit your investment to $2,000 per year, and there's no 10 percent penalty if you make a withdrawal—just normal taxes on any gains you realize by selling the fund. There's nothing wrong with holding an index fund in an IRA (or other retirement account), but if you have stock fund investments in a retirement account, and others in a taxable account, it's best to put any index fund positions in the taxable account, and any actively managed funds in the retirement account. That way you'll defer the most taxes.

SEVENTEEN

Bond Funds

OK, I admit it—you don't really need to be all that concerned with bond funds. Not yet, anyway. But even for investors like you and me, at least one type of bond fund can play a positive role in our portfolio. And while I prefer a money market fund over most bond funds, it's important to know what types of bond funds you can invest in, and when you might want to do so.

Bonds funds are often mistakenly thought of as a safe, sure-thing, no-worries, income-producing investment. Except for funds that invest solely in shorter-term government bonds, this simply isn't so. In fact, many bond funds have a significant degree of risk, particularly because rising interest rates will reduce the value of the instruments they invest in. Only by examining both interest rate and credit risk in relation to how they affect a bond fund's performance in different market environments can you be assured that the bond fund you've selected (or are thinking about buying) matches your investment objective.

BOND FUND PRIMER

Even my 11-year-old nephew knows something about stock funds. Most of us have become well versed in the many types of stock funds—especially those who have just read the preceding chapters of this book. But bond funds remain a less known and less used universe for many fund investors, particularly younger investors. That's OK, since for the most part you really can afford to do without them.

Here's most of what you need to know about the types of bond funds and their objectives.

First, bonds and the funds that invest in them can be divided into two main categories: **government** and **corporate.** Government bonds are basically backed by the full faith and credit of Uncle Sam. Corporate bonds are debt instruments of corporations, which can run the gamut from AT&T (a top-rated bond) to some company in bankruptcy (a "junk bond").

Bonds within each category fall into the following basic types:

- **Short-term bond funds** can invest in government bonds, corporate bonds, or a mix of the two. "Short-term" means that the bonds in these funds should generally have maturities of 1 to under 5 years. Objective: income with limited exposure to interest rate risk. Use: stock market hedge and/or short-term parking place for near-term needs.
- **Intermediate-term bond funds** can invest singularly or in a mix of government and corporate bonds with maturities of 5 to under 10 years. Objective: higher immediate income. Interest rate risk is a potential thorn in the side of these funds.
- **Longer-term bond funds** invest in a mix of government and corporate bonds with maturities of 10 to 30 years. Objective: steady source of income. There's no need to consider this group until you need bifocals to read the financial pages.
- **High-yield bond funds** (a.k.a. "junk" bond funds) invest in bonds below investment-grade quality that offer potentially high profits at the expense of higher risk. Needless to say, these can be volatile, but they're the best type of bond fund for investors like you and me to consider. Objective: higher-than-average yield. Use: stock market hedge and total return generator.
- **Municipal bond funds** (better known as "munis") invest in bonds of state and local governments. Objective: tax-free income. (Note: Muni bond prices are hard to find. Muni bond fund prices are not.) Use: tax-advantage hedge against the stock market. (Note: Not for use in a retirement plan.)
- **Single-state funds** invest in bonds from only one state. Since interest earned from these funds is free of state (and often local) as well as federal income taxes, single-state funds often

Year	Vanguard	Vanguard	Vanguard	Vanguard	Fidelity Capital & Income	Vanguard $20,634	Vanguard $28,254	Vanguard $23,935	Vanguard $27,976	Fidelity Capital & Income $28,805
						10,000	10,000	10,000	10,000	10,000
1989	11.34	17.93	14.76	15.17	-3.22	11,134	11,793	11,476	11,517	9,678
1990	9.31	5.78	10.32	6.20	-3.85	12,171	12,475	12,660	12,231	9,305
1991	12.22	17.43	16.76	20.90	29.82	13,658	14,649	14,782	14,787	12,080
1992	6.19	7.41	6.85	9.78	28.05	14,503	15,734	15,795	16,234	15,469
1993	7.00	16.79	5.90	14.49	24.90	15,518	18,376	16,727	18,586	19,321
1994	-0.94	-7.04	-0.95	-5.30	-4.61	15,373	17,083	16,568	17,601	18,430
1995	12.26	30.09	17.04	26.40	16.74	17,257	22,223	19,391	22,247	21,515
1996	4.75	-1.26	5.24	1.20	11.41	18,077	21,943	20,407	22,514	23,970
1997	6.46	13.90	9.47	13.78	14.70	19,245	24,993	22,340	25,617	27,493
1998	7.22	13.05	7.14	9.21	4.77	20,634	28,254	23,935	27,976	28,805

$10,000 invested 12/31/88 for 10 years becomes:

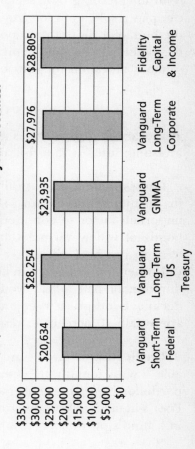

$20,634	$28,254	$23,935	$27,976	$28,805
Vanguard Short-Term Federal	Vanguard Long-Term US Treasury	Vanguard GNMA	Vanguard Long-Term Corporate	Fidelity Capital & Income

provide the highest tax-equivalent yields. Objective: double tax-free income.

THE ROLE OF BOND FUNDS IN YOUR PORTFOLIO

I don't think that bond funds should be the centerpiece of your solid long-term, growth-seeking investment strategy. But some types can play a role, even for growth investors like us, and may represent the bulk of a shorter-term portfolio's assets. The key is to recognize the potential risks and returns of each fund and choose the most suitable allocation for your own purposes.

RISKS OF BOND FUNDS

There are two main types of risks when it comes to bond fund investing: interest rate risk and credit risk.

Interest Rate Risk. Basically, a fund's duration reflects its sensitivity to interest rates—and so posits its interest-rate risk. This is an important factor to consider, given that different bond funds hold bonds of widely varying durations. For example, if interest rates were to rise by 1 percent, a fund with a duration of 10 years will (all other things being equal) fall 10 percent, while a fund with a duration of half a year would fall only 0.5 percent. (When rates decline, bond prices rise, and a fund with a 10-year duration would appreciate 10 percent in response to a 1 percent decline in rates.)

Credit Risk. A given fund's bond holding ratings provide a reliable way to identify the speculative and conservative bonds in its portfolio. Note the letter ratings from Moody's and Standard & Poor's in tandem with discerning the economic health of companies in a fund's portfolio.

GUIDELINES FOR INVESTING IN BOND FUNDS

The market offers many choices, but it isn't too hard to decide which—if any—bond fund is right for you. With bond funds, unlike stock funds, stated investment parameters are generally much more important than the fund manager or the specific holdings, except for funds holding junk bonds.

Credit Table

Moody's	Standard & Poor's	Meaning
Aaa	AAA	Best quality
Aa	AA	High quality
Baa	BBB	Medium quality
B	B	Minimal quality

Anything rated less than BBB/Baa is a junk bond.

First, if your money is held in a tax-deferred retirement account, or if your federal tax bracket is below 28 percent, you should probably choose a taxable bond fund. If your money is in a regular taxable account and you're in a federal tax bracket higher than 28 percent, you'll probably want to choose a tax-free municipal fund. (If you're right at the 28 percent bracket, the choice is apt to vary with market conditions and what state you live in.)

Among taxable funds (and likewise among municipal funds), there's a trade-off of higher yields for higher risks. But note that the income on most U.S. government securities (except for GNMAs and other mortgage securities), while federally taxable, is free of state and local income taxes, so if you're in a state with high income taxes, the funds with "government" in their name effectively yield a bit more than they appear to.

This doesn't mean that you should jump into long-term bond funds, especially in today's climate, where long-term rates are less than 1 percent above short-term rates. The risk associated with investing in long-term bond funds is well beyond what most investors would consider appropriate for their "cash reserves."

BUY CASH, NOT BONDS

Apart from junk bonds, which are closely tied to the economy and equities markets, bond prices mostly move inversely with interest rates. For the last few years, interest rates have been coming down and bonds have been performing well. But the fact that rates are near a 30-year low means we may be headed into a rising-rate environment. Moreover, with rates on even the longest-term (30-year) treasury bonds now down to about 5.6 percent, there is no longer much room for interest rates to fall, and there is a commensurately greater chance for rate increases.

I prefer cash. Using cash (in the form of a money market fund) can net you both a stock market *and* a bond market hedge, as well as liquidity, without giving up much in the way of return or yield.

Not to be confused with a money market account (found at your bank), a money market fund isn't FDIC insured but is typically safe, easy to use, and a smart alternative to today's bond market.

What is a money market fund? (See Chapter 18 for full details.) Money market funds invest your dollars in very, very short-term bank, corporate, and government debt securities, or IOUs. Because of the nature of these short-term securities, the price of a share in a money market mutual fund changes only infinitesimally from day to day, so your money market shares remain priced at a constant $1. Money market managers can't buy anything yielding much more than a 3-month treasury bill.

Money market funds are some of the safest and most convenient places to park your cash and can help you avoid an accounting nightmare when income taxes are due. So why would anyone want to try and earn a higher yield? Because the long-term gain in yield and return a bond fund can provide is often worth the additional volatility (short-term risk) that you take.

STRATEGY FOR SHORT-TERM BOND FUNDS

A fund that invests in individual U.S. treasuries offers virtually no credit risk, but depending on the duration of the treasuries in holds, it does present some level of interest rate risk. (The shorter the average duration, the less interest rate risk.) I prefer a money market fund or a short-term U.S. treasury fund (with an average duration under 2 years). But you may want to simply buy a CD or treasury on your own and avoid the bond fund's expenses. (Bond funds and bonds, of course, generally perform pretty similarly. Relative to individual bonds, bond funds of similar credit quality would tend to lag by approximately the value of their management and other expenses.)

SHOULD YOU BUY TREASURIES
OR A U.S. TREASURY FUND?

You can buy individual U.S. treasury securities in your brokerage account. If you don't have a brokerage account, I would strongly recommend getting one, even if you've been strictly a mutual fund customer. Even without a brokerage account, you can buy treasuries direct from the federal government. For complete information, call a Federal Reserve bank (e.g., at 617-973-3800 or 202-874-4000).

If you don't want to buy U.S. treasuries directly, you should buy a short-term U.S. bond fund. In fact, for most investors seeking a stable short-term place to park cash for upcoming objectives (such as a down payment on a new house or condo), I would recommend buying a money market fund or a short-term U.S. treasury fund.

Another advantage an individual treasury bond has over a bond fund is that the bond eventually matures, and you'll know exactly how much money you'll get when it matures. A bond fund, in contrast, never matures, and if rates go up between now and the time you sell it, you'll need to withdraw the money before rates rise too dramatically or you will face a loss of a part of your initial investment.

BE MODERATELY CONSERVATIVE

The first and most conservative step in boosting money market rates is to make sure you own the right money market fund. Look at your tax-equivalent yield. If you're invested in a taxable money market fund and you're in the 28 percent federal bracket or higher (and chances are you are), consider a municipal money market fund. Such funds invest in securities whose interest payments are exempt from federal income taxes. (In some cases a portion of the fund's income may also be exempt from state taxes as well.) And investors in Arizona, California, Connecticut, Florida, Massachusetts, Michigan, New Jersey, New York, Ohio, and Pennsylvania should consider a state-specific tax-free money market fund, whose interest is exempt from federal, state, and sometimes city taxes.

If the yield on the general municipal money fund or the money fund for your state is higher than the yield on your taxable money fund, make the switch.

EXTEND MATURITIES

When bond fund investors think about boosting yields, they almost instinctively think about extending the maturity of the funds they invest in. But the minute you move money into a bond fund, interest rate risks rise substantially. Remember that when interest rates fall, bond prices rise. That was the good news during the 1980s and early 1990s. But when interest rates rise, as they did in 1994 and may do in the next few years, bond prices fall.

With that caveat in mind, money market investors who feel compelled to boost their yields can do well by moving into short-term bond funds. The extra yield earned may be worth the additional risk. But in today's market you should not try to boost your money fund yield by moving into the longest-term bond funds. This is not a place for your rainy day cash. Even in bond bear markets, losses in short-term funds (unlike longer-term funds) have remained small and are usually recovered quickly. Stay short, stay safe.

THE ROLE OF THE JUNK BOND FUND
IN YOUR $10,000 PORTFOLIO

Yes, junk bonds are risky, but despite the popular impression to the contrary, they aren't any more risky than stocks. (In fact, junk bonds and the Fidelity funds that invest in them are generally significantly less risky.) They are too risky for short-term investors seeking income or a return of their assets in less than 5 years. Still, junk bonds are not an unworthy asset for investors who are mostly interested in stocks.

Junk bonds have potential returns and risks close to those found in the stock market. But junk bonds are only partially correlated with the stock market, so they can diversify a portfolio that's otherwise mostly in stocks. And at times (like after their 1989–1990 decline), junk will look particularly attractive relative to stocks and to high-quality bonds, and you may load up on it then and do quite well with a well-diversified portfolio of junk bonds. (I don't think now is such a time; junk bonds aren't yielding all that much more than good-quality bonds and thus aren't very attractive despite the strong economy.)

You really can't build your own junk bond portfolio with less than $250,000; and even at that level, you're unlikely to find a better

	Fidelity	Lehman	Wilshire 5000 Index
1990	-3.85	8.96	-6.18
1991	29.82	16.00	34.21
1992	28.05	7.40	8.97
1993	24.90	9.75	11.28
1994	-4.61	-2.92	-0.06
1995	16.74	18.47	36.45
1996	11.41	3.63	21.21
1997	14.70	9.65	31.29
1998	4.77	8.69	23.43
1999	11.46	-1.05	6.37

	Fidelity	Lehman	Wilshire 5000 Index
1989	10,000	10,000	10,000
1990	9,615	10,896	9,382
1991	12,482	12,639	12,591
1992	15,983	13,575	13,720
1993	19,963	14,898	15,268
1994	19,043	14,463	15,258
1995	22,231	17,135	20,820
1996	24,767	17,757	25,237
1997	28,408	19,470	33,133
1998	29,763	21,162	40,896
1999	33,174	20,940	43,501

Junk in the 1990s

$10,000 invested at the end of 1989

Returns for the Fidelity Capital and Income junk bond fund are generally intermediate between those of quality bonds and the stock market.

Legend:
- Fidelity Capital and Income
- Lehman Brothers Aggregate Bond Index
- Wilshire 5000 Index

adviser than can be had in a junk bond mutual fund, or to pay much less in expenses either, after accounting for the spreads in these illiquid securities, unless you are a passive index-like junk bond investor. And you will be doubly hard-pressed to find a manager who is: (1) excellent at picking bonds; (2) low-cost, in terms of both transactions and annual fees; and (3) willing to keep turnover in your portfolio quite low—say, under 20 percent per year.

THINK CAPITAL AND INCOME

Many investors think that "income" and "cash" are one and the same. As a result, they've held their investment accounts hostage, earning unnecessarily low overall returns on their savings. There's a better way.

Ask yourself this question: As an investor, should you care whether you've earned cash through stock dividends and bond interest (things we normally associate with income), or as a capital gain on a high-growth investment? The answer: yes, you should. In fact, most investors (investing for "income" or for "growth") are often better off going for capital gains rather than income. The reason is that the IRS, by keeping long-term capital gains tax rates far below many income-tax rates, makes it advantageous to invest for growth.

First, there are big tax advantages to investing for growth: income tax rates for middle-class taxpayers start at 28 percent while the capital gains tax on assets held more than 18 months is only 20 percent. You pay no taxes on capital gains until you sell the appreciated assets; the tax bill you get when that time comes around—assuming you held the assets for at least a year and a half—will thus be considerably smaller than what you would owe for same amount of income. Second, and more important, over periods longer than 7 years income-paying investments have virtually never performed as well as their growth-oriented counterparts. Here's why.

Suppose you have $10,000 invested in a corporate bond fund that pays you a 6 percent yield. You're being paid interest every month, and at the end of the year you've earned about $600 in interest. If you're in the 31 percent federal tax bracket (I won't even bother with state taxes, which only add to the validity of this argument) you'll owe the government $186 in taxes. So, really, you've earned just $414 in spendable "income."

Now suppose, instead, that you put the $10,000 into a stock fund, which gained 6 percent in value during the course of the year. At the end of the year, you'll have $10,600. If the fund distributed that much to you, the entire $600 would be taxable, but while the dividend income and short-term gains would be taxed at 31 percent, the long-term (over 18-month) gains would be taxed at 20 percent, and the medium-term (12- to 18-month) gains would be taxed at 28 percent. In this case, you probably won't owe more than $150 in taxes.

Now let's take the example of a fund or a stock that has essentially no distributions. (An index fund would approximate this situation, since it typically distributes only about 2 percent in dividend income, and individual growth stocks might distribute nothing.) To get your hands on $600 of "income," you have to sell $600 of the stocks or stock fund. From a tax standpoint, of that $600 only 6 percent (or $36) is a taxable gain; the rest is a nontaxable withdrawal of principal. If you wait until 366 days after purchase to sell the fund, the $36 gain is taxed only at the 28 percent rate, and you only pay $10.08 in taxes!

Under the new tax law you would have an even lower tax rate (20 percent) in subsequent years, as those sales would all be more than 18 months after purchase, but a larger proportion of your sale would be taxable gains. As I stated above, an S&P Index fund would probably distribute about 2 percent in dividend income. If you take $200 per year in income (taxed at 31 percent) and $400 per year of principal and gains, you're still talking about only $70 in taxes. (Further, if your aim is to leave an estate for your heirs, they generally won't have to pay taxes on your gains either, as they will inherit the shares with a cost basis "stepped up" to their value on the day you die.)

What if the stock fund doesn't earn 6 percent? Obviously, there's no guarantee that a stock fund will earn 6 percent or even lose nothing in any given year. But bond funds can also lose money in a given year; only money markets are pretty much assured of earning their stated (but rather paltry) yield. And month-to-month or year-to-year returns are relevant only to investors who will need their principal in the next year or so.

As long as you expect to live for at least several more years, what matters to you is how much your investments will probably be up after several years. History shows that stocks traditionally earn greater returns than bonds and money markets (on the order of 10 percent per year). Therefore, it is a good bet that you'll ultimately make more money by putting at least some of your "income" investments into stock funds.

If the stock fund pays out big dividends, you're still paying income taxes on that anyway, so what's the advantage? If you can afford growth-stock volatility and taxes are a big concern for you, you should be keeping your portfolio focused on good long-term growth funds. But even if your equity-income fund pays out big dividends, it still gets a substantial portion of its expected returns from capital gains, and you'll still benefit from the long-term growth advantage that comes from investing in stocks. So you're ahead both in terms of tax efficiency and in terms of pretax returns.

What if you're investing tax-deferred money—in an IRA, for example? In terms of taxes it doesn't matter what you do, because all the distributions you take from the IRA are taxed as income. It doesn't make any difference whether you buy income-producing or gains-producing funds in your IRA. The tax collector doesn't care.

QUICK TIP

Once you've decided to take the "growth" strategy to heart and you begin investing at least a portion of your "income" portfolio in equity funds, I've got one more piece of advice. Automatically put all your bond and equity fund income and capital gains distributions into a money-market account rather than reinvesting.

The advantages are twofold. First, funds must pay out income dividends and capital gains at least once a year; you have no control over these taxable distributions. So call your fund family and instruct the representative to pay all distributions automatically into a money market account. This will provide you with ready cash available for writing checks.

There's a second benefit from this maneuver. Because you aren't reinvesting in additional shares of your fund, you aren't creating a further tax mess down the road when you eventually want to sell those shares. In fact, you'll probably be doing a little bit of selling each quarter or month anyway, to supplement the "income" you receive from your holdings.

Then it's purely a matter of deciding where you want to fall on the continuum of low risk, low return versus high risk, high expected return. And unless you really need to spend that money in 5 years or less, you should probably place a good portion of your investments in a diversified portfolio of growth and income or capital and income funds, or both.

EIGHTEEN

Money Market Funds

Whether you're saving money for a rainy day or just looking for a place to park your spare dollars between investments, money market funds combine the convenience of a checking account with some of the safest, highest-yielding choices available. Not only can you write checks against funds in your money market account; you can also have dividend and interest income directly deposited there.

MONEY MARKET FUNDS VERSUS MONEY MARKET ACCOUNTS

Banks. Who needs them? Not you. True, you can find a money market account at your local bank; but, unless your bank is a big-money bank, you won't be able to invest in a money market fund there. However, while money market accounts are covered by the same FDIC insurance that protects your conventional checking and savings accounts, money market funds have no more protection than any other mutual fund investment. If the investment company goes belly up, you are just as likely to lose your money market fund dollars as your stock fund dollars. A money market fund is thus exactly as safe as the company sponsoring it, and when it comes to security, bigger is generally better. This is why I would suggest you open your money market fund with a giant like Fidelity or Vanguard.

How do money market funds work? Their core principle is that a money market fund share is always worth one dollar—no more, no less. But while the share price remains fixed, the interest rate paid fluctuates in response to the varying yields on the short-term bank, corporate, and government debt securities in the fund's portfolio. The fund managers aren't allowed to let their average maturity exceed 90 days, because that would imperil their ability to keep share prices at $1. Nor can managers buy anything yielding much more than a 3-month treasury bill. And they can gain only marginally more yield—certainly not more than 1 percent—by going to corporates, since 95 percent of their corporate holdings must have the equivalent of an AAA rating. All these strictures give money market fund managers precious little room to maneuver when it comes to boosting yields.

BENEFITS OF MONEY MARKET FUNDS

Convenient Checking. Unlike some analysts, I think that having a money market fund available to you is a smart investing move. First, though writing checks is an option available in a host of other funds, you should avoid at all costs using any fund other than a money market as your checking account. The reason is that any time you write a check on a fund, you are in effect selling shares in the fund to cover the amount of your check. Write a check for $500, and when it is cashed the fund will sell as many shares as necessary to cover the amount. And each time shares are sold, that's a "taxable event" whose gain or loss will have to be calculated and reported to the Internal Revenue Service.

This problem does not exist in a money market. Since shares in a money market fund are always priced at exactly $1 per share, there is no profit and no loss on the transaction. Money market yields may look relatively low. However, with inflation almost nonexistent today, real returns on money markets are well over 3 percent, actually pretty good by historical standards. As a place to park your cash reserves, there isn't anything better. I have been watching the bond markets since the early 1980s and know the heights and the depths to which short-term interest rates have risen and fallen. At their peak in late 1980, 3-month treasury bills were yielding more than 16 percent. With a few bumps along the way they slid as low as 2.6 percent in late 1992. By 1999, they were up to 5 percent.

RISKS OF MONEY MARKET FUNDS

Even though your share price is virtually locked at $1 and interest is being paid every day, this doesn't mean that money market funds are risk-free. The two biggest risks are interest rate risk and credit risk (though neither is a major concern when you are investing in a money fund).

Interest Rate Risk. Interest rate risk refers to the impact of rising and falling interest rates on the value of the securities held by your money market fund. Interest rates on very short-term securities (those with maturities under a year or so) generally move up and down according to the policies and actions of the Federal Reserve. When the Fed wants to stimulate economic growth, it will lower some of its key lending rates. The yields on most short-term interest-bearing securities will then follow suit. When the Fed wants to rein in the economy to try to prevent runaway growth and, possibly, inflation, it will raise short-term lending rates. The six increases in the Federal Funds rate in 1994, from 3 percent in early February to 5.5 percent in November, were the major factor behind the rise in money market yields.

Despite its short average maturity, a sudden, severe rise in interest rates—combined with heavy shareholder redemptions—could have an impact on the value of your money market fund's portfolio. However, it would take an extraordinary event to push interest rates high enough fast enough to cause a problem. If the rise in rates experienced during 1994 didn't cause a problem for these funds, it's a good bet that nothing so dramatic will occur at any time soon. Given the conservative manner in which money funds are managed, I don't think this problem is worth losing any sleep over. You can be sure that before any fund was forced to price its shares below $1, many other fund complexes and banks would have already failed.

Credit Risk. Credit risk can be a bigger problem for some money market funds. Credit risk is the possibility that debt issuers could go into default and leave the fund companies who bought their IOUs holding the bag. During the 1980s one well-publicized corporate default did force a couple of fund complexes to dip into their reserves so their money market funds would not be forced to "break the buck," i.e., let the price of a share sink below $1. But as that example shows, you can rest assured that most fund companies would move heaven and earth to head off any such buck-breaking, because they know that it would irreparably damage investors' confidence in their operations. Of course, by investing in a government-only money market fund, such as Spartan US Treasury, you can eliminate virtually any possibility of credit risk.

YOU CAN ENHANCE YOUR YIELD

The first and most conservative step in boosting money market rates is to make sure you own the right money market. Some money market funds invest in securities whose interest payments are exempt from federal income taxes. (In some cases a portion of the

---

QUICK TIP

How safe are money market funds today? Answer: not as safe as an FDIC-insured bank money market account—but, still, pretty close. The key is to ensure that your money market fund isn't propping itself up on a house of derivative cards. Derivatives can be highly speculative bets on, for example, the direction interest rates might go. (See Glossary.) How can you tell? The following considerations should help you answer this question for yourself.

1. Does your money provide an unusually high yield? If it does, or if it has high expenses (as revealed in the prospectus), then it could be using derivatives. Call and find out.
2. If your fund does use derivatives, what types does it use? Steer clear of funds that are swollen with exotic varieties of interest-rate floaters such as capped, CMTs, dual-index, inverse, leveraged, and ranged floaters.
3. Regardless of what your money market fund invests in, the best thing you can do is stick with a fund that is part of a large fund complex. A large firm is more likely to have the financial strength to compensate a fund for any losses. More important, a large fund group would have more incentive to help out a troubled fund, if only to pacify its existing clients in other funds.

---

fund's income may also be exempt from state taxes as well.) And (as noted in Chapter 17) if you live in Arizona, California, Connecticut, Florida, Massachusetts, Michigan, New Jersey, New York, Ohio, or Pennsylvania, chances are you should consider a state-specific tax-free money market fund, whose interest is exempt from federal, state, and sometimes city taxes.

You may feel insecure about investing in a single-state money fund. Given the default by Orange County in 1994, you may be inclined to stay away from single-state money funds, but most major fund families' conservative money market policies make this a fairly minor issue. For example, Fidelity CA and Fidelity Spartan CA money markets rode through the Orange County debacle unscathed. If the yield on the general municipal money fund or the money fund for your state is higher than the yield on your taxable money fund, think about making the switch.

NINETEEN

Global Diversification
and International Funds

While, taken individually, foreign markets are at least as risky as U.S. markets, a mix of foreign stocks in one diversified international fund, or in a pool of funds, when added to an all-U.S. stock portfolio, can actually reduce risk without reducing expected long-term returns. This is because foreign markets don't move in lockstep with the U.S. market. (Sudden market crashes in the United States do usually unsettle overseas markets, especially in English-speaking Canada, Australia, and Britain; but over periods of a few months or more they tend to go their own way.)

This intermediate level of correlation makes sense from a fundamental standpoint: foreign economic growth and foreign interest rates are only somewhat tied to growth and rates in the United States. For this reason—as well as the foreign markets' relatively good values—I believe that all but the most conservative investors should have a portion of their assets overseas. To repeat, such international diversification can reduce risk while maintaining (or even increasing) expected returns—something that is not true for defensive moves into cash or bonds.

International stock funds, like U.S. stock funds, present a wide variety of investment opportunities and, as the events of the late 1990s have shown, risks. Some international funds concentrate their assets in established European markets; others in concentrate on Japanese securities; still others participate wholly or partly in the combustible emerging markets. Given the economic, political, and currency risks that investing abroad entails, you'll need to keep your eye on country and portfolio diversification in order to rest assured that you've selected the best international fund for your overall goals.

DO INTERNATIONAL FUNDS MAKE SENSE?

American stocks are expensive. The S&P 500 is selling for over 30 times trailing earnings. This is markedly higher than the market's historical postwar average P/E ratio of about 12. While foreign markets generally aren't a lot cheaper in these terms—Japan, in fact, is more expensive relative to its trailing earnings—their stocks are more promising because they are looking forward at a long period of growth (more on this below). Foreign stocks are also starting to benefit from cash inflows from U.S. investors. To sustain above-average multiples, a market needs good news: falling interest rates, rising earnings, strong capital flows. In all three areas, the United States is not likely to show continued improvements, whereas many foreign markets look more promising.

FUNDAMENTALS FAVOR FOREIGN STOCKS
FOR OUR LIFETIME

1: Interest rates. American rates are more likely to climb than to fall. The Federal Reserve Board is walking a knife-edge between the twin precipices of inflation and recession, looking to economic figures to guide it. If the economy grows too fast, the Fed will tighten; if not, it won't. But barring actual recession or market panic, the Fed is unlikely to actually loosen its purse strings this year. In short, none of these scenarios makes a good bullish case for U.S. stocks.

Overseas, however, rates have room to come down in many markets. Inflation rates are generally lower in Europe, and trending downward—and much lower in Japan. European countries have high unemployment and should start easing interest rates soon to help pick up some slack. Japan will have to tighten a bit as it slowly exits what passes for a bad recession in that country, but Japanese rates will be coming off almost absurdly low levels (now 0.4 percent for 3-month government bills) and shouldn't hurt their stock markets much.

2: Growth. Corporate earnings have grown strongly in the United States since we started to come out of the 1990 recession. But the

United States is in its sixth year of expansion, and that expansion is inevitably slowing. Profits seem unlikely to continue growing at above-average rates. Few analysts saw 1996 or 1997 growth rates much above 10 percent. European, and especially Japanese, stocks looked more promising because Europe and Japan seemed to be looking forward, not back, at such a potentially long period of higher growth. They were half right. Europe remained robust. Japan's market continued to tank through 1998. But in 1999, the tables turned in favor of Japan.

While Japan still isn't cheap compared with other countries (relative to trailing earnings), its future earnings show a lot of promise as the country emerges from a long recession. As Mike Gerding states, Japan's economy is due for the greatest amount of acceleration precisely "because it's coming off the worst 5-year period in its history." And while I think the transformation of this leading industrial economy to a leading consumer-driven economy bodes well for several sectors, I think caution is the byword in the months ahead.

In fact, the entire Pacific region seems poised for continued strong growth, as Japan emerges from recession and the Asian tigers continue to grow toward developed-country status. All of these countries have shown enormous (often double-digit) growth rates over the past decade, and all seem likely to continue to do so. Still, these companies are not cheap, and all these markets are volatile. This area should be reserved for a modest portion of assets in the portfolios of speculative investors.

Hong Kong and China have perhaps the greatest upside potential. But since China has no real established rule of law (or property), political risks in this area are considerable, at least until I see what sort of people (and ideologies) take over in the next few years. It is not in China's interest for it to kill the "golden goose," Hong Kong, as several money managers have pointed out recently. On the other hand, China has not generally been known for wise and humane leadership these past few centuries.

While Latin America also shows great promise for future growth, it has similarly shown great potential for political risk and self-destruction. Even speculative investors should hold this area in moderation.

3: Capital Flows. One of the biggest arguments for investing in U.S. stocks has rested on the idea that baby boomers have to invest in stocks for their retirement, and that this will continue to drive the market upward. This argument is not without validity. It is, however, not a sure thing.

First, boomers really don't have to invest in stocks. They can sit on their hands for rather extended periods, invest in bonds or bank accounts even if the rates are low. An income of 7 percent (or even 5 percent) looks pretty good when you're comparing it with negative returns in the stock market.

Second, even if boomers do invest in stocks, they can put much of these new assets into foreign stocks. (Foreign stock funds are a growing portion of the mutual fund universe.) Foreign stock markets can also, of course, benefit from cash inflows from local as well as U.S. investors.

QUICK TIP

Understand the currency risk of your international funds. Currency movements are a big part of the risk for most foreign funds. As the U.S. dollar goes up, securities valued in foreign currencies tend to drop in terms of U.S. dollars. This will prove a drag on foreign mutual funds that don't hedge against currencies—most foreign funds. But foreign exporters benefit from a stronger dollar; their stocks will go up even in dollar terms as exports climb or their economies improve from monetary easing.

INTERNATIONAL FUNDS

Why invest abroad at all? It's profitable, to a degree—sometimes to a very large degree. A globally diversified portfolio can help you guard against a potential U.S. market correction, as well as benefit from a rebounding market beyond the United States. In fact, as the chart below shows, investing a portion of your assets abroad long-term can give you risk-adjusted returns that prove to be better than a purely U.S. portfolio. But it can also place your portfolio in harm's way if you attempt to time the markets or overconcentrate in one market. First, let's look at the potential benefits of diversifying your U.S. portfolio to include some international exposure.

Efficient Frontier Curves. For most of the past decade, the U.S. market has beaten the bulk of international markets. And combining the two areas into a diversified portfolio can't change that basic fact. However, over other time periods foreign markets have beaten the U.S. market. Further, over any significant time period, a portfolio holding both U.S. and foreign stocks has been less volatile—less risky—than an all-U.S. portfolio.

On page 154 are two graphs showing what would have happened to portfolios holding different blends of foreign and domestic stocks. The first graph shows the period from 1983 through 1988, when foreign markets (as measured by the Morgan Stanley Europe, Australasia, Far East Index, EAFE) handily beat the U.S. S&P 500 Index. The second graph shows 1989 through 1998, a period when U.S. markets were the stronger performers. Each graph includes an efficient frontier curve that shows the risk (monthly volatility) and return (annualized) of holding various amounts in the S&P 500 and EAFE indices, with the portfolio's foreign percentage varying from 0 percent to 100 percent in 10 percent increments.

Note that diversification reduces volatility for each time period. In the first period, although the EAFE has slightly more volatility than the S&P 500 (1.03 for the EAFE, while the S&P 500 is, by definition, always 1), a blend of U.S. and foreign stocks has less risk than an all-U.S. portfolio, with the least volatile portfolio having about 50 percent in the United States and 50 percent overseas. In the second time period, the EAFE Index has also shown a much higher relative volatility, 1.30. Nevertheless, portfolios holding a mix of 20 percent or 30 percent in the EAFE and 60 percent or 70 percent in the S&P 500 have shown slightly lower volatility (0.96) than the U.S. market. This is because foreign markets do not move in perfect tandem with U.S. markets.

Outlook for Foreign Markets. Unfortunately, while diversification can predictably reduce risk, it cannot change the fact that foreign markets have lagged the U.S. for the past dozen years. Why, you may ask, should you invest in foreign stocks if they lag? The answer is that they aren't likely to continue to lag. To assume otherwise is to make the same mistake as buying Japanese stocks in 1989 because they had been doing great: chasing momentum. (The Tokyo market is, in 1999, at less than half its peak level, and certainly a much better bargain than it was then.)

Percent foreign

	0%	10%	20%	30%	40%	50%	60%	70%	80%	90%	100%
1983–1988											
Volume	1.00	0.95	0.92	0.89	0.87	0.87	0.88	0.90	0.93	0.98	1.03
Return	16.48	18.27	20.05	21.82	23.58	25.32	27.05	28.77	30.46	32.14	33.80
1989–1998											
Volume	1.00	0.97	0.96	0.96	0.98	1.01	1.05	1.10	1.16	1.23	1.30
Return	17.33	16.16	14.97	13.77	12.56	11.34	10.10	8.86	7.60	6.34	5.07

EFC Charts

Graphs show risk versus return for portfolios holding 0 percent to 100 percent in foreign stocks, the remainder in U.S. In 1983–1988 the foreign EAFE Index beat the domestic S&P 500. In 1989–1998 the S&P 500 beat the EAFE.

In each case, a portfolio with at least 20 percent in foreign stocks had less risk than an all-U.S. portfolio, despite the fact that the foreign EAFE was more risky than the domestic S&P 500.

After such a long period of U.S. market dominance, it's more likely than not that foreign markets will do at least as well as the United States in the next decade. At any rate, most investors seeking longer-term growth, who should own a portfolio composed mostly of stock funds, should have at least 20 percent of those stock assets invested in foreign funds.

FOREIGN DIVERSIFICATION

The same benefits of diversification apply abroad or at home. But with an international or global fund, you'll need to focus on diversifying countries as well as stocks. When it comes to diversification, investors often think of global or diversified international funds. Geographical diversification is the main benefit. You can also add to your diversification by putting together two or more narrowly drawn international funds, but in that case you'll need to determine how closely the international funds correlate. Of course, funds with "Europe" in their name tend to perform relatively similarly, and downright differently from, for example, Japan or emerging market funds. However, this is not always clear-cut, especially among funds with more generic designations: "international" or "worldwide."

FUND WORLD

In general, I think investors like us would do well to hold two international funds: one European, one invested in Japan. These cover the bulk of the world's foreign markets, while allowing the fund manager to specialize in an organic and economically linked region. This method also gives you the ability to change the relative balance of the two regions in accordance with your objectives, or to rebalance the areas after major market moves. Somewhat more conservative investors, and those with smaller portfolios, may decide to opt for the simplicity of a one-fund approach. That fund should be able to invest, at a minimum, in the established markets of Europe and Japan.

GLOBAL FUNDS

Global stock funds invest in a combination of foreign and U.S. stocks to take advantage of both foreign and domestic investment opportunities, often hedging against currency risk. They usually have the word "global" or "worldwide" in their name.

Global investing is not a terrible concept, as a fund manager can move assets into the United States if foreign markets look less promising. A global fund would have the advantage of simplicity, as it gives the investor a "one-fund" approach, at least for stock positions; but most global funds have too much overseas to make sense as a one-fund stock portfolio. (They typically have two-thirds or three-fourths invested in foreign markets, whereas one-third or one-fourth would be more appropriate for most investors.) You could offset the global fund with a U.S. stock fund, but then why not just hold an international fund and a U.S. fund, with separate managers who are expert in each area? I think it's generally a better idea to allocate the money yourself between domestic and foreign funds, since the entire world is likely to be too much for one fund manager to really follow closely.

DIVERSIFIED INTERNATIONAL FUNDS

International stock funds invest only overseas in the stocks of several countries or regions. Objective: to take advantage of foreign stock market opportunities. You can usually tell a lot about foreign funds by their names. If the name includes the word "international" or "overseas," without reference to a specific country or region, it's likely to be a diversified international fund. These funds almost always have the bulk of their assets in a mix of European and Japanese stocks, as these areas represent the bulk of the non-U.S. markets. (Emerging markets are not typically a big part, because their market caps are much smaller and they are generally seen as much riskier; and Canada is not a big part, because it is not generally seen as a truly "foreign" economy.)

Diversified international funds should be benchmarked against the EAFE Index (Morgan Stanley's Europe, Australasia, Far East index) of established markets. For most of the 1990s, it was relatively easy for these funds to beat the index, merely by underweighting positions in Japan and overweighting Europe. That formula for success seemed to have changed by the second half of 1998, as Japan's markets, especially its small-cap markets, started to stir.

NONDIVERSIFIED INTERNATIONAL FUNDS

Whereas most international and global funds invest in several countries on one or more continents, regional funds narrow their sites to a portion of the globe, typically Europe or the Pacific basin, and single-country funds focus on one particular country's stocks and bonds. Most international investors should consider holding a regional fund or two but should not look too closely at the plethora of single-country funds. By far the most volatile of the bunch, single-country funds are generally best avoided unless, as in the case of Japan, the country is the largest market outside the United States, with well established markets, industries, and accounting practices.

EUROPEAN FUNDS

Most funds with "Europe" in their name cover all of Western Europe but tend to exclude (or have relatively small positions in) those Eastern European nations that were formerly part of the Soviet bloc. The European stock markets are dominated by the United Kingdom, Germany, France, Switzerland, Italy, the Netherlands, and Denmark.

Europe's progress in restructuring lags several years behind America's, but restructuring is now a factor in corporate success (and failure) and is accelerating, owing to the common market and the creation of a common currency (the euro), as well as the move from family and state ownership toward public shareholders. Spinoffs of unrelated businesses; mergers of other, better-fitted, divisions; and other forms of cost-cutting are all improving corporate profitability.

In general, the risks in Europe don't come from instability; they come from stagnation, high tax rates, and continued resistance to needed reforms in areas like agricultural policy. While market reforms have made headway, much work still lies ahead. The direction of European integration presents one major cause for concern. Will Brussels's policy of convergence mean that continental tax and social policies will be reformed to mesh with the more business-friendly practices of the United Kingdom? Or will Britain be forced to raise taxes and government spending to the higher levels prevailing on the other side of the Channel? The answer will have a major effect on the European business climate in the new century. The answer will be spelled out in the next several years.

PACIFIC BASIN FUNDS

This area is about as important to the global economy as Europe. But the Pacific basin is much more dominated by a single country (Japan, of course). While Japan's stock market has stagnated for most of the 1990s, it's still much larger than the rest of the region's combined markets. Hence most of the "Pacific" funds have more than 70 percent of their assets in Japanese stocks, and they closely follow the Japanese markets. (Moveover, the other countries' economies are heavily dependent on trade with each other and with Japan, and so they tend to move up and down together.) While the region has had a couple of tough years (more than that, in the case of Japan), it's likely to eventually resume its trend of rapid economic growth. Most growth-seeking investors should consider holding some assets in this region, through a "Pacific" fund, a "Japan" fund, or—for more conservative or smaller investors—a diversified "international" fund.

JAPAN FUNDS

Japan is the investment site for the most common single-country funds. That's because Japan dominates the Asian economic sphere to a greater extent than any nation dominates Europe, and the Japanese stock market is still the second-largest in the world after that of the United States. (For a brief time, a decade ago, all of Japan's stocks were actually selling for more than all those in the United States; that was when the emperor's palace in Tokyo was in theory worth more than California. These prices reflected Japanese market euphoria more than any real global dominance.) The other Asian economies (e.g., Australia, New Zealand, Malaysia) are much smaller than Japan, or are considered emerging markets rather than established industrial powers, or both.

OTHER SINGLE-COUNTRY FUNDS

One can find single-country funds covering most established markets, and also for many emerging markets, especially if one considers closed-end funds. But unless you actually like holding a dozen different international funds (on top of your U.S. funds), why bother? Of course, you may just happen to have a strong hunch that Austria is the one country to be in right now. But for most investors, it would be wiser to stick to a couple of overseas funds and let the fund manager make the country-specific market calls.

EMERGING MARKET FUNDS

While the majority of international funds invest in countries with well-established markets and economies, emerging market funds concentrate on developing markets, countries, and economies. The results can be spectacularly good or bad, and we've seen both kinds of markets in recent years.

What are emerging markets? They are countries that, until fairly recently, had relatively static economies, dominated by agricultural and artisanal production ("third world" countries), or communist-controlled economies, or both. To qualify as emerging markets, not just backward markets, and to keep "emerging markets" from being seen as a euphemism for backwardness, the term is generally reserved for countries that have at least started to show the following: considerable growth in industry and the economy; capital markets which, while they may retain examples of crony capitalism, are also at least somewhat open to free, transparent investments; and achievements or improvements in education and literacy. Some previously emerging markets (such as Malaysia) have achieved such a level of prosperity that they may be considered developed markets.

Where are the emerging markets? They are generally divided into three areas: (1) East Asia and the Pacific Rim—except for Japan, Australia, and New Zealand, which are clearly developed countries. (2) Eastern Europe, most of which was formerly dominated by the Soviet Union. (3) Latin America, with most of these investments in Mexico and South America. In addition, India, Turkey, Israel, North Africa, and the rest of the Middle East are often found in emerging markets funds. The nations of sub-Saharan Africa, with the exception of South Africa, are rarely represented, owing to considerable backwardness in political, market, and educational structures.

There are over 100 mutual funds invested in "emerging markets" in general, without sticking to one of these subregions. There are also about 60 funds invested in Pacific basin emerging markets (i.e., without significant positions in Japan or Australia). And there are about 40 funds invested primarily in Latin America. There are a few (but very few) open-end mutual funds invested primarily in Eastern Europe (e.g., Kaminsky Poland, Lexington Troika Dialog Russia, U.S. Global Investors Regent Eastern Europe). Generally one must buy a European fund, which will probably have less than 10 percent of its assets in Eastern Europe. There is a Calvert New Africa fund, and there are some single-country emerging markets funds (although there are more such options among closed-end funds).

PACIFIC RIM

The major emerging nations in this area are, in approximate order of decreasing prosperity: Malaysia, Hong Kong, Taiwan, Singapore, South Korea, Indonesia, the Philippines, Thailand, China. ("Prosperity" is a somewhat subjective concept. Hong Kong is of course now part of China but still has a very different economy and markets. Malaysia is included in Morgan Stanley's EAFE Index of established markets, as are Japan, Australia, and New Zealand; but I include Malaysia here because most "emerging markets" funds include Malaysia.)

Until 1997, the Pacific Rim was the fastest-growing part of the world, with many countries showing annual GDP growth rates of 10 percent or more. Unfortunately, that prosperity was partly due to a "bubble" of foreign investment, and after Thailand devalued its currency, and devaluation spread to most of the rest of the region (with the exception of Hong Kong–China), investors pulled out suddenly, leaving many companies undercapitalized and expansion and building projects halted.

This instability spread to emerging markets throughout the world. It hurt Russia and Latin America—not because of any actual problems with trade or other economic ties but because market sentiment led to a pullback from risky credits throughout the world. It was also expected to hurt the United States, but it had little effect here, perhaps the Federal Reserve Board skillfully eased interest rates precisely to ward off such an effect. (Lower prices on Asian imports, and in the global oil markets, provided deflationary pressures which allowed easing in the United States with little fear of causing domestic inflation.)

LATIN AMERICA

Economically, the most significant nations in this area are Mexico, Brazil, Argentina, Chile, Venezuela, Peru, and Colombia.

The biggest investment risks in this area come from the frequent success of statist politics, with heavy regulation of capital flows and employment, and the occasionally popular expropriation of private assets.

After strong performances in 1996 and 1997, most Latin American markets were hurt in 1998. The reason? Primarily an overflow of fear from the market's decline in the Pacific basin markets, and the resulting global breakdown of liquidity.

While NAFTA has greatly increased the United States' trade with Mexico, it isn't likely to be expanded to other South American nations any time soon. (Free trade has so many powerful enemies, ranging from organized labor on the left to Pat Buchanan on the right, that it will no doubt be a contentious issue for years to come.)

EASTERN EUROPE AND RUSSIA

By some measures Russia, Poland, Hungary, and the Czech Republic are more advanced than other emerging markets. But although heavy industry and education were built up under communism, much of that industry is now obsolete, and capital markets were essentially nonexistent until recently.

Russia is, in the long run, likely to return to its position as the dominant power in the region, but so far it has had more trouble converting to capitalism than the three next largest economies. The problems? The people who used to run the country, nominally ex-communists, are still largely in charge, often alongside gangsters and military elements, and corrupt cronyism isn't conducive to capitalism. Bullets aren't mightier than the dollar—just more persuasive in the short term. With the global credit shocks of 1998, the Russian stock market declined almost 90 percent.

Is there a potential light at the end of the Russian tunnel? Yes— if you squint your eyes. The country's gas, oil, and minerals aren't going anywhere. That's precisely the problem in the short term, but as world demand grows and the Russians sort out who owns what, production and trade of these commodities should help considerably. While the elimination of corruption—or even a reduction to

European or U.S. levels—seems impossible, the country can reasonably hope for a more moderate Asian-style corruption, which benefits from building things and growing the economy, rather than
an African-style corruption, which steals from the country without
spreading any wealth around.

Currently, Poland, Hungary, and the Czech Republic are much
further along than Russia in the conversion to free markets, helped
by heavy investments from European multinationals seeking new
markets and labor. (The former East Germany is even further along,
but it is of course now combined with the former West Germany.)
These Eastern nations will not join the euro currency union any
time soon, but they are becoming more and more integrated with
the West.

This is a promising area, but I think, in line with the limited
pure investment choices here, it makes more sense to have a
broader European fund. None of the "Europe" funds have more
than a small minority of investments in the East, but most do hold
a lot of multinationals with exposure there. This is a safer way to
invest in the area, especially given that much of the investment in
the East is coming from the West, and that Eastern bourses are
relatively small and thinly capitalized.

SHOULD YOU INVEST IN EMERGING MARKETS?

Both established and emerging foreign markets have badly lagged
the U.S. market for most of the past decade. But just as it was a
mistake to rush into emerging markets at the end of 1993 (when
the Morgan Stanley Emerging Markets Index gained 73.2 percent),
it's also a mistake to assume that the United States is the place to
be on the basis of its past performance.

INTERNATIONAL BOND FUNDS

I fear debt—and I fear foreign debt (especially in less-developed
countries) most of all. Like U.S. bonds, foreign bonds have interest
rate risk and credit risk. But foreign bonds also have currency risk
and political risk. With emerging-market bonds there's often some
yield advantage over the United States; but it is not, in my opinion,
enough to justify purchase. In fact, I can't run away fast enough.
Have you ever tried to collect an IOU outside of our borders? I

thought not. If you wouldn't trust the leaders of Russia or South America to safeguard your credit cards while on holiday, why would you lend them money that may never see the light of repay? (And even apart from actual defaults, market risk is considerable: 1998 saw steep declines in emerging markets debt as the summer's global credit crunch caused a collapse in illiquid third-world securities; U.S. junk bonds went down only about one-fourth as much.)

In the established countries of Europe and Japan, you won't run into disastrous political risk scenarios, but you won't find high yields there either. Since bonds don't have a lot of potential for growth, I prefer my bond funds to be as plain-vanilla as possible. In other words, if you're going to take on the risks of international markets, you should at least get the greater upside of their stock markets. My preference for income investing: U.S. bond funds, individual U.S. treasuries, or—for those who like to walk on the wild side— domestic junk bonds.

No one really knows where world markets are going. But the same can be said about the United States. After having been told for a decade that with each passing year the world was becoming more economically interconnected—a contention the spread of the "Asian contagion" seemed to prove—we are experiencing an American economy that thus far has proved remarkably robust. Are we just experiencing a delayed reaction due to the differential between world and U.S market cycles? Will the other shoe be dropping soon? Or is the United States, as some economists assert, actually a much more autonomous economy than most free-traders and globalists would have us believe? My sense is that in the new millennium, the big story for us will be the comeback of the global market—and the relative strength of a handful of international funds.

PART V

TAX SMARTS

TWENTY

Tax Planning
for Your Funds

About as much fun as having your teeth drilled, tax planning is an important aspect of fund investing that many younger (and older) investors ignore to their detriment. If your only investing is in a tax-advantage retirement plan (see Chapters 21 and 22 for details), you can ignore most tax issues for at least the next 30 years. However, if you have a taxable account, you'll want to dig into this chapter, which discusses how smarter tax planning can actually help you save money.

While it would be a mistake to let tax considerations dominate your investment planning decisions, it still pays to strategize: there are high-tax and low-tax ways to reach almost every investing objective. This chapter shows you tax-wise fund investing strategies (like using capital losses in one fund to offset gains in another), unveils a trick or two for avoiding those pesky capital gains distributions, and shows how to structure your portfolio in the most tax-savvy manner possible.

To repeat, if most of your fund assets are happily ensconced in a 401(k) plan or an IRA account, you can happily disregard the tax factor: gains and income generated by assets in these retirement plans are tax-free. In fact, I suggest that you keep pumping money into your IRA even if you have to use after-tax dollars, because you can reinvest distributions made by funds held in your IRA tax-free. Unless you shelter your distributions from taxes, the fund you own will never match the performance of the virtual fund whose numbers are tracked in the financial press.

Why? Because those impressive charts showing the fate of an

initial $10,000 investment over 5, 10, and 20 years assume reinvestment of all distributions. They conveniently ignore the fact that in the real world, unless your fund is in a tax-advantage retirement account, you will lose ground in comparison with the chart every time the fund makes a distribution.

TAX BASICS

Each time your mutual fund sends you a check—or keeps your earnings in house to buy more shares for you—the payout is called a distribution. Distributions consist of capital gains, dividend income, or often a combination of the two. The proportion of gains to dividends, or even whether a distribution is all gain or all dividend, depends on the type of fund and what sort of trades its management has been making. (The distribution period may be monthly, quarterly, or annual.)

When a fund manager sells portfolio assets for more than they cost, if the resulting gains outweigh losses accumulated from other trades, the law stipulates that gains must be passed along to shareholders. Thus, although you obviously make the decision when to buy and sell your shares, the actions of fund managers, not your own tax-planning savvy, determine when gains generated by the fund's underlying portfolio are passed on to you. As I'll explain in a moment, these distributed gains are one real drawback of funds, in comparison with directly owned investments. Under current law, the capital gains portion of your mutual fund distribution, as well as gains you may realize from selling shares, is taxed on the basis of whether it was a short-term or a long-term capital gain. Short-term gains are now taxed at 39 percent, while long-term gains are taxed at 20 percent.

The dividend portion of your fund distribution represents your share of the income generated by all the stocks, bonds, and money-market instruments held by the fund. It is taxed, straightforwardly enough, as ordinary income.

GAINING FROM LOSSES

If some of the funds in your portfolio have posted capital losses for the year, liquidating these investments can provide some needed tax relief. Be careful: don't bail out of a good fund just because it

---

QUICK TIP

Before you buy shares in a fund, call the investment company and find out when the next distribution will be made. If the next distribution will be made in the near future, I would recommend postponing your fund investment until after it occurs—this is one boat you would do well to miss.

---

has experienced short-term reverses. (Unless you're already well into retirement, 1 year is generally too short a time span upon which to base a sell decision.) But assuming you've come to the considered conclusion that a particular fund really is a dog, selling it can have benefits if you've realized capital gains in other areas of your portfolio.

For example, suppose you bought 500 shares in XYZ Capital Appreciation Fund 5 years ago at $100 and, now that the fund is selling for $90, you decide to sell the shares. If one of your other funds had a $4,000 capital gains distribution for the year, your $5,000 capital loss on the XYZ Cap App shares would erase those capital gains as far as the IRS is concerned. Tax owed: $0. As for the $1,000 of excess losses, they can be used to reduce your amount of taxable income or carried forward to reduce income in subsequent years; just be aware that there is a $3,000 ceiling on the amount of loss you can use to offset other income in any subsequent year. In fact, the tax code allows you to carry unused capital losses forward for as many as 15 years into the future, so if you had $45,000 in losses, you could use up to $3,000 to reduce your tax bill in each of the subsequent 15 years.

Another wrinkle is what might be called "tax-loss shorting." Suppose that you sell your XYZ Cap App shares on December 15, 2000, and then use the capital loss to offset other gains. Then, by mid-February, you feel that the fund, which is now selling at $75 a share, has good enough long-term prospects to look attractive at that price. You could buy back the shares at the lower price without jeopardizing the tax advantages of the capital loss you took, as long as a 30-day period separates the sale and the repurchase. You now own the same shares for $75 that you sold at $90 plus getting the tax advantages of the capital loss. Or, without waiting for the 30-day period to expire, you could buy shares in another, better-performing fund with the same investment objective as the fund you dumped. Just don't get too fancy and do something like switching within the 30-day period from one fund company's S&P 500 index fund to one sponsored by another firm's: such nimbleness might cause the IRS to disallow your capital loss offset.

Generally, if you've lost less than $1,000 or under 10 percent of your initial investment, selling for tax purposes will hardly be worth the bother. Also, timing is everything: if the losing fund still has some capital gains distribution to make at year-end, be sure to make the sale before the distribution occurs.

CALCULATING YOUR CAPITAL GAINS (OR LOSSES) ON SALES OF FUND SHARES

As you grow older, and as your goals and objectives evolve, your portfolio will need periodic adjusting. Eventually, no matter how inspired your fund picks may have been, the time will come to sell some or all of your shares in one or more of them. If the fund you are selling is one which you've owned a long time and in which you reinvested dividends, selling shares could be a bit of a tax headache. Why? Because each batch of shares you bought over all those years had a unique cost basis and therefore will realize a unique amount of capital gains. Suppose you've owned Gilt-Edge Growth Fund for 20 years and religiously reinvested your distributions each quarter. Even during periods when the market was treading water, you can be sure that, day-to-day price fluctuations being what they are, each share purchase would have had a slightly different cost basis.

For better or worse, the IRS allows you to use several different methods to calculate the amount of taxable capital gains on sales of shares. If you want, you can treat each fund share you purchased as though it were a separate share of stock and calculate the gains accordingly. This is called the "specific share method" and requires that you obtain written confirmation from the fund company as to which shares you sold and when the shares sold were purchased. Fortunately, there are also several ways of determining your average cost basis that provide a detour around such endless exercises in bean counting. They are as follows.

Another wrinkle. By now, you probably realize that the one thing I really hate about mutual funds is those involuntary capital gains distributions they saddle you with. Wait a minute, I hear you saying. I thought that capital gains, having each of my shares grow in value, were the whole point of investing. Right you are. But paying capital gains taxes is not. The problem is that even if you use every penny of the capital gains the fund company distributes to buy more shares—in other words, if your money never leaves the fund—the IRS treats the distributions as realized capital gains taxable to you. The SEC requires investment companies to distribute both capital gains and dividends to shareholders at least once each year. This is a major contrast with what happens when you buy shares on your own: in that case, you are required to pay the capital gains tax only on shares that you sell.

There's worse to come. Believe it or not, when you get your Form 1099-DIV, you could end up paying capital gains taxes on a fund that had a negative return for the year. How could that be? Even if the bulk of the stocks in the portfolio did badly enough to drag down the fund's return into negative territory, chances are that at least some holdings rose in value. If the managers choose to sell some of these appreciated stocks—say, to meet redemptions triggered by the fund's poor performance—the gains thus realized must be distributed to the hapless shareholders. The result is a fund delivering a negative return *and* a capital gains tax bill. Yuck. Of course, if the fund sold some of its losing shares as well, the capital losses thus generated would offset those gains.

Investment companies are fully aware of the tax traps this whole issue sets for shareholders. And guess what—they've devised a product to address this problem (or at least to make a buck from people's fears and concerns). These relatively new funds (most were launched in the 1990s) are managed with a "buy-and-hold" philosophy that keeps portfolio turnover low relative to the average stock fund: in a given year, tax-efficient funds generally sell less than 20 percent of the stocks with which they began that year. These funds typically use redemption fees to discourage shareholders from making short-term investments, thus making it less likely that managers will have to sell appreciated shares to raise cash. Vanguard's Tax Managed Fund: Capital Appreciation Fund is another index-type fund that gives itself room to deviate from its index enough to avoid realizing capital gains. Fidelity also has an entrant in this category, the Tax Managed Fund.

Like every other fund product, the features that make tax-efficient funds distinctive have their drawbacks. For one thing, it could be argued that restricting portfolio turnover cramps a fund manager's style. Rules that limit the number of trades the manager can make in a given year could tie his or her hands while choice buying and selling opportunities sail by. Especially in a volatile marketplace, this loss of freedom may be too high a price to pay for tax minimization. (On the other hand, given the continued poor performance of actively managed equity funds against their relevant indices, perhaps restricting the manager's flexibility isn't such a bad idea!) To be honest, tax-efficient funds have not been in operation long enough for a meaningful performance assessment to be possible: the category has been around only since the early 1990s.

QUICK TIP

Standard and Poor's has produced statistics suggesting that the low-turnover management style of tax-efficient funds may not be the best route to long-term high returns. High-turnover portfolios did quite well during the 10 years from 1988 to 1998, according to the folks at S&P: the 50 best domestic stock funds had an average portfolio turnover rate of 80 percent. This could mean that better performance and frequent trading go hand in hand; but as something of a buy-and-holder, I wonder whether that isn't a rather specious conclusion.

Municipal Bond Funds. An obvious way to keep the tax collector at bay is to invest in a fund consisting of municipal bonds (see Chapter 17 for details), issued by the state where you are a legal resident. The income you earn from a single-state muni bond fund is generally exempt from local, state, and federal taxes, although capital gains distributions—and even these income-oriented funds can generate them—are subject to the usual tax. (If you invest in a fund owning municipal bonds from a variety of states, your dividends are still exempt from federal taxes.) Municipal bond funds should become a major element of your portfolio when you've reached retirement age and need tax-free current income, but they are not intended for a long-term investment, although a moderate dose of muni bonds may be a good hedge against the advent of a protracted bear market or a period of deflation. Outside of this potential hedging function, putting your money into muni bond funds when you still need to build your retirement portfolio is a perfect example of misplaced priorities.

Deducting Investment-Related Expenses. You may not realize that Uncle Sam lets you claim as miscellaneous itemized deductions a whole raft of investment-related expenses. In 1998, if your miscellaneous itemized deductions exceeded 2 percent of your adjusted gross income, you could deduct a wide array of costs associated with building and maintaining your mutual fund portfolio. Of course, if you are pretty sure that your total itemized deductions are likely to be less than the amount of your standard deduction (for 1998, $7,100 for married couples filing jointly and $4,250 for single taxpayers), you'd be wise to skip the paperwork and take the standard deduction instead. If you're married, however, and there is a marked disparity between your two incomes, it might make sense to file separate returns if the lower-income spouse can claim most of the investment-related deductions.

What exactly are you allowed to deduct? It's really quite surprising how widely you can cast your net. According to Section 212 of the Internal Revenue Code, "In the case of an individual, there shall be allowed as a deduction all the ordinary and necessary expenses paid or incurred during the taxable year for the production or collection of income; for the management, conservation, or maintenance of property held for the production of income; or in connection with the determination, collection, or refund of any tax." As far as the IRS is concerned, even expenses related to losing investments come under this definition of deductibility.

Do you use your home PC to track your investment portfolio via on-line services or with software of your own? You can deduct depreciation for the equipment, the purchase price of the software, and any subscription fees you pay to on-line financial service providers. Do you use a broker or pay for financial or tax-planning assistance? You can deduct fees paid to these financial professionals. Do you spend a lot of time on the phone with your financial advisers? You can deduct the cost of those calls. If you are confident enough to dispense with costly investment advice—and you should be after reading this book—you can deduct the cost of the magazines, newsletters, and newspapers you buy to help shape your investment strategy.

You can also deduct any trustee, custodial, administrative, and management fees for your IRA or 401(k) plan, provided you pay them directly rather than have the plan sponsor deduct them from the account. If the fees are going to come to a substantial amount, you should request that these fees be billed directly. All these and other potential investment-related deductions are detailed in IRS Publication 529 "Miscellaneous Deductions." It's a publication worth getting.

All in all, my advice about deducting investment-related expenses is as follows. Be sure you have an idea of how much your time is worth before you spend inordinate amounts of time accounting for every nickel and dime you spend on investment-related expenses. You may come to the conclusion that the time spent on paperwork and tax returns does not warrant the savings your diligence may enable you to wring out of your tax bill. On the other hand, you may conclude that you already have sufficient miscellaneous deductions from other sources to warrant taking the time to track your investment-related expenses.

TAX STRATEGY

As I said at the outset of this chapter, don't allow tax avoidance to become an all-consuming passion. That said, it pays to keep an eye on the tax implications of your investment decisions. While you have no control over the timing and amount of the capital gains distributions fund managers make, you should take tax considerations into account when weighing whether and when to buy or sell shares in a particular fund. You might also want to take a look at the growing group of tax-advantage funds to see whether any meet your investment objectives. And when you're comparing the merits of funds within the various conventional categories, it might not be a bad idea to take a look at their portfolio turnover rates. Not only should a very high turnover rate suggest that the management style might be frenetic, but it means that investing in the fund will expose you to frequent capital gains distributions, a sure recipe for indigestion at tax time.

TWENTY-ONE

Funding Your 401(k)

We've got a long way to travel before we pull into retirement town. As a result, we can take on some added risk in order to increase our potential returns. Doing so will entail building a $10,000 portfolio which has small- and large-cap funds invested primarily in domestic growth (and maybe value) stocks, and international stock funds. Forget about cash or bonds unless you're within a decade of retirement. Also, remember that the stock funds you select will already have a small position in cash. Finally, don't ignore your biggest potential asset: your 401(k) plan.

Treat your 401(k) or other tax-deferred retirement plan like you would any other long-term investment portfolio, and as an integral part of your $10,000 portfolio. The exact retirement vehicle you have chosen—such as a 401(k), 403(b), IRA, or Roth IRA—will determine specific guidelines for when you can invest and withdraw assets and what amounts to invest and withdraw, and it may affect your exact menu of investment choices; but it has essentially no bearing on what sort of investments you should choose to build your $10,000 portfolio. In fact, your 401(k) or IRA (see Chapter 22 for details on IRAs and Roth IRAs) is an excellent place to invest in the more aggressive—and probably most traded—growth funds in your $10,000 portfolio.

By now, we know that diversifying across industries, stocks, and countries is the best way to deliver solid long-term, risk-adjusted returns. But you'll need to pay attention to the funds on your 401(k) menu, which may or may not be name brand funds that are easily tracked. For each fund, request a copy of the prospectus from your employer's human resources department, or from the fund itself. The prospectus will describe the fund's various investments and overall objective. You can also read the fund's semiannual reports, which list all of its holdings. (Check out Chapter 10 for my crib notes on how to read a prospectus, or check out Chapter 23 for a review of the best fund research sites on-line.)

Chances are that your plan offers, at the least, some growth, balanced, bond (income), and money market options. Which should you concentrate on? Aggressive growth and growth funds. You can afford to take on some additional risk in the form of an aggressive small-cap value or large-cap growth concentration, with some foreign exposure added to your mix. Remember, the risk of taking no risk (i.e., putting your retirement money into a money market account) is that, over the long run, you'll almost certainly see minimal gains after accounting for inflation.

KEEP TABS ON YOUR 401(K)

Reviewing your portfolio is essential. Some people will buy the *Star Wars* trilogy and watch it over and over again. But when it comes to their 401(k) statement (which typically arrives quarterly), do they review it even once? Many people don't—and that's a mistake. Every time you receive a statement involving your finances you should review it to ensure that (1) it's your account, (2) it shows the right amount invested, and (3) it reflects any trades that you authorized—and none that you didn't authorize.

I also keep a running portfolio of my 401(k) funds, checking their performance regularly by turning to the fund section of my local paper. (I also create a personal "daily" sheet which tracks performance of every fund I own or might own—see Chapter 25 for details on creating one for yourself.) I like to know how the funds I have selected are performing relative to certain meaningful benchmarks, like the S&P 500 (for my large-cap stock funds), the Russell 2000 (for my small-cap funds), and the EAFE (for international funds). If the performance of particular fund or stock is steadily deteriorating over several quarters relative to similar funds or stocks (i.e., those within the same industry), then it's probably time to consider an alternative fund.

I find this a great way to stay up to speed on the overall market as well—after all, the stocks each fund invests in come from different industries. Keeping track of each fund lets me connect industry and economic news to down-to-earth terms that mean something about my own financial condition. Developing a general awareness of the economy and how it affects your investments' performance is something I encourage you to do.

TRADE, EVEN OFTEN

Of course, having said all this, I'm not advocating trading in and out of funds on a regular basis. In fact, frequent trading in and out of the market doesn't work. What does work is selecting the best funds available for the long haul (note that I didn't say this year's best-performing funds) for your $10,000 portfolio. Since some 401(k) plans provide a limited menu of investment possibilities, this may prove to be very difficult indeed. What you'll need to look at most is investment style (value versus growth, and small-cap versus large-cap) and country allocation (U.S., established markets, emerging markets) in order to ensure diversification and find the best in your limited lot. If, on the other hand, you've got a menu that's a mile long, you'll need to sift the wheat from the chaff. Once that's done, you'll need to establish a way to determine (on a regular basis) whether and when to readjust your 401(k) portfolio.

Some employers may restrict your ability to actively manage your own 401(k) investments, while others encourage you to manage it. The more you know about your plan's rules, the more likely your 401(k) will be to perform in accordance with your expectations and objectives. The rules regarding such trades are specific to your company's plan, but most allow trades quarterly. (Of course, you're restricted to the menu of funds offered by your employer.) Your employee benefits department is the best place to go for all the details.

FUNDING YOUR 401(K) PLAN

While only a small minority of firms with fewer than 50 employees sponsor 401(k) plans, nearly all companies employing over 5,000 people offer them. By the time you read this, that number may be 100 percent. So, chances are you're already one of millions of American workers who have an opportunity to participate in one of these tax-advantage employer-subsidized plans. Even if you think you already understand how your plan works and are planning to take maximum advantage of it, be sure to read the fine print. When you receive your 401(k) packet or are alerted about a mandatory presentation about retirement plans, fight the impulse to toss the paperwork into a drawer or call in sick. The truth is that this is one of the best ways in which you can build at least a piece of your $10,000 portfolio.

Although investing in a 401(k) plan couldn't be easier from a mechanical point of view, many 401(k) fund menus are limited and even limiting. The first thing you'll need to do is answer the basic question of whether and to what extent you should participate in the 401(k) plan offered by your employer.

What? Isn't it obvious? Everyone should! Well, I don't think the answer is a simple yes. Chances are it *is* yes. But you need to be sure.

In fact, there's so much positive press about investing in a 401(k) that I think I'll start in on the potential downsides first, and then move on to the well-traveled path of positives. That way, you'll be thinking along lines that should help you secure the best retirement option for you—whether it's a 401(k) or opening up your own retirement plan (using an IRA or Roth IRA, for example—see Chapter 22 for details).

NOT ALL 401(K)S ARE CREATED EQUAL

Some 401(k) plans are downright dangerous. For one thing, many don't provide you with a menu of potential investments that are suited to your objectives. Or yours may provide funds in market areas with poor performance records or excessive loads or fees. In fact, if your employer's 401(k) fund menu offers less than eight options, and within those options offers no no-load funds from a fund family you have heard of, you're probably better off investing on your own—even if your employer matches a percentage of your own investment in the 401(k).

If you think that your plan is too restrictive, don't be afraid to just say no. True, 401(k)s are addictive—and, if the menu of investment choices is solid, it's worth getting in the habit of contributing. But just because everyone says 401(k) plans are the best thing to invest in doesn't mean that your particular plan is. Scrutinize the plan the way you would any menu of potential investments. If there isn't a way to build a portfolio you can live with and prosper by, consider opening an IRA or some other retirement account instead.

WHO CONTROLS YOUR MONEY

There are four main players in every 401(k) plan. In retirement-plan jargon, your employer is the plan's sponsor, but this doesn't mean your company has any real involvement in running it. That is the province of the administrator, the company your employer has hired to process the paperwork; and the adviser, the company selling the financial products in which you, the participant, can invest your 401(k) funds. In many cases the administrator and the adviser are the same entity. Sometimes the administrator contracts with an independent adviser to sell a package of investment products to participants. When the options on your 401(k) menu are restricted to only those products that the administrator has prepackaged, it is called "bundling." The main problem with bundled plans is that the choice is not always the greatest. In fact, according to Spectrem, in 1997 the average 401(k) plan offered participants 7.2 mutual funds to choose from—hardly the epitome of diversity in an investment universe now encompassing upward of 7,000 funds. Furthermore, funds sold through bundled plans often have higher expense ratios than publicly sold funds.

Some administrators—those that do not have a relationship with fund companies—offer unbundled 401(k) plans that can be customized for the plan sponsor. The problem is that such plans are more expensive for employers to establish: because only 401(k) plans with more than $1 million in assets are big enough to be unbundled, most small companies can't afford to take this route. Fortunately, plan administrators seem to be moving in the direction of offering larger fund menus; if your company's menu is on the scanty side, it certainly wouldn't hurt matters to voice your dissatisfaction to the employee benefits department.

Some administrators include in their menus so-called institutional funds—mutual funds sold only through particular 401(k) plans. The benefit of such tailor-made products is that they are generally cheaper for both administrator and participant than equivalent funds sold to the general public. But low cost can equal low service: because institutional funds are not marketed to consumers at large, they aren't even required to publish prospectuses. This makes it hard to live by the investment maxim: know what you own.

MATCHMAKER

For many of us, a big component of our decision-making process regarding a 401(k) is the employer's contribution, or "match." It's typical for a company to match a percentage of your contribution, up to a certain maximum. Some companies will contribute to your 401(k) account even if you don't. A company might contribute 5 percent of your pay, for example. If you, too, are contributing 5 percent, that's 10 percent of your pay, a good goal. If your employer matches your contributions, you'd be leaving big money on the table if you invested nothing.

Under U.S. tax laws, the maximum amount you can direct into your 401(k) plan per year is 15 percent of your pay, to a ceiling of $10,000. Combined with your employer's match, the maximum is $30,000 a year, or 25 percent of your taxable compensation, whichever is less.

A word of caution here: Don't invest more than you can afford. Make sure you're able to save some current money, in addition to your tax-deferred retirement investment.

DON'T CRACK YOUR NEST EGG

As crucial as it is to start investing for retirement as early as possible, many young professionals fail to save other money outside their 401(k), whether in a bank account, a money market, or taxable mutual funds. While they're building an impressive nest egg they can use after age 59½, some find they have little or no liquid savings to tap when they want to get married or buy a house.

While most companies permit you to borrow from your own 401(k) account, these loans are not recommended. Your assets aren't earning returns for you while they're withdrawn from your account. You have to pay yourself back, with interest, and often quickly. Bottom line: it's better to save some money in a bank than to plan on borrowing from your retirement plan for a down payment on a house.

That said, it is much better to save in a 401(k) plan—before taxes and through payroll deductions—than it is to save after taxes. With a 401(k), investing is automatic. You never see the money, and you rarely feel the pain of setting aside income instead of bringing it home. With after-tax savings, it's different. The $50 or $100 you move from your checking account to your savings account feels like real money, money that you could use for clothes or sporting gear or beer or a weekend on a sandy beach.

So look closely at your budget and your goals. If you're putting 15 percent away for retirement, but you have to use credit cards to pay for groceries, then you may be working against yourself. Maybe at this stage you should contribute 10 percent or 7 percent of your pay to your 401(k) in order to leave yourself enough cash to pay your bills, put something into your savings account, and go out on Saturday nights.

When it comes to choosing investment options for your 401(k), think long-term, but also think "niche." After all, your 401(k) is an integral part of your total $10,000 portfolio. You're young. You should be mostly in stock funds that shoot for growth over time. Don't be too conservative or too worried about the short-term ups and downs of the market. If you invest too conservatively, you won't reach your goals by the time you retire.

Your investment should be spread out among large-stock funds and smaller-stock funds. You may own a small amount of a bond fund to reap possible upside gains when bonds do well and stocks falter. You should consider putting a portion of your money, 10 percent to 20 percent, in an international or global stock fund.

VESTING

As with traditional pensions, it's important to understand your company's 401(k) vesting schedule. You will always own your personal contributions to the plan, and they will go with you should you ever leave the company. The employer's contribution, however, may become yours over a period of time. For example, you might be 25 percent vested in 2 years, 50 percent vested in 4 years, 75 percent vested in 6 years, and so on.

Finally, consider making an IRA (individual retirement account) contribution. If you don't have a 401(k) plan, the contribution may be a tax deduction for you. And it will set you off on the right path for long-term investing. If you max out on your 401(k) and you still have enough money left over to stash away more for retirement,

---

QUICK TIP

You've worked for your company for 5 years. In that time you have put $25,000, or $5,000 a year, into your 401(k) account. Your company has matched 50 percent of that, with full vesting in 10 years. If you leave to take a new job now, you take your own $25,000—plus market gains—and half the $12,500 the company has contributed. That's $6,250 on top of the $25,000 or $31,250, plus market gains (or minus any losses). If you had stayed the full 10 years, however, you'd clearly have more in your 401(k). You should figure this into your pay negotiations at your new job.

---

you could open a Roth IRA. There's no up-front tax deduction, but you don't pay taxes down the line either, when you withdraw the money.

WHAT TO AVOID IN YOUR 401(K)

Avoid tax-free investments, particularly municipal bond funds, since taxable bonds deliver a higher yield and are just as tax-free when held within a tax-deferred retirement plan. Guaranteed investment contracts (GICs) are rarely the best investment choice. They deliver bond-like performance when you probably should have most of your assets in stocks. When you buy a GIC, the insurance company promises to pay a specified interest rate over a specified period of time; but, as with a single corporate bond, there's nothing truly guaranteed about it. (Insurance companies that offer these products can fail, just like an S&L, but without the $100,000 in federal insurance.)

I would also avoid putting shares of your own company's stock in your 401(k). As one of my personal finance mentors was fond of saying, "As optimistic as you might be about your company's financial future and fortunes, you never know what's going to happen to its stock price." You may want or need to own your company's shares, either because you are optimistic, because you get a significant employee discount, or because of "political" pressure to do so. But don't let them account for more than 20 percent of your overall retirement portfolio. The last thing you want is for the bottom to fall out of the company's stock price and your 401(k), too (especially since such a happening might coincide with the end of your career there).

WHEN TO QUESTION YOUR 401(K)

Fraud still happens, and it happens more where large sums of money are involved. In 1995, the U.S. Labor Department investigated over 300 cases of possible 401(k) fraud, out of the more than 250,000 401(k) plans that were up and running at the time. While the 300 problem cases represented a thin 0.1 percent of all plans, the increase in plans may bring about an increase in the number of employers who might dip into this retirement pool. Here are some clear warning signs that can alert you to potential problems with your 401(k):

- You notice a steep drop in the value of your account that can't be explained by the performance of the funds (or other types of investments) you hold.

403(B) PLANS

The same tax law that established corporate 401(k) pension plans also created 403(b) plans for public employees and workers in nonprofit organizations. The 403(b) rules are particularly complex.

The key distinction is that moneys in 403(b) accounts before December 31, 1986, must be withdrawn beginning at age 75—not 70½—using the term certain method. Funds that went into the account after that date are subject to the 70½ rule and the recalculation method. Another wrinkle: college professors who continue teaching after age 70 are allowed to continue making contributions to their 403(b)—but they've also got to make minimum withdrawals.

Special tax booby traps have been set for people who have large balances in so-called qualified, or company, pension plans, like a 401(k). But you can worry about that when the time comes—40 years hence.

- The deductions from your paycheck don't match the contributions on your 401(k) statements.
- Your 401(k) statements should arrive on a regularly scheduled date, four times per year. If your quarterly statement arrives late or at irregular times during the year, get an explanation from your benefits administrator—and be on guard.
- You have heard that former employees had difficulty when it came to receiving their benefits.

If any of these problems seem to be occurring in your plan, and you can't get a reasonable (and understandable) explanation from your plan administrator, then by all means contact the Pension and Welfare Benefit Administration (202-219-8776). Be discreet, since you don't want to be in the position of angering a thief or wrongly accusing someone at your company.

TWENTY-TWO

Funding Your IRA

TWO STONES, ONE BIRD

Whether you invest in an IRA or a Roth IRA, many of the same rules apply. However, there are significant differences you need to know about. This chapter will help you leap into the thick of the debate about which type of account is most appropriate for you. Suffice it to say, however, that even if you participate in your employer's 401(k) plan (and thus you lose the deductibility factor in either the IRA or the Roth IRA), you should consider placing any money you have left on the table in one or the other plan. That's because both plans provide deferral of taxes owed until the day (way, way down the road), when you decide to make a withdrawal.

THE DEBATE

Ask a simple IRA question, get a Roth answer. The Roth IRA, named for Senator Roth of Delaware, is the new IRA that everyone is talking about but few understand. And while you should talk directly with your accountant to be sure that a Roth is or is not for you, I think it's important to understand its basic advantages and disadvantages.

The difference between a Roth IRA and a regular IRA amounts to paying your taxes now or later. All IRAs offer tax deferral, which means there are no tax consequences for trading any kind of funds or other securities. For all IRAs, you are taxed once on the money. With a regular IRA, you are taxed on the money when you withdraw it; with the Roth version, because you contribute after-tax dollars to your account, you get to withdraw the money tax-free. For a deductible regular IRA, withdrawals are taxable as income. For a nondeductible regular IRA, a portion of the withdrawals are considered "return of contributions" and are therefore exempt from tax, but most of the withdrawals are taxable. But for a Roth IRA (since contributions are nondeductible and thus were taxed like your other income), withdrawals are generally not taxed at all.

IS THE ROTH IRA BETTER?

There are really two different questions here.
1. If you already have an IRA, is it a good idea to roll the money over into a Roth IRA?
2. For new money, is a Roth IRA better than a traditional IRA?

The answers to these questions are more complicated than you might imagine and, no matter how carefully they are considered, will always be uncertain because they depend in part on unknowable factors, such as what income tax rates will be like in the future. People who are prone to worry may never relax with the decision they make, no matter how many lawyers they hire to help; those with a more devil-may-care attitude are not likely to regret either decision. Certainly, the question of what type of IRA to fund is much less important than the decision to fund an IRA, a 401(k), or some other retirement account.

In general, the advantages of the Roth IRA do not come from the fact that there's an advantage to paying your taxes now, rather than after retirement, when you'll (hopefully) have much more money as a result of market gains. (A 28 percent tax payment cuts your assets by 28 percent whether it happens at the front end or after investment.) The Roth advantage really comes from the fact that a Roth IRA is like a bigger IRA. For a person paying 33 percent in taxes, a $2,000 (nondeductible) Roth IRA is effectively like a $3,000 deductible regular IRA—but regular IRAs, like Roths, are limited to $2,000 per person, so a Roth IRA is, to repeat, like a bigger regular IRA. (More on this below.)

The Roth IRA is generally superior to the regular IRA, except for people who will be in a lower marginal tax bracket after retirement. For example, under the current tax code, many workingpeople at the lower end of the 28 percent marginal tax bracket will probably fall to the 15 percent bracket after retirement. They should probably stick to a deductible regular IRA, deferring taxes now but paying them upon withdrawal. On the other hand, many younger workers who are now in the 15 percent or 28 percent tax bracket can expect to be paying a higher tax rate in retirement. They should generally choose the Roth IRA.

Of course, no one really knows what will happen to tax rates more than a few years from now. If, to take an extreme example, we move from an income tax system to a "consumption tax," then all investments will essentially act like a regular IRA, with contributions deductible but withdrawals subject to tax. But even then, it's highly improbable that people would be taxed on their "consumption" of proceeds from Roth IRAs, because hordes of seniors would vote out the offending members of Congress. In short, the Roth IRA is likely to become as sacred a cow as its more established brethren.

1: Rollovers. You can roll over your 401(k) into an IRA—if you change employers, for example—without triggering a tax event. But a conversion or rollover from a traditional to a Roth IRA can be a taxable event. Thus if you move a $100,000 IRA into a Roth IRA, that $100,000 is taxable income. Sounds bad—but, of course, it also means you won't have to pay taxes on the (hopefully much higher) amount you'll be withdrawing after retirement.

If your modified adjusted gross income (AGI) is under $100,000 in a give year, you may roll regular IRA money over into a Roth IRA. You don't need to have earned income, and it doesn't matter how old you are or how much money is in your IRA (the conversion amount does not count toward the $100,000 AGI limit). The rolled-over IRA money is taxed like income, as it would be if you were withdrawing from your IRA now, but without the 10 percent penalty. Nondeductible IRA contributions are not taxed on the conversion, but earnings and deductible contributions are.

This may be worth doing if you have—outside of any retirement-type account—enough money to pay the taxes. In essence, the effect of paying taxes now with nonretirement money is to increase the effective amount you have invested in your IRA. But if, in order to pay the taxes on the Roth conversion, you have to withdraw some of the money, paying a 10 percent penalty in addition to income taxes now, then conversion probably does not make sense for you.

Starting with 1999, conversion is payable in the year the conversion is made. But you can always convert just a part of your IRA each year, to keep tax payments down and perhaps avoid bumping yourself into a higher marginal bracket.

Note that if you pay the income tax on a conversion from within the IRA funds, you are effectively making no real difference in the size of your IRA, since you will have eliminated tax owed on withdrawals. But if you are under age 59½, you will also owe a 10 percent penalty on this tax-driven withdrawal. For this reason, you should consider delaying any conversion until you are past that age or until you can afford to make the income tax payment with other funds. If you use other (taxable money) resources to pay the income tax on a conversion, you have effectively made a large contribution into your IRA moneys, even though the government doesn't describe it that way. (This is related to the fact that a Roth IRA is in effect a *bigger* IRA, as noted above and discussed on page 189.)

To avoid taking an IRA distribution after age 70½, you may convert to a Roth IRA. You will be paying the same taxes as with other IRA withdrawals, but the advantage of the Roth conversion is that you will continue avoiding taxes on future growth. By contrast, if you move your IRA money into a taxable account, all future income and realized capital gains are taxed each year.

Both the taxable and the tax-free portion of a regular IRA may be rolled over to a Roth IRA. If you have made nondeductible contributions to a regular IRA, the standard IRA basis recovery rules (requiring a prorated calculation on all your regular IRA assets) must be applied to determine the taxable amount of the transaction. This can be a little complicated if you're not rolling over all of your regular IRA money.

Convert if all the following are true:

1. You can pay the conversion taxes with money that is not in a retirement plan.
2. You can leave the money in the plan for at least 5 years.
3. You expect your retirement tax rate to be the same as or higher than your present rate. This last depends on guesswork, generally including the assumption of an unchanging tax code. It's hardly a certainty unless you're in the 15 percent tax bracket this year.

2: New IRA Money. In a given year you can make contributions to any combination of regular IRA (both nondeductible and deductible) and Roth IRA, as long as the total amount does not exceed $2,000, and as long as you have made at least as much earned income as you are contributing. (Married couples can make a $4,000 contribution, as long as their total earned income is at least that much.)

The ability to contribute to a Roth IRA phases out for singles at an AGI (adjusted gross income) of $95,000 to $110,000, and for married couples filing jointly at an AGI of $150,000 to $160,000. Above these levels, you must use a regular IRA (which at these income levels would be nondeductible if you also participate in a retirement plan at work).

IS BIGGER BETTER?

If you expect to be in the same tax bracket after retirement, then the Roth IRA is still probably the best way to go. Once again, that's because in essence, a Roth IRA is like a *bigger* deductible regular IRA. Here's why: the IRA is limited to $2,000 per year ($4,000 for married couples). Most people should be putting away more money than that if they can. If you're paying 33 percent in combined federal and state income taxes, and you will pay the same rate in retirement, then a $2,000 Roth IRA is just like a $3,000 deductible regular IRA. The $2,000 Roth costs you $2,000 out of pocket. Say it grows to $20,000. You get the $20,000 tax-free.

If, instead, you had a $3,000 deductible regular IRA, it would also cost you $2,000 out of pocket (since it would cut your income taxes by $1,000). It would grow tax-deferred to $30,000. After you paid the 33 percent taxes on that money, you'd be left with the same $20,000. So in this example the Roth IRA is just as good as the regular IRA. However, the Roth has the following advantage: you can make a bigger effective contribution. A single person can make a $2,000 Roth IRA contribution but simply cannot make a $3,000 regular IRA contribution.

If you're comparing a Roth IRA and a nondeductible regular IRA, the Roth is favored even more. In each case, you deposit $2,000, which is $2,000 out of your own pocket. If it grows to $20,000 in a Roth IRA, you get the $20,000 tax-free. If it grows to $20,000 in a nondeductible regular IRA, you'll owe taxes on the gains upon withdrawal ($18,000). After paying $6,000 in taxes (remember, we're assuming a 33 percent tax rate), you're left with $14,000. So if you cannot deduct your contribution to a traditional IRA, you should definitely contribute to a Roth IRA if you can.

ROTH WITHDRAWALS

A distribution from a Roth IRA is completely tax-free if you meet the following rules:

1. At least 5 years have passed from the time of your Roth contribution or converstion; withdrawals are considered to come first from your oldest contributions.
2. The distribution is made for an approved reason—you're over age 59½, or you're taking out up to $10,000 for "first-time" home-buying expenses, or you're disabled or dead.

Note that if you don't meet these rules, you're generally subject to normal taxes and a 10 percent penalty on withdrawals. The penalties for not following the rules can thus be more severe with a Roth IRA than with a regular IRA, since with a regular IRA only the 10 percent penalty is at stake—income taxes are generally due regardless of your age or the reason for withdrawal.

Because older-age distributions from a Roth IRA are not taxable, the government has no financial interest in forcing you to make Roth withdrawals, so it doesn't. (Regular IRAs have withdrawal requirements after age 70½.) You can keep your Roth IRA intact no matter how old you are. Indeed, with a Roth IRA you can make new contributions or conversions at any age!

Of course, although the Roth IRA and the regular IRA are pretty certain to remain in effect in close to their present form, details of the law can change, often unpredictably. Recently there has been talk in Congress of raising the IRA maximum contribution to $5,000, and also to create a Roth 401(k), but no one is confident that either change will occur.

Bottom line: don't wait for the light to change. Just put your pedal to the Roth IRA's metal.

Websites:
Fidelity Investments
http://www.fidelity.com

Has an IRA Evaluator to help you pick the right type of IRA (Roth, or deductible/nondeductible traditional IRA).

Roth IRA Website Home Page
http://www.rothira.com
Contains more technical information.

PART VI

NET SMARTS

TWENTY-THREE

Funds On-Line

You know the drill. Type "investing." Click enter. 840,000,000 matches. Type "funds." Click enter. 146,900,000 matches. Type "stock funds." Click enter. 25,600,000 matches. Type "Help." Click enter. Get nowhere. Type "What am I doing here?" Click control, alt, delete. Scream. Break the last remaining pencil on planet Earth. Grab yourself a Bud Lite. Grab two. Grab another, and another.

Today, there are those who proclaim that we live in an informed age. The truth? We live in an age of information—overwhelming information—where smart guys finish first and losers suck their tail-pipes' dust. This is perhaps most true in the realm of on-line investing, where there's an avalanche of information about mutual funds just waiting to bury you. Fortunately for us, there are also a handful of fund sites that you simply can't afford to do without. This guide will help you ferret them out.

Let's face it, the smart investors (including you) will know how to rule the information that is most relevant to them—whereas the foolish investors will let information rule them. In these turbo-charged times for fund investing, survival of the swiftest (both in terms of getting the right information at the right time and in terms of knowing how to apply it) determines who will thrive in the market—and who will merely get by. One key: get plugged in.

You've got to get plugged in. Otherwise, your trades will be left to the mercy of someone else's research, recommendations, and timing. (It's only money.) Plugging into on-line investing can give you total control over your own investments. It's easy once you know how.

It's no secret that the Internet and services like America On-line provide a way to keep fully current with your fund invest-ments, as well as with the range of themes affecting them. But beyond the info glut, the net also provides the most efficient way to invest in funds (and the most cost-effective way; almost every fund family offers web traders substantial cost cuts, since they're doing all the work). Sure, there are some disconnects along the way—a busy day in the markets can leave you out of the action (as many customers on most on-line trading sites have already discovered at one time or another)—but who said the web world was perfect?

Despite the glitches, no one I know of can afford to remain clueless when it comes to on-line fund investing. To get (and stay) ahead of the deadheads, you'll have to become a net head. Clicking into the following will get you your digerati diploma.

If you are completely new to the world of the web, perhaps the best way to begin is to select the only viable major on-line services still in existence: America Online (AOL) and Microsoft Network. On-line services are cost-competitive with straight web servers (around $20 per month for unlimited access time) and offer a more tailored, user-friendly environment in which to pursue research-related work. Also, such services provide access to the web itself. The major on-line services generally give you a good start, with financial news, portfolios, quotes, articles offering general advice on money management and investments, and live forums where you can participate in question-and-answer sessions, often with money management experts and investment notables, such as mutual fund managers, market gurus, and authors.

The Internet servers provide access to a wider array of investment sources right off the bat—and many investment sites on the web are mimicking the on-line services' chat format. Such servers are growing in number, and the basic difference between them is cost and accessibility. Many servers are behind the times in terms of speed and user-capability. This can translate into busy signals, dis-connects, and slow searches.

Once you've selected your server, you'll need to choose a searcher. You know the names: Netscape, Yahoo, Alta Vista, and Lycos are now brands as familiar to most of us as Coca Cola, McDon-ald's, and Midas. You can test-drive these searchers, and the rest of the following, by logging onto:

Netscape:	http://www.netscape.com
Yahoo:	http://www.yahoo.com
Alta Vista:	http://www.altavista.com
Lycos:	http://www.lycos.com

Once your system is set up, and your server and searcher are selected, you'll need to select a primary site from which to get the bulk of the your investment-related information. (If you're using an on-line service, this will be much easier to do.)

To begin with, I recommend a downloadable device called Real Audio (found at realaudio.com). This is web TV on your PC. The result is the equivalent of a picture-in-picture (PIP) effect on your PC screen. The image is a bit fuzzy compared with an actual TV broadcast. But there are the expected moving-bit-stream images, as well as high-quality sound. I have my audiovisual preference set to Fox's business channel (but could as easily have it set to an entertainment or sports channel). The source of the feed is Fox.com, and the experience alone is worth the price of admission (a one-time $29 charge for the Real Audio Plus version).

Next, don't only use searchers like Yahoo and Lycos. (But do use at least one of them.) Beyond the searchers' more traveled path lies push technology. That's right: since 1984 Big Brother hasn't been watching—he's been pushing. Today, push technology is beginning to make real headway with investors. Push technology's hip city hub is still PointCast.com, which is like a customized news and business channel for your computer. You tell the program what stocks, industries, and topics you're interested in; it grabs the info off the Internet and presents it on a flashy screen. One drawback: PointCast is dominated by press releases, so you will definitely meet all the hype that's fit to type, but the pluses easily override this concern. Besides, many other investment sites are committed to pushing news you can use through your E-mail—or finding only the fund news you can use (see zinezone.com for this). In less than a year, all you will need to do is to select the themes, regions, industries, and individual issues of interest to you. For now, however, using the name brand searchers to "hot-list" remains the mainstream way to locate the best investment resources.

Hot-listing a handful of active financial news sites creates a virtual resource room that can rival a business library's stacks—and it puts you in the driver's seat rather than at the mercy of whoever is pushing information your way. Such websites are modeled on magazines or newsletters: each "page" is a screen on your computer. Some are virtual mirrors of their hard-copy progenitors, while others are distinctly unique siblings with novel ideas all their own, like filling out worksheets wherein the web server performs calculations and dishes out answers or advice. These are very cool, most are free to visit, and none of them has any magic way of charging you money without your knowledge. (More and more sites are starting to charge customers for a password needed to access the most interesting or most recently published parts of the site. Fortunately, however, as of now you can still access some of the best sites at no cost.)

Bottom line: Access to information doesn't guarantee successful use of it. Investing with these sites in mind does.

Bloomberg.com. A more conventional and more comprehensive source of financial facts and overall market views is found at Bloomberg.com. But you get much more than mere coverage—you get in-depth analysis, market quotes, and access to a range of market experts and money managers that frequent Bloomberg's site on a daily basis. You can also zip into a number of market and industry comparison charts, which can give you a snapshot of how your overall portfolio may be doing.

CNNfn.com. A comprehensive one-stop shop. Here you'll find all the news headlines, as well as a comprehensive market watch. Trying to keep in rhythm with the daily pulse of regional and international markets may leave you crying in your beer. But staying fully informed is one way to stay ahead of the herd—and it's not hard to do. Of course, if you're interested only in regular checkups, you can turn to the weekly overviews.

EIU.com. EIU stands for Economist Intelligence Unit. If you invest in foreign stocks or international stock funds, you can't afford to overlook this site. EIU.com covers 190 countries, including emerging and newly emerging markets. EIU's core value is its consistent, objective analysis of trends in these countries, with uniquely informed commentators and commentary. EIU's network of more than 500 analysts, consultants, and researchers provides reliable and accurate intelligence to a client base that consists of the world's leading businesses, financial institutions, and government agencies.

If other sites offer more expertise, greater coverage, or a stronger reputation for accuracy and insight, they're hard to find.

FundAlarm.com. This is a noncommercial site dedicated to putting underperforming funds in the spotlight, as a consumer service. Besides tracking funds that lag their category benchmarks, Fund-Alarm.com also alerts fund shareholders about changes in management.

Morningstar.net (or fundsinteractive.com). There's nothing new under the fund sun that these two sites don't know about first. Completely reversing the old way of gleaning fund info—waiting for a monthly magazine or newsletter—these sites offer you the ability to leapfrog ahead of the unplugged investor. In fact, these two leading mutual-fund-focused sites each provide an informed and efficient way to judge the funds you're investing in and the funds you might want to check out—or check out of.

Stocksmart.com and CBSMarketwatch.com. Two stock-steeped sites that deliver more meat than most are Stocksmart.com and CBSMarketwatch.com. In this case, as in the case above, two sites are better than one. These sites cover every stock you could hope to trade—and they offer real-time quotes, analysis, trends, and forecasts. In fact, if you want only one site to hot-list for all your investment resource needs, you could choose either one of these sites and fare well. For example, beyond stocks, these sites also cover funds. If you're looking for the top- and bottom-performing mutual funds, the best and worst fund managers, the largest funds, and fund ownership of stocks, as well as sector and fund-by-sector performance numbers, you can turn to Stocksmart. If you want to look beyond a single rating system for funds, and for more commentary on individual funds in relation to their peers, you can turn to CBSMarketwatch.com's SuperStar Funds review. This directory of the top-250 SuperStar Funds is a consensus-based derivative of 25 "best funds" lists published in financial periodicals that regularly cover funds for investors. (For those wary of consensus, this site still proves invaluable in that it establishes what the consensus is.) This section monitors all the major "best funds" lists, including national financial magazines and newspapers publishing "best funds" directories monthly, quarterly, and annually. (The funds and fund managers selected have solid track records of 3 to 10 years.) The consensus is viewed as balancing out any statistical biases. One significant advantage is that all the major rating agencies are represented in the decisions of the editors this area is monitoring.

TheStreet.com. This site wails and regales. Its leader, Jim Cramer, is the Howard Stern of Internet investment sites—but don't let his blather bowl you over. He's a sharp reader of the markets and has built up a team of streetwise reporters to rival the best of any bunch. If you are going to pay for any investment site, this is my pick.

Together, these sites provide the most efficient, comprehensive sources for fund information on the web. But there's much more you'll need to learn about the web before you can consider yourself its master.

TWENTY-FOUR

Your Portfolio On-Line

Sometimes, even the World Wide Web doesn't get it. And when it comes to tracking one portfolio of funds (let alone a multiple mutual fund portfolio or a portfolio consisting of funds, stocks, and bonds), there are plenty of placebos to be found—but no real solution to the problem. So, although you can look for more advanced, more comprehensive, friendlier portfolio trackers in the near future, today, if you want to track portfolios at home, Infofund.com, Morningstar.net, Mutualfundsinteractive.com, and Stocksmart.com are your best current options.

The Net is often at its best when it provides a niche service that the megasites have overlooked or when the megasites provide a comprehensive toolbox to tackle your specific investment problem. Surprisingly, this isn't as clearly the case with a subject that's near and dear to our hearts—tracking multiple mutual fund portfolios. In fact, if you're looking for a niche on the Net that is being tapped but has yet to be fully developed, creating a comprehensive mutual fund portfolio analysis site could be your ticket to virtual success. Why? No matter what the hyperlinks suggest, there isn't a site that fits that bill, yet the demand for fund portfolio tracking (let alone a portfolio of multiple investment instruments) is clearly here today—and to stay.

Since I don't have a Bloomberg terminal in my house (and why Bloomberg doesn't join forces with Oracle and create a low-priced Bloomberg plug-in laptop, I don't know), I rely on the web to net all the fund-related data I need to survey the broad landscape of funds I invest in. But, even more important, I like to be able to click into model portfolios (my testing ground) whether it's a Saturday morning or a Tuesday night.

There are a handful of sites that provide mutual fund portfolio management abilities (albeit none comprehensive or user-friendly enough to corner the market). At least three sites have mutual fund portfolio tracking systems that are well worth trying out. These sites are (in order of my preference) Infofund.com, Morningstar.net, and CBSMarketwatch.com. You can click into each of them and find a similar mechanical rite of passage: no money down, but registration is required. And while not one site is a portfolio paradise, for reasons I'll get into below, they're all heading in the right direction, and one or two may even end up as an essential resource for anyone who wants to track a portfolio.

A quick tour through one site can help you get a sense of what you'll find elsewhere. Infofund.com is perhaps the best example, since its sole function is to track mutual fund portfolios. Infofund.com (unlike Morningstar.net, CNNFN.com, Stocksmart.com, etc.) is not a news service site, but it does exhibit a portfolio paradigm that all other sites seem to be following. As such, it makes an excellent case study of what is useful and what isn't when it comes to existing portfolio tracking sites on the web.

At Infofund, the emphasis is on personalization. It's easy to create a portfolio (once you've registered) and it's free; but it's limited to eight funds, and the technology is limited in that you will find it hard to create multiple portfolios without having to click out of the members' area, then log back in. Log-in time creates downtime—that's annoying. Nevertheless, the benefit of tracking your portfolio on-line is that you can get up on a Saturday morning (or any morning, for that matter) and automatically update your mutual fund portfolio to reflect the previous evening's close. You can then click on one of several function buttons to see your portfolio's asset and industry allocation. You can also quickly click and see how your particular funds have performed over time compared with a relevant industry or market benchmark. There is no downloading of cumbersome software and no use of spreadsheets, and you don't have to reinput your information each time you log in.

From there, you can begin to create your portfolios. The funds included in your core portfolio are valued each business day. The month-end portfolio value is automatically tracked in chart form so you can review your portfolio's 30-day performance record. You can click into a daily comparison of your core portfolio and a host of indices. You can also access a pie chart that neatly illustrates your portfolio breakdown. (The month-end unit price of each fund in your core portfolio is charted so that you can see price fluctuations over time in one snapshot.)

You can also check on the current value of your funds on a daily basis, and compare that price with their cost basis. (There's a graph that pops up, together with some textual commentary delivering a contextual picture of your funds' performance.) You can also easily compare the historical performance of each fund in the portfolios with its industry. You can make changes in your core portfolio easily and as often as you wish. In addition to your core portfolio of up to 8 funds, choose any number of funds to build your monitored funds list to keep track of price changes. Add funds to your core portfolio or remove funds from it with a simple click.

For viewing the top- and bottom-performing funds on the basis of different time periods, Morningstar.net is superior to Inforfund and Mutualfundsinteractive.com. They are also all better at providing analysis and research than Infofund, but Infofund holds its own in terms of being focused solely on tracking fund portfolios.

Beyond Infofund, there are sites that provide more information but don't allow you to track your portfolio: FundAlarm.com, Morningstar.net, Mutualfundsinteractive.com, Stockmaster.com, Stocksmart.com, and CBSMarketwatch.com. Each site offers substantially more information about mutual funds' performance and fund particulars, nested within its overall investment site. Morningstar obviously has a lock on funds, but although it offers excellent tracking software (Principia, for example), the on-line version simply pales. The main drawback for Morningstar, which should be the leader here, is that it has this crazy notion of wanting to make money (or at least not lose money by giving away its products).

The competition among fund sites is fierce—meaning that you're likely to get more bang for your Internet buck for many years to come. Bottom line: these sites already provide enough return on investment (ROI) to make them worth your while. Chapter 25 will show you how to maximize your return on your Net investment.

TWENTY-FIVE

Create Your Own On-Line Fund Tracking System

If you want to get technical and be in greater control of a broader number of funds (and the markets, industries, and stocks they invest in), you can move beyond the obvious fund sites and create your own spreadsheet.

Now, I know that the very word "spreadsheet" probably has the hair on the back of your neck standing on end. But making a spreadsheet is easy to do. It enables you to gain a broader and more meaningful picture of your funds' performance. And, after taking 10 minutes to read this, and 10 minutes to set it up, you will need only 10 minutes a day to update a top-level tip sheet.

Creating your own fund tracking system recognizes that the Internet is our friend. In fact, it's a crowded house of friends: resources all designed to make our professional life more efficient and informed. But while most market strategists and journalists (I include myself in both camps) focus on the latest and greatest sites that you and I can use to enhance our insights into markets and personal financial planning issues—which are the yeast of our daily bread—the truth is that most of us are still not using the web to the degree of personalized proficiency that would mark it as an invaluable tool.

Although there are many portfolio management programs available (see Chapter 24), I have long preferred the flexibility and control that come from working with raw data and a spreadsheet program. It's also far more hip than bringing a copy of the *WSJ* to the café—it's your proprietary report on the markets.

All I use to keep track of the daily performance of 200 or so funds, their top 50 stocks, and the most relevant market indices is a web browser to cull the data (I use Yahoo), and Microsoft Excel to manage the data.

Here's how I do what I do; call it a mini-lesson in how to excel on the web. To show returns I use a spreadsheet that keeps track of a month's worth of daily prices. The spreadsheet includes the investment's year-to-date return through the end of the previous month, and its share price (or net asset value, NAV) on the last day of the previous month.

To calculate total returns for periods shorter than a month, I divide the fund's most recent day-end share price by its most recent month-end share price and then multiply the result by a factor for any dividends paid within the month. So if a fund's share price rose from $10 to $10.45 during the month but the fund did not pay out any dividends, then its return is 4.5 percent. $100 \times ((10.45/10.00-1) \times$ the dividend multiplier), which, since no dividends were paid, is simply 1. Year-to-date (YTD) returns are shown by compounding the previous end-of-month YTD return by the present month-to-date return.

Distributions can be hard to keep track of and, as a result, are a potential glitch in my system, but I've learned to look for them and integrate them when they occur. Fortunately, most are on a fairly regular schedule available from the fund companies. Barron's also shows distributions after the fact; and sizable distributions can usually be spotted by an unexpectedly negative one-day return for a fund, and then the size can be confirmed with a call to the fund company or a check of its website.

In the spreadsheet, the aforementioned distribution multiplier is simply 1 + (dividend/reinvestment price). My "daily report" spreadsheet has separate distribution multiplier columns for the month-to-date, week, and day returns. The dividends of the month-to-date multipliers are of course cleared out at the beginning of each month; the others are cleared more often, as the affected time periods elapse.

For bond funds, which have gradually accrued interest instead of occasional distributions that lower share price, there is a further multiplier that estimates income accrued for month-to-date, using the funds' yield and the date of the month. I do not bother to show week-to-date or one-day income accrual, as these small numbers will rarely affect returns much.

Return errors are almost always the result of a missed distribution or a stock split. To make sure I'm not carrying forward errors from one month to the next, I do check my end-of-month YTD returns against another published source such as the newspaper listings or the relevant fund company.

Stock splits, like dividends, lead to unexpectedly negative returns. Splits are generally easier to catch, because most are 2-to-1 or greater, leading to one-day returns on the order of −50 percent. Usually a check of company news by ticker will quickly confirm the split (or will mention the stock's devastating decline). There are many such sources for recent company news. I tend to use two free ones: Bloomberg.com, and the one that AOL has on its main "quotes" screen. There are also websites featuring news of stock splits, for example, www.2-for-1.com. Or search Yahoo with "stock splits" for other sites.

Yahoo has many indices in its database (e.g., S&P 500, Dow 30, and NASDAQ Composite), but these are raw index values, not total return numbers. You'll either have to forget about index income or, like me, estimate accruing income intramonth, and correct for exact figures on a monthly basis. Barra.com shows exact monthly total returns for the S&P 500, 400, and 600 indices, including growth and value indices, usually on the second business day of the month.

On the Morgan Stanley site (ms.com) go to MSCI (for Morgan Stanley Capital International). There, under "World Stock Market Performance," you'll find daily index values for its famous EAFE index, as well as all the country and regional indices you could possible desire. They're generally available each weekday by 9:00 A.M. Eastern time but are sometimes several hours late, especially with crucial end-of-month data. Be patient. Be persistent.

If you have one or more model portfolios, it's a relatively simple matter to track their values, and thus their returns, with a row of your spreadsheet. For each day, the value of the portfolio is simply given by a formula summing up the number of shares in each relevant fund or stock. These formulas will of course have to be updated to account for any distributions and trading. The following page shows what my daily looks like.

So that's it in a nutshell—or should I say a web shell? Ten minutes a day can provide a low-tech way to ensure that I'm on my way to being able to see strong and troubling signs in every investment

Snap of Daily

		YTD %	MTD %	Week+ %	Day %	Day $	Jun 28
^SPX	S&P 500	9.0	2.4	-0.9	1.2	16.04	1331.35
^DJI	Dow 30	16.8	1.0	-1.8	1.0	102.59	10655.15
^IXIC	NASDAQ Comp	18.9	5.4	1.5	2.0	49.79	2602.44
^SLXA	S&P 400	4.8	3.3	0.3	1.2	4.73	408.52
^RUT	Russell 2K	7.0	2.3	0.8	1.2	5.50	448.61
^SML	S&P 600	3.1	3.7	1.6	1.5	2.61	182.07
^WIL5	Wilshire 5K	8.4	1.9	-0.6	1.1	131.59	12192.43
	MS EAFE	4.6	4.5	-1.0	-0.2	-3.12	1458.11
	MS Europe	-1.6	2.8	-1.8	-0.7	-9.05	1304.39
	MS Japan	20.6	8.5	0.4	1.1	28.05	2669.39
	MS Far East Free ex Jpn	47.7	18.7	4.3	1.0	3.04	302.77
dia	Dow Diamonds	17.3	1.6	-1.6	0.9	0.95	106.69
spy	S&P SPDRs	8.6	2.5	-0.7	1.2	1.61	133.31
mdy	S&P Mid-Cap	6.1	2.9	-0.2	0.7	0.53	76.88
qqq	NASDAQ 100	22.2	7.6	1.7	2.4	2.59	111.97
xlb	S&P Basic Industries	19.5	6.2	-3.1	1.9	0.48	26.17
xlp	S&P Consumer Staples	-9.6	-2.7	-1.9	0.1	0.02	24.56
xlv	S&P Consumer Services	10.3	2.1	-1.1	1.1	0.31	28.69
xly	S&P Cyclical/Transport	10.0	2.6	1.0	1.9	0.55	28.73
xle	S&P Energy	16.8	-1.3	-5.6	-0.6	-0.17	27.27
xlf	S&P Financial	8.9	1.6	-0.5	2.3	0.58	25.48
xli	S&P Industrial	18.8	3.6	-3.0	0.2	0.05	29.14
xlk	S&P Technology	20.7	6.6	0.8	1.7	0.64	39.38
xlu	S&P Utilities	-0.6	1.3	-2.0	1.1	0.31	29.98
Large-Cap fdegx	324 Aggressive Growth	27.9	4.5	1.1	2.0	0.76	39.73
fbgrx	312 Blue Chip	4.8	2.4	-0.4	1.3	0.68	52.79
fdcax	307 Capital Appreciation	14.1	2.6	-0.2	1.4	0.35	25.19
fcntx	22 Contrafund	9.6	3.6	-0.3	1.3	0.79	61.70
fconx	339 Contrafund II	9.7	1.2	-0.8	1.2	0.15	12.22
fdesx	6 Destiny I	4.3	1.9	-0.8	1.1	0.30	28.12
fdetx	306 Destiny II	7.7	2.9	-0.8	1.2	0.18	15.35
fdeqx	315 Disciplined Equity	7.0	2.8	-0.1	1.1	0.33	31.37
fdgfx	330 **Dividend Growth**	**7.7**	**1.3**	-0.5	1.0	0.30	30.95
fexpx	332 Export & Multinational	9.8	1.7	-0.1	1.4	0.31	21.83
fftyx	500 Fifty	23.3	1.5	-1.0	0.9	0.18	20.77
fdgrx	25 Growth Co	15.4	5.9	0.5	1.3	0.76	58.39
flcsx	338 Large-Cap Stock	7.7	2.4	1.2	1.2	0.21	18.02
fmagx	21 Magellan	10.2	3.2	-0.4	1.3	1.66	125.76
fdffx	73 Retirement Growth	9.9	3.9	0.5	1.4	0.31	21.90
fsmkx	317 Sp Mkt Indx	8.8	2.4	0.0	1.2	1.12	91.94
fstmx	397 Sp Total Mkt Idx	8.6	2.0	-0.6	1.3	0.42	33.96
ftxmx	343 Tax Managed Stock	5.9	2.4	-1.0	1.0	0.12	11.79
ftqgx	333 TechnoQuant Growth	7.6	3.0	-0.6	1.4	0.20	14.38
Mid-Cap fmcsx	337 **Mid-Cap Stock**	**11.0**	**3.7**	6.9	1.1	0.21	18.48
fmilx	300 New Millennium	33.2	1.2	-1.1	1.6	0.55	34.90
focpx	93 OTC	16.3	3.6	0.3	1.8	0.92	50.72
fsemx	398 **Sp Ext Mkt Idx**	**8.4**	**1.2**	0.3	1.3	0.35	28.13
fdssx	320 Stock Selector	8.8	3.4	-0.2	1.3	0.39	31.25

I own and track. If one stock or fund takes a significant nosedive, I first look for a distribution or split. If that hasn't been the culprit, I review Yahoo's daily news and also click into Bloomberg.com for the thin read. If the fund or stock is losing ground relative to the industry benchmark over 5 trading days, even if there's no punishing news, I know my manager isn't making the grade. And I need to review the possible reasons for this by going to FundAlarm.com.

TWENTY-SIX

Fund Trading On-Line

Beyond information lies action.

Gulp.

After all, what good does a bunch of investment news do you if you can't turn it to your advantage and make money with it? Today, you can create your own trading desk—without having to pony up over $1 million to secure a seat on the New York Stock Exchange. Not bad.

There are several on-line trading sites worth clicking into: Ceres, Fidelity's FOX software, PCN, Quick & Reilley, Schwab's E*Trade, Suretrade, and Jack White. These sites offer differing price structures for your trades, as well as differing investment menus. The quickest way to assess which one is for you is to glance at the table below. But before you do, make a mental note of the following: Fidelity and Schwab currently offer the most comprehensive (and within the low-cost universe, the most expensive) cyber floors for all types of trades and analyses. If bare bones are what you're after (and you meet the account minimums) Ceres, PCN, and Quick & Reilley may be your ticket. Suretrade is the new kid in town, but I have high hopes for this site in the near future since it offers advice packs; full stock, bond, and fund menus; and deep discount trading costs.

The reality is that all these deep-discounters are moving in the direction of bountiful research, trendy analysis, and efficient real-time quotes and trades. The upshot? I'd opt for "less is more" and click into Suretrade.com. It may be the new kid on the block, but it's a great litmus test for other on-line investing sites. It offers a market-tested and proven Internet securities trading system, developed in partnership with Reuters. Suretrade's system is one of the fastest, easiest to use, and most comprehensive securities trading systems on the Internet. It's one of the best, most competitive trading systems, and it gives you hands-on trading and research, and commissions among the lowest available. (At Suretrade, there are no hidden charges such as inactivity fees or postage and handling fees.) Its low $7.95 price per trade isn't achieved by jacking up an account minimum. Suretrade has no minimum account size, minimum number of trades, or qualification on the type of stock traded, unlike others that place such restrictions on their so-called low pricing, or that offer a headlined price only for trades in over-the-counter stocks.

Putting your money where your mouse is, is no easy task—it tests one's nerves as well as one's wires. But the time saved, the research gleaned, and the advice pooled and sifted make the advent of on-line investing much more than a cool trend. In fact, with a mere flick of your wrist, you can take on the brokerage house giants and score a market-beating $10,000 portfolio for less money and with more control.

When you are choosing an on-line investing service, be sure you know both the advantages and the limitations of the sites you're considering. The following list will help you do this at a glance. Be sure to get answers to these questions before you make your final move.

1. Does the site allow you to trade stocks, bonds, mutual funds, and options?
2. What is the site's cost per trade for transactions involving fewer than 5,000 shares? What is the cost for market or limit orders conducted over the Internet? Is there a discount for using the Internet as opposed to your touch-tone phone to make trades?
3. Are any hidden charges imposed, like inactivity fees and postage and handling fees?
4. Does the site have account insurance in case of company failure? For example, one site offers up to $50 million per customer ($500,000 under SIPC, including $100,000 for cash claims) and an additional $49.5 million in protection provided by Aetna Casualty and Surety Company. (Note: this coverage isn't for market losses; it's more like FDIC insurance at you bank.)

Brokerage Site/Phone	Cost/Trade	Additional Costs	Account Minimum	Perks
Ameritrade www.ameritrade.com 800-669-3900	Stocks: $8 flat fee. $5 additional fee for limit, stop and stop limit orders. Options: $29 min. No-load funds: $18. Bonds: $40 min.	Moderate	$2,000	Limited real-time quotes; some advice
DLJdirect www.dljdirect.com 800-825-5723	Stocks: $20 (up to 1,000 shares). Options: $40 min. No- and low-load funds: $35. Bonds: no commission (may be marked up or down).	Minimal	$0 initial min., but $10,000 check min.	Can open account and trade in minutes; real-time quotes; news; research
E*Trade www.etrade.com 800-786-2575	Stocks: $19.95 (up to 3,000 shares). Options: $40 min. No- and low-load funds: $24.95. Bonds: no.	Moderate	$1,000 cash $2,000 margin	Intra-day charts; interactive charts
Fidelity WebXpress www.fidelity.com 800-544-7272	Stocks: $19.95 (up to 1,000 shares). $3 add'l for limit/stop orders. Options: $28.75 min. Fidelity and NTF funds: zero; other funds: $28.95. Bonds: $40	Minimal	$5,000	Limited real-time quotes; news; some advice
e.Schwab www.eschwab.com 800-435-4000	Stocks: $29.95 (up to 1,000 shares). Options, most funds and bonds: $31.20 min.	Minimal	$5,000 ($2,000 for IRAs)	Limited real-time quotes; news; research
SureTrade www.suretrade.com 212-566-2031	Stocks: $7.95 (up to 5,000 shares). Options: $27 min. No-load funds: $25. Bonds: $37.50 min.	Minimal	No minimum ($2,000 for margin accts.)	Many real-time quotes; news; research

5. How quickly does the site confirm trades? Does confirmation occur within seconds of execution, or do you have to wait hours or even days for this information? Is your portfolio updated automatically as trades are made?

6. What sort of free services and information does the site offer? A good site will give you a certain number of free real-time quotes each day, sometimes as many as 100. It will offer free unlimited portfolio access and returns-charting services, allow you to monitor your investments in real time, and provide free financial news services and free access to fundamental, technical, and earnings estimates.

TWENTY-SEVEN

Model $10,000 Portfolios

The bulk of this book has brought you up to speed on almost everything under the mutual fund sun. But there's one aspect that we haven't explored yet: putting our theoretical understanding of mutual funds into real-life investment practice.

This section does just that. In fact, it provides 10 model $10,000 portfolios. The first—"core $10,000 portfolio"—is meant to be one in which you can invest and forget the rest; but the remaining nine account for the fact that we, being only human, become restless and, more important, the market itself is restless and ever-changing. The subsequent nine $10,000 portfolios, then, represent strategic moves that take advantage of the specific market condition in which you may find yourself today, tomorrow, or years down the road. While I'm a big advocate of not letting the daily market turn you around, I also recognize that there are times when even your core portfolio will need to be revised to account for the market's twists, turns and detours. There are also more specific signals that change may be needed (like a change of fund managers) within one or more funds you originally thought could last a lifetime.

Markets change. Our objectives change. Our portfolios change. But, surprisingly, the basic components of a solid portfolio don't change all that much—what does change is the funds you pick to represent each of the following five components, and how you weight your assets in each of those funds.

QUICK TIP

The most basic job any $10,000 portfolio must accomplish is to beat inflation; it has to ensure that, in the very worst-case scenario, your savings grow at least as fast as the CPI. (Right now, we're fortunate that inflation is on vacation. But don't count on that lasting forever.) The point is, of course, to do much better than merely keeping pace with prices. How much better? Over the long term, 10 years at a minimum, your core portfolio should generate a total return (capital gains plus dividends) of between 4 percent and 7 percent above inflation. A so-called "60-40" portfolio—60 percent in the S&P 500 and 40 percent in U.S government bonds—has historically returned about 4 percent over inflation. A more aggressive all-stock core portfolio should return something in the vicinity of inflation plus 7 percent.

GROWTH FUND COMPONENT

As you now know, growth companies are focused on expansion: they reinvest their profits instead of paying them out to shareholders who anticipate rewards in the form of large long-term gains in value. When you invest in a growth stock fund, you leave current dividend income on someone else's table for what you hope will be steep increases in the share prices of the stocks it invests in. Because growth stocks tend to be relatively volatile, the growth component is the part of your core portfolio with the longest time horizon. In conjunction with the value component, growth funds are what will generate the returns you need for far-off goals like retirement.

VALUE FUND COMPONENT

Value companies are firms that are considered inexpensive relative to their earnings or to the value of their assets. When you invest in a value-oriented stock fund, you are—as with growth companies—investing for the long term, but from a different perspective. When you buy shares in a value fund, you are investing in companies you hope will exceed the marketplace's low expectations; this provides a foil to growth stocks, which face the greater challenge of meeting sometimes wildly inflated hopes.

Think of it this way. Suppose you had two siblings and thought one was sure to fail math this semester. You would probably be rather pleased to see him come home with a C. If you were convinced that your other sibling was bound to get an A in her math course, you would probably be disappointed if she ended up with a C. A value company is the child who was expected to fail but surprised you by achieving mediocrity; a growth company is the child you thought would ace the course. Even though, on an absolute basis, a C is a C, the market views things relatively. As a result, the value of one C is perceived to be much higher than the other—and the high-value C is the one that exceeded, rather than failed to live up to, expectations. There's no recipe for disappointment like hopes that soar too high. But despite the perils of disappointed expectations, growth companies do get A's often enough to justify the risk. Growth and value funds are really the two sides of the stock investment coin: together, they are your core portfolio's engine of long-term capital appreciation.

INDEX FUND COMPONENT

Perhaps the biggest investment story of the 1990s is the debate that's been raging between the partisans of passive investing and active management. The activist camp argues that it is difficult but not impossible for the well-equipped investor to achieve above-average returns; the passive crowd says that beating the market is a delusion and wants us all to throw in the towel. The indexers recommend investing in a mutual fund that comes as close as possible to providing total market exposure, or, if a more focused portfolio is required, a fund tracking a particular subsection of the market like small companies or large-caps. While I tend to think that the jury is still out on the active-passive debate, I do think that index funds belong in your core portfolio. The proportion of index to actively managed funds you choose depends on how much faith you have in your chances of picking a market-beating fund. (As you can tell from the following portfolios, I think our odds are better than even.)

INTERNATIONAL FUND COMPONENT

Investors like you and me have enough time to accept the risks involved in investing in an international stock fund. While some international markets are more established and solid than others, the truth is that they're not only a good way to profit from the new millennium's global economy but also a great way to hedge against our own U.S. stock market. I advocate avoiding emerging markets for the most part, and concentrating your money in Europe and Japan-based international stock funds.

BOND FUND COMPONENT

As noted in Chapter 17, bond funds are often mistakenly thought of as a safe, sure-thing, no worry, income-producing investment. Except for funds that invest solely in shorter-term government bonds, this simply isn't so. In fact, many bond funds have a significant degree of risk, particularly from rising interest rates, which reduce the value of the instruments they invest in. Only by examining both interest rate risk and credit risk in relation to a bond fund's performance in different market environments can you be assured that the bond fund you've selected (or are thinking about buying) matches your investment objective. Since your objective is long-term growth, you can rest assured that bond funds will play a minor role—so minor, in fact, that you don't need to consider them so long as you invest in a money market fund for short-term goals (and to hedge against a declining stock market wherein cash is king).

There is one exception: high-yield or "junk bond" funds, which are less sensitive to interest rates and more sensitive to economic factors. Long-term, these hybrid bonds have proved to be less risky than stocks, with about the equivalent hedge-factor you'd get from bonds while, at the same time, generating decent total returns.

THE $10,000 PORTFOLIOS

The following $10,000 portfolios will help you rule market changes rather than be ruled by them.

1: Core Actively Managed $10,000 Portfolio. A well-designed core portfolio should have one rock-solid, diversified, core fund. That's right. One. Once you've locked into your core fund, you can build in funds that take advantage of regions, markets, capitalizations, and industries.

Your core fund will serve as the base from which you launch your core $10,000 portfolio. It's the aircraft carrier among your fleet of battleships. Or perhaps it is the cruiser among your torpedo boats. The point is that it's the biggest and strongest component of your portfolio.

Your core fund should be a well diversified growth fund that blends both the value component and the growth component above. It should be one that invests in a broad range of large-, mid-, and small-cap companies on both sides of the fence: growth and value. In this category I'd place Fidelity Dividend Growth and Janus. These are funds run by deeply experienced, committed managers who have demonstrated that they have the right stuff when it comes to managing through good and bad markets. Like any good core fund managers, they diversify in terms of the size of companies they invest in as well as the percentage of the fund's assets they place in any given single stock. But they don't buy the whole market (and all the rewards and risks therein). Instead, they concentrate their portfolios on less than 200 issues. This means that, if they do their job right, their stock picks will have a greater impact on performance and lead to long-term market-beating results. I would place 40 percent of my assets in either fund.

Once you have your core fund, you can begin to add the index components. I would add both the Vanguard Extended Market Index fund (30 percent) to cover the markets from mid- to small-cap, stem to stern. Next up, consider Vanguard International Growth (5 percent) and Fidelity Pacific Basin (5 percent; this fund concentrates on Japanese stocks, with a smattering around the Pacific Rim), and Fidelity Europe Cap App (5 percent). Pluses of this tripartite exposure to the international markets: relatively low expenses, broad-based international market coverage, and one of the top-performing and most experienced managers on the international fund circuit. Finally, Fidelity Capital & Income (15 percent), whose junk bond portfolio will serve as a hedge against stock market downturns and bond market stumbles, as well as provide some significant upside potential.

2: $10,000 Index Fund Portfolio. Fidelity and Vanguard offer the best range of index funds for this portfolio. But don't make the common mistake of thinking that there's only one type of index fund in town—namely, the S&P 500 Index (a fund that owns the largest 500 U.S. stocks). In fact, this portfolio creates a more defensive index fund by simply purchasing Fidelity's Four-in-One index fund. This fund consists of 55 percent Spartan Market Index (which is an S&P 500 index fund); 15 percent Fidelity Spartan Extended Market Index (which matches the Wilshire 4500 or most U.S. stocks excepting the S&P 500); 15 percent Fidelity Spartan International Index (mirrors the EAFA); and 15 percent Fidelity U.S. Bond Index (which tracks the Lehman Brothers U.S. Bond Index). You could invest in all four index funds separately and adjust your weightings in each category, too. That would make you an active manager of a passive portfolio. This may sound contradictory, but actually it is a smart money move.

3: $10,000 Survivalist Portfolio. Word on the street (be it Wall Street or Main Street) is that index funds are the best route to investment success. But if the market takes a nosedive, those who bought the index will be in for a theme park ride from hell. Here's the glitch. In times of a market correction, an index fund falls as much as the market does. For example, if you had thrown all your assets into the Vanguard Index 500 fund on September 1, 1987, you would have suffered a nearly 30 percent loss by November 1, 1987. Crash!

In the rush to get a good ride, everyone seems to ignore the roller coaster's height restriction bar. Sentiment indicators suggest that the majority of people are more bullish today than ever before—and consensus makes me nervous. But if an index fund isn't the place to go, where should you turn? A $10,000 portfolio that could secure potential profits, and at the same time suffer less than an index fund if the market takes a nasty spill, would do the trick.

First, rent the video *The Lost World.* You'll find the missing metaphorical link between reality checks and the bull market. The biggest dinosaurs dominated the food chain. No one stepped on their toes. In the real world, the market tells the same tale. In the past 10 years, the odds were approximately 18 to 1 against selecting a large-cap fund that provided a return materially greater than that of the Rex of all index funds, the Vanguard Index 500 fund. But the index funds rely on large-cap growth stocks for superior returns, and large-cap growth stocks depend on big earnings to sustain their ability to run ahead of the pack. When earnings dry up, these stocks, and the index funds that invest in them, fall faster than a Tyrannosaurus that has run out of digestible theme park visitors. After years of bullish earnings, there's an increased risk of falling earnings.

You could have survived unharmed in *The Lost World*: by not relying on the carnivores' food source; by being smaller than all the rest so as to be overlooked; by moving to a less hostile locale. Consider investing in Vanguard Index Growth (30 percent), Vanguard Index Value (20 percent), Vanguard Index Small Cap (15 percent), Vanguard International Growth (15 percent), and Fidelity Aggressive Growth (20 percent). That way, you're better armed for bear, and ready to run with the bulls without getting trampled in the process. If times continue to be good, this portfolio should deliver solid returns that can still give you bragging rights at the bar. Even more important, if S&P 500 index funds get stopped in their tracks, this portfolio should deliver the defense you need to survive the big chill—and last until the thaw—relatively unscathed.

4: $10,000 Niche Fund Portfolio. Sector funds, as we learned, can burn a hole in your pocket or spice up an otherwise insipid portfolio by concentrating on the stocks of one specific industry. For example, a technology sector fund would invest only in technology issues and, moreover, might invest only in software issues or semiconductor issues. However, while sector funds break the golden rule of fund investing (which emphasizes diversification across industries), they nevertheless provide diversification within an industry. Constructing a portfolio out of several sector funds can give you diversification as well as depth. Remember, diversification derives not from the number of funds in which you invest, but from the number of industries and regions your total portfolio covers. If you have five growth funds, chances are they may invest in much the same sorts of companies. However, recognizing that the overall market can be divided into main industries and subsectors, and knowing what you do about sector funds, you can diversify your portfolio by gaining exposure to different parts of the economy, some of which are almost guaranteed to do well when others are flagging. To net solid results, put 10 percent in one sector fund per major industry. Note: Fidelity is the only fund family with a menu of sector funds big enough to accomplish this task. Rydex comes close.

5: $10,000 Info-Tech Portfolio. New age. New economy. New portfolio. Three years ago, if I had said that Internet funds would exist, I would have been handed another large martini and told to go smoke a cigar. This portfolio isn't for the faint of heart. In fact, even the lionhearted might tremble at the sight of it. The reason for the fear? Pulse-pounding risk. Nosebleed volatility. The reason for the portfolio? The potential to set a new land speed record for total return. Here, timing is everything. This portfolio is a pure adrenaline mix of new economy stocks. Place one-third in each of the following funds: (1) Mundner Net Net fund is almost all Internet. (2) Guinness Flight Wired Index fund is a far more diversified portfolio of technology stocks. (3) Finally, Fidelity Select Developing Communications nets you the best-of-breed tech and telecom stocks. Put this portfolio plan into action after a major correction in the technology sector: these high-flying funds are best bought when their share prices temporarily tank. Together, these three funds put into one sector-packed portfolio the Internet, the computers and software that bring you there, and the wrist pads to kill the pain. Note: it might be even better to consider this as a piece of your $10,000 portfolio—say about 10 percent.

6: $10,000 Saint Portfolio. You're hip. Happening. Know it all. Been there, done that. You're down with the people and down on big business. Suddenly, you find you're making real money instead of daily bread for some local Salvation Army. You like the way that feels. (It's OK.) But a voice inside your head keeps telling you that if you don't watch out, you'll be buying a gas-guzzling cherry BMW 2002 with a faded bumper sticker reading "Die yuppie scum!"

If you're convinced that money is the root of all evil despite the obvious fact that it's hard to build a church or an animal shelter without it, this portfolio is for you. Socially responsible investing (SRI) funds provide a way to invest your money in companies that aren't capitalizing on child labor in Kuala Lumpur or deforesting the planet to make better soap. True, there's enough PC PR in some new entrants' names—the Cruelty-Free Value, Green Century, and Noah funds come to mind in this regard—to make Madison Avenue blush. But while investing in SRI funds may be nothing more than a placebo for your postcapitalist mind, some funds can, in fact, help you profit without feeling as though you have just switched from the Democratic to the Republican party. In fact, the following portfolio will help you answer for yourself the primary question about the ethics of investing: can you do well by doing good?

The performance benchmark for SRI funds is the Domini Social

Index 400 (DSI 400). It reflects some recurring themes that most SRI fund managers adhere to. The index monitors the performance of 400 companies that successfully pass the following PC litmus tests. How does a company treat its employees? Typically, SRI examines whether a company "exploits" a labor force in terms of wages, benefits, or discriminatory hiring or promoting practices. Also, SRI tend to avoid "sin" stocks like tobacco, alcohol, and gambling companies. Other SRI funds seek to impart their political take on the world by avoiding stocks in companies that make products for the defense industry.

The $10,000 "saint portfolio" can be well diversified in terms of types of assets, industry, region, company size, and fund managers' investment styles. To get there, consider cash (as green as you can get) at 5 percent, meaning both some defense and some potential offense (if the managers see opportunity rather than chaos in the markets): Ariel Appreciation (20 percent), Bridgeway Social Responsibility (25 percent), Citizens Income (10 percent), Domini Social Equity (25 percent), and Pax World (15 percent).

7: $10,000 Sinner Portfolio. "Green" and "socially responsible" funds have become fashionable in certain quarters of the investing public as people have tried to square concerns about corporate practices with investment performance. A case can be made for turning this relationship on its head, however: investing in companies that cater to our weaknesses rather than appeal to our better angels. In their defense, these so-called "sin" stocks have earned their name not by exploiting their employees or the environment but exploiting our own desires and lack of discipline. Sin stocks typically have one thing in common: they are shares in companies involved in habit-forming industries like tobacco, liquor, and gambling.

Surprisingly, "sin" stocks tend to hold up better in down markets and also rally with similar market-beating strength in good times. When times are tough, we all need some form of escape, and when the market is booming, how better to celebrate than with a martini and a cigar?

Consider combining a core sin fund with three more diversified habit-forming focused ones. Allocate equally among these four funds. Morgan Fund Shares (MFUN), a closed-end fund, is the closest thing to a pure sin fund available; its holdings include the distiller Seagram's, the condom manufacturer Carter-Wallace, the lingerie emporium Frederick's of Hollywood, and several gaming concerns. The other three funds are Invesco Strategic Leisure, which holds some tobacco companies and brewers but focuses on less controversial sectors like entertainment, recreation, restaurants, retailing, toys, newspapers, cable, and broadcasting; Fidelity Consumer Industries, which holds such companies as Coca Cola, Philip Morris, and Sara Lee; and GT Global Consumer Products fund (GTSBS), which invests for long-term growth in companies throughout the world that manufacture, market, retail, or distribute consumer products and services. This last offering is a relatively new fund and has a fee structure that no-load fund proponents would certainly find sinful. But GT Global's comprehensive coverage of the world's merrymaking markets gives us seamless exposure to global good-time spending.

8: $10,000 Wimp Portfolio. What if you could let someone else— and I don't mean your broker!—pick funds for you? You could hire a money manager to run your account. But if you have less than $250,000 invested, you'll probably have to pay 2 percent or more per year for this management. You could buy a balanced fund that invests in many individual stocks and bonds, hopefully diversifying across asset classes and internationally. But few, if any, fund managers are so expert that they are equally knowledgeable about the markets for U.S treasury bonds, medical device start-ups, and Swiss cuckoo-clock makers. The other option is to invest in a fund of funds (FOF), a mutual fund that invests in a basket of other mutual funds. That way, each asset class in your portfolio can be managed by an expert. FOFs were trendy in the late 1960s, but high expenses and lack of real diversification killed most of them off. In recent years, however, they've become trendy again. Take a close look at the expense ratios: since these FOFs hold managed mutual funds, each with its own layer of fund expenses, management costs can really start to multiply.

One rule of thumb: Funds of funds with an average annual expense ratio of 1 percent or more (which is levied on top of the underlying funds' expenses) should be avoided. For one thing, paying 1 percent per year may not sound like much, but after 30 years, it means 26 percent less money in your pocket. More important, I've discovered that most funds with 1 percent expense ratios have significantly underperformed compared with their less expensive peers.

Another key consideration about funds of funds is their past performance. That's right. Past performance. No, it won't guarantee that you'll have a similar run in the future, but the truth is that these instruments lay bare the manager's underlying ability to select a diversified bag of funds for past market conditions—which is an indicator of how a manager will fare in future markets.

One more word of caution. Sometimes, you need to compare apples and oranges in order to get the right answer about investments. This is certainly the case with this month's fund investment vehicle du jour. If there's good and bad news about funds of funds, there's also the ugly fact that funds of funds have fallen far short of the simplest fund investment option we have: Vanguard Index 500.

9: $10,000 Small Potatoes Portfolio. Small companies may seem a riskier proposition than their big-board brethren, but for long-term investing they can't be beat. According to Ibbotson Associates, the Chicago-based analytical firm famous for its chart "Stocks, Bonds, Bills and Inflation," small-caps have earned annualized returns of 12.7 percent since 1926, versus 11 percent for the crowd-pleasing large-cap S&P 500 stocks. Needless to say, those 2.7 percentage points compound considerably over time: $1 invested in your great-grandfather's favorite large-cap stocks in 1926 would now be worth $1,828; the same investment in small-cap stocks would be worth $5,520—nearly three times as much. And since 1975, small-cap value stocks have netted more than double the cumulative return of their better-loved sibling, small-cap growth stocks. And they've done it without the hype and sizzle of technology issues.

Investors can't live by sizzle alone. You've got to get the steak (and eat it) too. That's why I think you can be better served by avoiding today's high-flyers and going to the bargain basement instead. For this reason, the funds in the portfolio below tend to avoid stocks found in the index we typically think of when the buzz is small-cap funds, namely, NASDAQ. Instead, my picks prospect the Russell 2000 Index, composed of companies representing approximately 7 percent of the U.S. market's total capitalization. This index is used to measure other small companies, whose stock performance might not have the NASDAQ sizzle but certainly has the earnings steak.

The four funds that make up this sample small-cap value portfolio are Fidelity Small Cap Selector, Jurika & Voyles Mini-Cap, Weitz Hickory (which includes some real-estate investment trusts in addition to its small-company equities), and Berger Small Company Value.

10: $10,000 Defensive Portfolio. Defense. Defense. Defense. We all know that investing has its risks as well as its rewards: you don't have to be a Cassandra to recognize that the American economy continues to be prone to periodic recessions. One way to build a stormproof, or at least storm-protected, portfolio is to look for mutual funds with lower-than-average volatility. Such funds may move more sluggishly when the market is rocketing ahead, but they are also much slower to start sinking when the market tanks. A common way of calculating the relative volatility of a group of funds is to see how each fund's "beta," which measures its volatility against the S&P 500, compares with its fellows. (As the measurement's benchmark, the S&P 500 Index is assigned a beta of 1.) An aggressive growth fund like PBHG Growth with a beta of 1.15 would most likely go up 11.5 percent when the market as a whole is up 10 percent and sink 11.5 percent in conditions when the market is down 10 percent. Conversely, a more conservative fund like Dividend Growth, which has a beta of 0.89, will probably rise or fall 8.9 percent.

This sample portfolio is built from a group of low-beta (i.e., low-volatility) funds for high-risk times. Fidelity Dividend Growth (40 percent), is arguably one of the best large-cap growth funds in any market. Fidelity Low-Priced Stock (15 percent) has an even lower low beta; it concentrates on beaten-down equities whose strong current earnings and promising future have escaped the market's notice. Fidelity Puritan (25 percent), with the lowest beta in this unwild bunch, gives the portfolio its conservative ballast. With just over 60 percent in stocks, and 40 percent in mostly investment-grade bonds, this fund is also a solid pick for the one fund to own even if you can own only a single (defensive?) fund. The fund's stock component concentrates on financials, pharmaceuticals, energy, and consumer staples—all defensive industries that are also well positioned to take advantage of a recovering economy. On the bond side, the fund concentrates on higher-yielding bonds that are rated below AAA but stand well above the junk category.

Investors in this fund can expect a stable ride if things remain bumpy. International exposure—a key component of defensive investing, for when the American economy is bad, there are almost invariably good times somewhere on the planet—is provided by Invesco European Small Company (5 percent) and Fidelity Japan Small Companies (5 percent). The betas (relative to the U.S. market) show the extent to which European and Japanese markets have historically marched to the beat of a different drummer from the S&P 500 Index. Fidelity Utilities (10 percent) may seem a rather staid choice, but it has a modest correlation with the stock market and should reduce total portfolio risk while providing possibilities for growth—the essence of this portfolio.

TWENTY-EIGHT

Mini-History
of Mutual Funds

Being informed is what being a better investor is all about. Yet, surprisingly, few people take the time to learn even some rudimentary lessons about the most popular investment vehicle of our age—mutual funds.

While we dedicate ourselves throughout this book to learning how to invest in mutual funds, we can all benefit from learning about their history. It's a recent history. Basically, it's an all-American story. And it's a history that reflects the way market uncertainty—as opposed to fear of being flimflammed—has developed into the key concern for fund investors like you and me. That wasn't always the case. In fact, as recently as the 1960s fraudulent funds papered Wall Street.

NOT YOUR GRANDFATHER'S MUTUAL FUND

The history of mutual funds is enmeshed in the general history of twentieth-century American capitalism: the products available to us today are offspring of two great trends in U.S. economic history—the rise of the individual investor and the advent of the federally regulated financial marketplace.

The first of the conditions necessary for the flourishing fund industry—large numbers of motivated small investors—appeared in the 1920s, but a truly well-policed financial services sector has become a reality only relatively recently.

The early investment trusts, as the forerunners of mutual funds were known, were characterized by a great deal of fraudulent conduct. And while the famous market crash of 1929 put plenty of fund sponsors out of business, the housecleaning wasn't thorough. Two decades after the reforms of the securities industry in the 1930s, a rash of financial scandals, including several involving mutual fund promoters, made funds look like the last place you'd want to invest your hard-earned money.

Today, the opposite is true. This has less to do with performance than with the fact that the markets are well regulated. Today, fund investors like you and me can be highly confident that the risks we face are economic, not fiduciary.

THE INVESTMENT TRUST

When was the first American mutual fund launched—and where did the idea behind it originate? As in many other areas of history, coming up with a neat "first" in this area is not easy, because the fund format so popular today evolved over a fairly long period of time. Most accounts identify the British investment trust, a vehicle developed in the third quarter of the nineteenth century, as being the great-grandfather of the American mutual fund.

Of course, American investors had banded together to pool their assets long before the late nineteenth century. The Massachusetts Hospital Life Insurance Company trust fund, a fund organized in the 1820s, was one example. That this was developed in Massachusetts is suggestive: Boston would later play a central role in the industry's development.

It would take the post–World War I transformation of the U.S. economy to transform investment trusts into a product with mass appeal. In the 1920s, as is well known, the stock market became a national sport: historians have estimated that the number of Americans investing in shares rose from perhaps 500,000 in the prewar years to anywhere from 5 to 20 million in the 1920s, and many of these newcomers participated in the market through investment trusts.

Boston, which could draw upon a long tradition of trusteeship, played a central role in this development. Not only did several major modern-day fund houses—Fidelity, Putnam, Scudder, State Street Management, and Research and Mass Financial Services—have their origins in Boston, but what is generally considered the prototype of the modern open-end fund was launched there as well. This was the Massachusetts Investors' Trust, now the flagship fund of Mass Financial Services. It was the brainchild of Edward G. Leffler, a transplanted midwesterner who had become convinced that what investors wanted was a fund offering share redemption on demand. Disagreements with his partners prompted Leffler to set out on his own again; eventually, he joined forces with a well-connected Boston broker named William Amory Parker and a prominent lawyer named George Putnam to launch a second open-end fund called Incorporated Investors.

Leffler and his new partners managed this fund's operation through a structure that would become the industry standard. The Incorporated Investors fund was technically an independent corporation run by a board of trustees, who in turn contracted with an outside firm to manage their portfolio and market their shares. But the fund's board members were partners in the advisory firm that they hired to manage and market their fund. One other aspect of Incorporated Investors deserves notice: the identity of the man who would become its general counsel. His name was Edward C. Johnson, II, and in 1943 he would take control of a small, young Boston investment trust named Fidelity Fund.

One other concept dating from the 1920s would come to have enormous importance for the shape of the industry today. In 1925, one year after Leffler had succeeded in founding his first open-end fund, Incorporated Investors, *Barrons* ran a series of articles by Kenneth Van Strum with equally profound implications for the future of the mutual fund industry. After comparing the long-term movement of stock, bond, and commodity prices, Van Strum concluded that bond investing—long the preferred strategy of risk-averse wealthy investors—was not a safe haven but a "disastrous speculation on the trend of commodity prices." In the near term, these influential articles helped persuade many elite investors and their advisers that stock investing made sense. The events of 1929–1932 would discredit this notion for a long time to come, but Van Strum articulated the principle that guides fund investors today.

THE CRASH AND ITS CONSEQUENCES

The innovations of the 1920s occurred against a backdrop of incredible manipulation and fraud. Regulation was practically nonexistent: only individual states had securities laws with real teeth, and state officials were hardly up to the task of solving national problems. The industry was rife with unsavory practices: capital was used to make dividend payments that portfolio holdings couldn't generate; bonds were used to raise cash, creating a class of creditors who had the first claim on a fund's assets should it run into cash flow problems; portfolios were saddled with doggy stocks that the open market refused to buy; and sales gimmicks like contractual plans were used to milk customers. Even among the better funds, the sort of disclosure today's investors take for granted was unheard of: many investment trusts refused to reveal the components of their portfolios, claiming that to do so would give their competitors valuable proprietary information.

The stock market crash, or rather the downward spiral that started in October 1929 and continued, with only a short pause, into 1932, did more than wipe out billions of dollars of American wealth. It also exposed the fraud and the questionable practices that riddled the securities industry.

Like the banking sector, the securities industry was desperately in need of a complete overhaul: reform of the entire financial services sector was a priority of the New Deal. Beginning in 1933, Congress enacted a series of laws regulating securities, including the 1934 act that established the Securities and Exchange Commission. From the standpoint of the fund industry, the most important of these reforms was the Investment Company Act of 1940, which governs the mutual fund landscape we invest in to this day.

The 1930s are popularly seen as a period of unremitting depression, but open-end investment trusts fared quite well, especially compared with the closed-end funds so popular in the preceding decade. In 1940, the total value of assets in closed-end funds was only a quarter of what it had been in 1929, whereas open-end assets tripled during the same period. One mutual fund that fared especially well was Walter L. Morgan's Philadelphia-based Wellington Fund (today, Wellington remains the key subadviser for many leading Vanguard funds), which had been founded in 1928 as the very first balanced fund. The high-quality corporate bonds in the Wellington portfolio, as well as some timely "sell" recommendations made by Morgan's advisers, helped keep the fund afloat at a time when equity prices were sinking. In the summer of 1929, Wellington scaled back its equity exposure from 75 percent to 33 percent of its portfolio.

THE POSTWAR ERA TO 1970

Although the fund industry managed to do modestly well during the 1930s, it took World War II to pull America as a whole out of the Great Depression. For the United States, the conflict was a tremendous stimulus; the nation came through the war with its manufacturing capacity at an all-time high. Not only had wartime spending enabled companies to dig themselves out of the hole of the 1930s, but technologies developed for military purposes—jet propulsion, radar, nylon, atomic energy, television, and FM radio— were marketed to the consumer. And the combination of high savings and wartime shortages of consumer goods had created a huge reservoir of pent-up demand.

In a trend that can be traced back to the days following the crash, open-end funds drew further and further ahead of the old-style closed-end trusts that had dominated the 1920s: between 1945 and 1958, assets of open-end funds went from under $2 billion to nearly $15 billion.

As the industry expanded exponentially, Boston's dominance began eroding: the city's share of the nation's mutual fund assets slipped from more than half in 1940 to about one-third in 1950, although Boston still managed more fund dollars than New York. By 1959, an eighteen-year-old firm from the Minnesota-based Investor's Diversified Services (now American Express Advisors), had succeeded in using its door-to-door sales force to muscle its way to the top of the heap. Its $1.5 billion in assets eclipsed the old number-one fund, the Massachusetts Investors' Trust. Newcomers that would become household names included Chicago's Stein Rowe, launched in 1949; and New York's Dreyfus Corporation, which entered the fund business in 1951. With its now-famous lion as a symbol in its early television advertisements, Dreyfus made a splash: in the 1970s, the company would gain fame and fortune with money market funds.

The most famous fund to hit its stride in the 1950s was, of course, Fidelity. In 1951, Fidelity managed 2 percent of the nation's mutual fund assets. Four decades later it was America's—and thus the world's—biggest fund company, with 12 percent of fund assets under its management.

Unfortunately, growth in assets was not matched by fiduciary responsibility. On the contrary, it seems as though the lessons of the

1920s were being conveniently forgotten. Symptomatic of the industry's willful amnesia was the revival of one of the worst features of the post-crash era, the contractual sales plan. This device allowed the investor to make a fund purchase over the course of several months, but while it may resemble today's dollar-cost averaging, in fact it was designed for the benefit of the sales representative, not the consumer. The sales charge had to be paid up front, so under a typical contractual plan the investor had made several monthly payments before any of his or her money had actually purchased any shares. In the worst cases, high fees could eat up almost half of the total sum contracted.

FUND MANIA

The last years of the great postwar boom saw the arrival of the go-go market and the aggressive growth mutual fund. From 1955 to 1966 sales of so-called "high-performance" funds—aggressive growth funds, as we would call them today—went from 21 percent to 64 percent of new mutual fund sales. These funds became the driving force of an industry that saw total assets under management grow from $25 to $35 billion from 1963 to 1965. In 1968–1969, on the eve of the collapse, 96 new aggressive growth funds were launched. Nowadays funds that seem to engage in excessive trading generally raise investors' suspicions, but in the heyday of the 1960s, some funds actually bragged about their high portfolio turnover. In tandem with hotshot funds came hotshot fund managers: the celebrity of Gerald Tsai, manager of Fidelity Capital Fund from 1957 to 1965, was an entirely new phenomenon in an industry known for its pinstripe conservativism. At about the time you were being born, the fund industry was overheating.

THE 1970S: SHAKE YOUR BOOTY

Decades as measures of time and decades as historical periods rarely coincide, but the hot market of the 1960s obligingly sputtered out at the end of 1968. Thereafter, stocks and the funds that held them began a downward slide, and brokerage houses closed left and right; the downturn became a crisis in April 1970, during what one chronicle of the era describes as the "worst stock market panic since World War Two." As divisions between the middle-aged and the young, black and white, and supporters and opponents of the Vietnam War grew ever more bitter, the bears took up long-term residence on Wall Street. The term "stagflation" says it all: high inflation rates—which by the late 1970s were in double digits—were combined with sluggish economic growth. Western Europe and Japan were emerging as potent international competitors, and their exports to the United States were putting relentless pressure on domestic producers. Growing unemployment, an increasing trade deficit, and ballooning federal budget deficits led to a market collapse that few investors now seem to recall.

The first half of the 1970s was especially bleak for equities—the stock market itself lost nearly 40 percent of its value during 1973–1974; and in an era when bond funds were relatively rare, this was poison for the fund industry as a whole. The numbers tell the story: between market losses and redemptions, the amount of money invested in mutual funds sank from a total of $48 billion in 1970 to a total of $36 billion in 1974, a loss of 25 percent.

In 1971, the National Association of Securities Dealers took a long overdue step, adopting new accounting rules that all but proscribed the future use of contractual plans, while Fidelity lost on appeal a major case regarding the centerpiece of reciprocity (the steering of rebated commissions on portfolio transactions to reward sales representatives). This meant that fund companies had to find new distribution channels: some, like Vanguard's maverick president John Bogle, took the radical step of abolishing loads altogether and marketing funds directly to the public.

FUNDS AS WE NOW KNOW THEM

Besides these reforms, the 1970s saw three major innovations sweep the industry: the money market mutual fund, the bond fund, and the rise of the no-load philosophy. The first of these developments, the money market mutual fund, was the most important. As a product tailor-made for an environment combining high inflation and moribund stock prices, it arrived just in time to save the industry. In this new type of fund—unlike regular open-end funds—shares were valued at $1 each, so that to the consumer they had the same "feel" as a conventional bank checking account. Since fund companies were not under the same regulatory constraints as federally insured banks, they were free to offer much higher interest rates than banks could pay. At a time when practically everyone could see how inflation was eroding purchasing power, high interest rates became the holy grail of financial survival. The Reserve Fund and the Benham Capital Preservation Fund (whose name says everything about those highly inflationary times) were first, but it took the marketing strength of Dreyfus to put the product on the national map. Between March and December 1974, the Dreyfus Liquid Assets fund went from a $7.5 million experiment to a $700 million powerhouse. Its success set off a stampede of investment companies into money funds, but a Boston firm introduced the innovation that allowed money funds to go head-to-head with the banking industry: in May 1974, Fidelity unveiled a money market fund with check-writing privileges.

Not only did these funds save the industry in its bleakest hour, but they marked a conceptual turning point: in the future, mutual funds would become more and more like other consumer products in terms of ease of use and the way they were marketed.

Another aspect of the money market fund with profound implications for the industry's future was the fact that it was really impossible for the fund to charge a sales fee. Since each customer dollar purchased a money market share worth $1, there was no way for the fund sponsor to skim off the top without "breaking the buck." As customers got accustomed to the idea of buying one kind of fund without coughing up a sales fee, it was only a matter of time before at least some customers, and some companies, would begin to wonder why other types of funds couldn't be sold in the same manner. For example, many municipal bond funds, which followed the money market funds as a quintessential 1970s fund product, also eschewed loads. Even today, while most funds are still load funds the no-load philosophy has become influential enough to exert an industrywide dampening effect on fund expenses: these days, it seems that just about every fund family has no-load or low-load funds to offer. (I may be being too Pollyannaish here: according to the Bogle study, the industrywide expense ratio has increased from 1.08 to 1.10 percent between 1974 and 1995. On the other hand, Vanguard's president Brennan is now ICI chair; perhaps this bodes a sea-change.)

One man deserves a considerable share of the credit for making no-load funds a visible, viable part of the industry: John Bogle, the former Wellington Fund executive who established the Vanguard Group in 1975. Bogle is a man of remarkable focus and prescience: as a senior at Princeton in 1951, he wrote an undergraduate thesis, "The Economic Problems of the Investment Company," in which he dissected the problems facing the industry with a perceptiveness that would have done credit to a senior SEC regulator. In 1977, after considerable wrestling with Vanguard's board, his fledgling (and struggling) company became a no-load fund distributor. By the late 1990s, Vanguard, despite its contrarian marketing philosophy and unique structure—it administers and distributes the funds bearing its name, but each fund is managed by a truly independent outside investment adviser—would be the number two fund group, after Fidelity.

The last development that stemmed from the bear market years was the rise of the bond fund. Once a negligible part of the industry, these funds grew—from 1974 to 1980—from $7.8 billion to $17.4 billion. Besides corporate bond funds, tax-free municipal bond funds became significant players. Fidelity opened its first municipal bond fund in 1976.

THE 1980S: GREED IS GOOD

The 1980s are famous, of course, for Reaganomics and the bull market that lasted from 1982 to 1987. The first seven years of the decade were so full of variegated developments that it is hard to catalogue them all. Corporate America was in a state of ferment, not to say turmoil, as mergers, leveraged buyouts, and corporate restructurings made it difficult just to keep up with who owned whom. One day a private company would be taken public; the next day a public company would be taken private. Sometimes the same company went in and out and back from one form of ownership to another.

DEVELOPMENT OF 401(K)S

Of course, with so many changes of ownership going on, the concept of long-term job security became more and more antiquated as the decade progressed. As companies and employees grappled with new realities, it became increasingly clear that it made sense for companies to relinquish control over employee retirement funds and put them into the hands of the employees themselves. From the company's standpoint, the transition from defined benefits plans (in which the company committed itself to long-term pension coverage) to defined contribution plans (in which the company agreed to contribute a certain amount to each employee's retirement fund) greatly simplified the administration of these plans. From the standpoint of the individual employee, the retirement revolution was both a great opportunity and a frightening challenge: the quality of an employee's retirement now rested largely on his or her own investment decisions.

From the fund industry's standpoint, the changing face of pension investing meant millions of new customers like you and me.

THE 1990S AND BEYOND

In the modern mutual fund landscape, regulatory concerns can become just the background: market-related concerns are the foreground. This isn't to say that some funds won't blow up—but if you've read this book, chances are you'll know how to spot those dogs a mile away. Of key concern for you and me, then, is the extent to which the markets at home and abroad will continue to be able to sustain the economic growth that we have come to take for granted. This is as much a political issue as an economic issue—and one that we, as individual fund investors, need to factor into any portfolio we think will stand the test of time.

Time will test us. The impact of our aging population on the markets and our fund investments is unknown. But what is known is that investors like you and me have to invest if we want our assets to grow beyond the rate of inflation. We certainly can't rely on social security. We can't rely on low taxes as we reach retirement age, either. In fact, we can rely only on ourselves. Fortunately, creating a $10,000 portfolio today remains the best way to secure a bright financial future for ourselves. As you now know, you can do it. So go to it.

Glossary

This glossary is designed to help you understand fundspeak. At times, fundspeak may sound like a foreign language. But it's easy to learn, and it's an essential part of this book's mission—to make sure we're among the articulate, informed fund investors on Main Street and Wall Street.

Active Management. Trying to surpass the return of the financial market. Active managers utilize their own knowledge and experience in making investment decisions while looking at market trends and company research.

Adjusted Gross Income (AGI). Utilized in deciding whether an IRA holder qualifies for an IRA deduction. This is shown on tax form 1040 or 1040a.

Advance/Decline Ratio. The number of stocks whose prices have advanced relative to those that have declined over a given day. Typically calculated at the close of the market, this ratio is used to represent the general direction of the market. Since, unlike most market indexes, it weighs all stocks evenly, it is heavily influenced by the performance of small-cap stocks.

After-Tax Contributions. Part of an employee's salary put into a retirement plan that is still subject to federal income tax.

Aggressive. Investing exclusively for growth and ignoring income from dividends or interest. Also used as a synonym for "risk-taking." While definitely risky, aggressive investing also has the most potential for profits. An aggressive strategy would include investing in small, fast-growing companies. Investing exclusively in long-term zero-coupon bonds is also considered aggressive, at least among bond investors.

American Depositary Receipt (ADR). Securities representing a fixed number of shares of stock in foreign companies. ADRs trade like regular common stocks and are much easier to buy and sell than overseas shares. Many fund managers prefer ADRs to foreign stocks for this reason alone. There are several hundred ADRs available in the United States.

American Stock Exchange (AMEX). This is the less well-known of the two stock exchanges domiciled in downtown Manhattan. The companies that trade on the AMEX are generally smaller than those on the New York Stock Exchange (NYSE).

Annual Report. Yearly report of the overall financial condition (from operations to balance sheet) of a company or mutual fund, which is sent to all shareholders.

Annuity. A form of life insurance policy which can provide tax deferral to underlying investments (however, usually at the cost of substantial fees). For retirees, annuities can usefully be structured to make payments for the life of the annuity holder—making them the exact opposite of life insurance. The advantage of such an arrangement is that the holder of such an annuity won't outlive his or her savings.

Asked Price. The price an investor is willing to pay for a security or commodity. This contrasts with the *bid price*, which is the price at which the seller of an asset is willing to part with it.

Asset. Value attributed to stocks, bonds, real estate, mutual funds, and, for a company, owned equipment or plants. (Contrast with *liability*.) A mutual fund's net asset value (NAV) is its assets minus its liabilities, usually expressed in dollars per share.

Asset Allocation. The process of diversifying the assets in a portfolio among the major investment categories and markets as well as among particular types of investments within each category.

Asset Allocation Fund. A mutual fund that invests in a wide variety of assets, such as stocks, bonds, money market securities, and sometimes gold bullion.

Asset Class. Different kinds of investments. Stocks, bonds, and cash reserves are the three main asset categories.

Automatic Investment. A method for investing in mutual funds that enables you to select a specific amount to be withdrawn from your bank savings or checking account on a regular, scheduled basis and invested in a mutual fund. It's a great low-cost way to start investing in mutual funds, since many funds are willing to waive their minimum in order to get your long-term participation.

Automatic Reinvestment. Typically, this refers to automatic reinvestment of dividends in new shares of a company's stock or a mutual fund. Some companies and almost all mutual funds allow automatic reinvestment. You have to pay taxes on distributed dividends and capital gains even if they are reinvested.

Average Annual Return. A measure of historical return. The amount per year you would have had to earn to achieve the same total return over the time period in question. If you were up 21 percent over the last 2 years, your average annual return was 10 percent, even if your returns were very different in each of the 2 years. (Confused by 10 percent + 10 percent = 21 percent? See *compound interest*.)

Average Maturity. The maturity of a bond is the date the debt is due and payable. The average maturity of a bond fund is the average of the maturities of the fund's holdings (weighted by size of holding). Typically, the longer a fund's average maturity, the greater its interest-rate risk. Not quite as meaningful a term as a bond fund's *duration*.

Balanced Fund. A fund that invests substantial portions in both stocks and bonds. A conservative type of growth and income fund.

Balance Sheet. A company's accounting of its current assets, liabilities, and owner's equity at a specified point in time. Found in the company's annual report.

Basis Point. One-hundredth (1/100) of a percentage point of yield or return.

Bear. An investor who expects a market decline.

Bear Market. A sustained period of falling stock or bond prices with a decline greater than or equal to 20 percent of value. (A "correction" is generally defined as a decline over 10 percent.)

Before-Tax Contributions. The allotted part of an employee's salary put into a retirement plan that is not taxed because it is not included in gross income.

Beneficiary. The person to whom death benefits are paid when the owner of an annuity dies.

Bequest. Under the terms of a will, property given to an inheritor.

Beta. The extent to which the value of a fund or a stock tends to go up or down as the market goes up or down. A growth fund with a beta of 1.5 would most likely go up 15 percent when the market as a whole is up 10 percent (or down 15 percent when the market is down 10 percent).

Bid Price. The price at which the owner of a security or a commodity wishes to sell that asset. This contrasts with the *asked price,* which is what a prospective purchaser is willing to pay for a security or commodity.

Big Board. The New York Stock Exchange.

Blue Chip. A large, well known, established company whose stock is considered to be a solid investment and safer than other companies' stocks, since a blue chip is unlikely to go bankrupt.

Bond. An IOU issued by a corporate, municipal, or government entity in return for a pledge of repayment of the original face value invested, plus interest payments to be paid on specified dates.

Bond Fund. A mutual fund that invests primarily in bonds.

Bull. An investor who expects a market rise.

Bull Market. A sustained period of rising stock or bond prices. While the market is trending upward, there will be volatility and shorter-term down days (but no declines of 20 percent or more from the market's peak).

Buy and Hold. A long-term strategy that, as its name implies, emphasizes ignoring short-term market moves and instead holding on for the long term.

Call. The act of paying off a bond issue before it reaches maturity. Bond issuers usually do this at the worst possible time for bondholders—when prevailing interest rates are lower than what the bond being called is paying.

Capital Appreciation. Profit made by selling a security for an amount of principal greater than when the security was purchased. Contrast with *income.*

Capital Gain. Profit made on the sale of securities or property. Federal capital gains taxes are currently capped at 28 percent for investments held over 12 months, and 20 percent for investments held over 18 months, even for investors whose income is taxed at a higher rate.

Capital Gains Distribution. A mutual fund's distribution to shareholders of gains realized on the sale of securities in the fund's portfolio. Typically, the distributions are made once per year, and they can affect the optimal timing of your own purchase or sale of the fund.

Capitalization. The total market value of all shares of a company's stock.

Capital Loss. Loss suffered by an investor when the amount realized on the sale of an asset is less than the amount originally paid for it.

Capital Preservation. Investors who have already grown their seed money into a harvestable crop want to protect what they've got. Capital preservation refers to the objective of ensuring that the amount of capital doesn't become reduced over time, which in turn means that risks are avoided in favor of a defensive portfolio. Nevertheless, some growth of capital must ensue, if only to be able to safeguard the capital from inflation. Income is also usually sought, to allow periodic withdrawals without depleting principal.

Cash. The most liquid asset, typically thought of as negotiable currency but also including stable interest-bearing short-term money market instruments like *commercial paper* or *treasury bills and notes* (see also those entries).

Cash Account. A brokerage account that has transactions recognized on a cash basis.

Cash Dividend. Taxable cash payments made to shareholders from a corporation's earnings. Some companies issue a stock dividend in lieu of a cash payout.

Cash Flow. A company's net income after expenses, but before accounting for abstract costs such as depreciation. Cash flow is one indicator used by stock analysts to evaluate a company's ability to pay off debt and keep paying dividends or expanding financially.

Certificate of Deposit (CD). A specified-term, fixed-interest earning debt instrument issued by a bank or a savings and loan. A good temporary parking place for cash you will need at a specified date in the near future. (CD maturities range from 3 months to 5 years.) Penalties apply for early withdrawal. Most CDs are insured by the Federal Deposit Insurance Corporation (FDIC).

Certified Financial Planner (CFP). This certificate, issued by the Institute of Certified Financial Planners, signifies that the holder has passed a series of tests showing the ability to advise clients on a host of financial concerns including banking, estate planning, insurance, investing, and taxes. Be advised that tests are no substitute for experience, intelligence, and integrity.

Certified Public Accountant (CPA). The designation CPA is an accountant's license to practice. It is the oldest and most meaningful of what is fast becoming an alphabet soup of proliferating professional designations for providers of financial services. Although CPAs must pass a rigorous examination covering accounting, auditing, and tax preparation, you should remember that investment management is *not* necessarily part of the accountant's curriculum.

Chartered Financial Analyst (CFA). A person who has passed a rigorous (3-year) examination process, coupled with relevant experience in economics, ethics, financial accounting, portfolio management, and hard-core security analysis. CFAs stand out among those who proclaim themselves qualified to analyze an investment's fundamental worth and its appropriateness to particular portfolios.

Chartered Financial Consultant (ChFC). An excellent addition to the designation CFP, this charter is offered to CFPs who have also passed a four-year program at Bryn Mawr College, which covers economics, insurance, investing, and taxes.

Chartered Mutual Fund Counselor (ChMFC). A new designation offered by the National Endowment for Financial Education, indicating a financial adviser's enhanced ability to advise clients on questions and concerns regarding mutual funds.

Closed-End Fund, Closed-End Investment Company. In contrast with an open-end mutual fund (See *mutual fund*), which issues new shares per new purchase, a closed-end fund sells a fixed number of shares in its portfolio of securities. Closed-end fund shares trade on the major U.S. exchanges and the over-the-counter market. Their market value is determined by supply and demand, which leads to shares being sold at either a premium or a discount relative to the actual *net asset value* of the fund's portfolio.

Commercial Paper. Short-term loans to corporations, usually of very high credit quality. Held by taxable money markets, except for those that stick to government securities.

Commission. A fee (usually expressed as a percentage of assets sold or amount managed) charged by a brokerage firm—be it real estate or investment.

Committee on Uniform Securities Identification Procedures (CUSIP). This committee supplies a numeral identification, called a "CUSIP number," for each mutual fund, stock, or other security. These lengthy numeric codes are not as well known as the letter codes used by *QUOTRON*.

Commodities. Generic goods, ranging from grains and other foods to metals, which are traded on several exchanges by traders speculating on the effect of supply and demand on the goods' prices.

Common Stock. A share of ownership in a company. Stock prices can rise or fall with the company's fortunes, or even with fluctuations, in stock market supply and demand (which may or may not be entirely rational).

Compound Interest. Interest earned on previously paid interest as well as on the original principal. Example: $500 principal at 10 percent annual interest would become $550 in one year; but going forward, that $550 at 10 percent compound interest would become $605, after realizing $55 in interest during the second year ($50 interest on the original principal, plus $5 on the first year's interest).

Consumer Price Index (CPI). A monthly measure of the cost of a fixed bundle of goods that are considered typical consumer purchases.

Contrarian. An investor who examines what investments and trends consensus wisdom is buying into, and invests in their opposite To a contrarian, the crowd is always wrong. But, you might ask, what happens if there's a crowd of contrarians?

Convertible Security. Convertible securities, or **convertibles,** are bonds and preferred stock that can be exchanged for a set number of common stocks, at a prestated price.

Corporate Bond. Debt instrument (IOU) issued by a private or public corporation, as opposed to a government entity. Corporate bonds typically share the following characteristics: their income is taxable; they have a par value of $1,000; they have a specified maturity; and they're traded (albeit thinly) on one of the major exchanges.

Correction. A modest but significant market decline, usually defined as one bringing the market down 10 percent to 20 percent lower than its high.

Correlation. The extent to which a fund and the stock market (usually as measured by the S&P 500 Index) tend to move together. An S&P 500 index fund would have a correlation of 99 percent or 100 percent. A fund which is invested in smaller stocks not found in the S&P 500, or which makes big bets on narrow sectors, or which invests heavily overseas would tend to have a much lower correlation (most likely less than 50 percent). See also R^2.

Cost Basis. An investment's original cost, which is subtracted from the sale price to see if there were capital gains or losses from the sale of the security. It is used for tax purposes.

Coupon. The original interest rate paid on a bond's face (or par) value. A $1,000 par bond paying $50 per year has a 5 percent coupon.

Credit Rating (Consumer). A report of a consumer's history of timely (and untimely) payment of bills, used to determine potential credit risk for mortgages, new credit cards, and other loans.

Credit Rating, Credit Quality (Bond). A letter grading of potential risk. Standard & Poor's (S&P) and Moody's are the top rating agencies, and both rate companies on the basis of ability to repay bondholders' interest and principal. Standard & Poor's ratings of AAA (Moody's Aaa) to BBB (Baa), signify a range of "investment grade" bonds, while ratings of BB (Ba) or lower denote "below-investment-grade" bonds, more commonly referred to as "junk bonds." The rating D signifies that a bond is in default.

Currency Risk. The likelihood that the dollar value of an international stock will fluctuate in reaction to a change in currency exchange rates.

Current Yield. Current yield is determined by dividing a bond's annual interest by its current market price. It differs from the coupon rate in that it accounts for the price paid for the bond (as opposed to its par value). For example, while the coupon rate of a $1,000 par bond paying $50 per year is 5 percent, the current yield of that same bond, if it is bought at $950, would be 5.26 percent.

Custodian. An organization in charge of and protecting financial assets. For example, a bank is a custodian.

Cyclical Stock. A stock whose performance is closely tied to the health of the economy. In tough economic times, these stocks falter. In good times, they typically rise rapidly. Housing, cars, and "deep cyclicals" (like steel manufacturers) are directly affected by the consumer's and the industry's willingness and ability to purchase goods.

Debt to Equity. A ratio that is calculated by dividing a company's total liabilities by the total amount of outstanding stock. It is used to help measure a company's ability to pay its creditors if business falters.

Default. Failure of a company or another debtor to make payments of principal, interest, or both on schedule. A bad thing.

Defensive Stocks. These stocks are the antonym of *cyclical stocks,* since the company's products tend to be staples (like food) that consumers can't do without (unlike a new car). As a result, their performance is less affected by economic downturns.

Defined Contribution Plan. A retirement plan proposing a benefit that relies on the total contribution from employer and employee and the return of the contribution. The employees bear the risk of the investments. This contrasts with defined benefit plans (DBPs), which offer a guaranteed return in which the employer assumes the risk. DBP benefits are guaranteed by a federal agency, the Pension Benefit Guaranty Corporation.

Deflation. Deflation (not to be confused with disinflation, which is a slowing down in the rate of price increases) is the opposite of inflation. Thus deflation is a decline in the general price level of goods and services.

Derivative. A bet on the direction of interest rates or the price of some other security or commodity. Some funds and investors use derivatives aggressively to enhance the yield or potential return of a portfolio, while others use them in an attempt to reduce the risk of a portfolio. Derivatives aren't all bad, but a fund that loads up on them may be drifting into high-risk territory.

Discount. Just like what you find at Wal-Mart, discounts reflect a price reduction in the product or security you're buying at market. For example, with regard to bonds, a discount is the difference between the bond's par value and its current market price, where that price is lower than the par value. (In contrast, buying a bond at a premium would mean that the current market price is higher than the par value.) For a closed-end fund, a discount is the amount by which the purchase price is less than *net asset value*.

Discount Broker. A broker that typically charges less (in comparison with full-service brokers) for services rendered—from trades transacted to reports and recommendations issued. There's a wide variance in such costs and services among discounters and deep discounters.

Discount Rate. The interest rate the Federal Reserve Board charges member banks on loans. This rate in turn affects the interest rates on loans to consumers, since banks use the discount rate as the benchmark from which they mark up the rate on their loans. The discount rate gets a lot of press only when the Fed is tightening (i.e., increasing interest rates).

Distribution. A payment made to a shareholder. Except for income from municipal funds, distributions are taxable events. Distributions amount to a return of your capital because (except for dividends of monthly bond funds) share prices are reduced by the same amount as the dividend. This reduction in share price occurs on the *ex-dividend date*.

Diversification. Spreading risk among many entities. To spread out their risk, fund managers may buy several stocks or bonds issued by several companies in a wide range of industries. The objective is to not let one investment have too much impact on the entire portfolio.

Dividend. A distribution of earnings to shareholders, either by an individual company or by a mutual fund.

Dividend Reinvestment Plan (DRIP). Like automatic reinvestment, the reinvestment of dividends in new shares of a stock or fund. A smart move, even though you will have to pay taxes on the dividend amount (even if you don't receive it in cash).

Dividend Yield. The current dividend paid on a single share of stock divided by the current price of that share. In terms of a portfolio, one would look at the weighted average dividend yield for the stocks held in it.

Dollar-Cost Averaging. A strategy in which the purchase of an investment like mutual fund shares is divided into a number of equal installments to be made at regular time intervals. The aim is to lower the average share price the investor ends up paying, but dollar-cost averaging doesn't always beat putting all your money to work at once.

Dow Jones Industrial Average (DJIA). A stock market index—also know simply as the **Dow**—that is calculated by adding up the prices of 30 large-cap stocks. This results in a potential flaw (according to some critics): its narrow definition excludes newer industries and companies. Nevertheless, this index is the most widely used measure of the market—and it has certainly earned its place as a standard worth watching.

Duration. A measure of a bond fund's sensitivity to interest rates, based on the maturities of the bonds in the portfolio. A fund with an effective duration of 4 should lose 4 percent if interest rates rise 1 percent, or gain 4 percent if interest rates fall 1 percent. A zero-coupon bond with a maturity of 4 years would have such a duration. Duration estimates are rather amorphous for mortgage-backed securities, whose effective duration can get considerably longer when rates go up and refinancings are slow—just when you don't want a longer duration.

Earnings per Share (EPS). Portion of a company's profit allocated to each outstanding share of common stock. (Total profits divided by number of shares of common stock.)

Economic Indicators. Statistics used to represent the current state of the economy and also to predict (with a meteorologist's accuracy) the direction of the economy.

Education IRA. An account started with the goal of paying a child's postsecondary education. Five hundred after-tax dollars can be contributed each year on the child's behalf.

Efficient Market Theory. A theory suggesting that market price reflects market value, meaning that dart throwers and analysts have an equal chance of selecting the best stocks. Contentious, but hardly groundless. See *index fund, inefficient market theory*.

Emerging Markets Fund. Emerging markets are also referred to as developing economies. An emerging markets fund is a mutual fund that mostly invests in countries in the process of being industrialized. These funds tend to be very risky, so fluctuations in values will most likely occur.

Employee Contribution. An employee's contribution to his or her retirement plan, normally made on a pretax basis.

Employer Matching Contribution. The employer's contribution to the employee's retirement plan.

Estate Planning. Formulation of a plan including a will, power of attorney, and trusts that execute a person's wishes concerning his or her property before or after death.

Estate Tax. Tax imposed for the right to reassign property because of death. The tax is imposed on the deceased's property, not on the inheritor receiving the estate. IRA assets can be included as part of an estate and are taxable.

Estimated Tax. A tax a person has to pay on income such as investment income, capital gains, alimony, and rent because it is not subject to withholding tax.

Equity. A fancy name for common stock. If you're in the habit of saying "*très* good," then by all means call stocks "equities."

Exchange. Transfer of money between one fund and another within the same fund complex. Usually accomplished by a single phone call. Investors should be aware that an exchange out of one fund constitutes a sale of that fund's shares and is taxable.

Ex-Dividend Date. The date on which stocks (or mutual funds) effectively pay out their dividends. On this date, shareholders receive the dividend, the share price tends to fall by the amount of the dividend, and automatic reinvestments are made. (However, actual dividend checks may be delayed by several days.)

Expense Ratio. The amount investors in a fund pay for expenses incurred in the operation and management of the fund during the year. This expense may be 1 percent or more. A higher expense ratio reduces the fund's total return; therefore, two funds of equal strength but with unequal expense ratios present a clear choice—opt for the one with the lower expense ratio. An expense ratio is even more important than load, since this figure is charged continually (it is expressed as an annual rate). Even if a fund has a decent past performance, it's likely to be handicapped looking forward if its expense ratio is high compared with funds with similar objectives. However, figures on fund performance already have these expenses subtracted, so don't double-count them by subtracting them from published returns. Note that the infamous *12b-1 fees* (which are paid to brokers and other fund sales representatives) are included in a fund's expense ratio; you should generally be more concerned with this total expense ratio than with its breakdown into 12b-1, management, administrative, and other expenses.

Face Value. Nominal worth of a bond or another security, as printed on its "face." Also known as *par*. The security may actually sell for considerably more or less than this figure, especially if it is a long way from maturity (see *average maturity*).

Family of Funds. Group of funds "owned" (that is, managed and operated) by the same investment management company. (Technically, each fund is owned by its shareholders, who could vote to move the fund to another fund family.)

Federal Funds Rate. The rate on short-term, overnight loans among commercial banks. The Federal Reserve influences the Fed Funds Rate by buying and selling treasuries in the open market and by changing reserve requirements for banks.

Federal Reserve Board. Also known as the **Fed.** Group of economists and bankers (led by a presidential appointee—currently Alan Greenspan—who in England might have the title "Lord of the Purse"). The Fed sets short-term interest rates and other factors affecting monetary supply.

Fees. Fees come in many forms. Here are the most common ones:

1. **Load.** Also called **front-end load.** A load is an up-front sales commission charged to and deducted from your initial investment amount. (Load charges range as high as 8.5 percent but are more commonly in the range of 3 percent to 4.5 percent.) There's little reason to purchase high-load funds when there are so many good no-load and low-load funds to choose from. Some load funds may become no-loads when purchased in a retirement plan.

2. **No-load.** No-load means no initial sales commission fee. No-load refers only to up-front sales commission charges. Many no-load funds have other fees (listed below). Nevertheless, no-load funds tend to be the best way to invest in mutual funds because more of your money is going to work for you.

3. **Back-end load.** Also known as a **redemption fee,** this is a fee charged when you sell your shares. Either your profit is cut or your loss is increased. No matter how you look at it, this load is just as bad as any other.

4. **Deferred loads (contingent deferred sales fees).** On the surface, a deferred load seems as lousy as a back-end load. But a deferred load is charged by some funds if and only if you redeem your shares before a specified time—typically a few years. While this may not be to your advantage if you're investing for the short-term, the principle of discouraging investors from jumping into and out of the market on impulse is a good one.

5. **Reinvestment loads.** Some fund companies (not Fidelity) dock your dividend, interest, and capital gains should you decide to reinvest them. Any fund that does this is discouraging a very wise investment choice—reinvesting dividends. Drop any of these funds from your list of possible investments.

6. **12b-1 fees.** Some funds deduct the costs associated with advertising and marketing from the fund's overall assets. The charge associated with such deductions is called a 12b-1 fee, and it ranges as high as 1.25 percent per year. Some funds feed a portion of the fee to the broker who sold you the fund. Many funds have 12b-1 plans established in case the SEC decides to call some of their sales-related expenses (such as mailing out prospectuses), but under current rules none of the funds in this book actually charges any 12b-1 fees.

7. **Early redemption fees.** These are charged only within a set period of purchase, usually 1 to 12 months. They differ from

deferred loads in that they are paid to the fund (not the management company) to reimburse the fund and its shareholders for the expenses associated with heavy shareholder turnover. These are actually a good thing for most shareholders.

Fee Table. A table showing the expenses and fees a shareholder will take on concerning a particular mutual fund. Usually located at the front of a fund's prospectus.

Fixed-Income Fund. A mutual fund that invests in fixed-income securities such as *corporate bonds, commercial paper,* or *Ginnie Maes (GNMAs).*

401(k) Plan. A retirement plan offered to employees of many for-profit companies. A 401(k) works a lot like a deductible IRA, but with higher contribution limits: $9,500 in 1997. One downside: the employing company chooses what investment options to offer, sometimes only a half-dozen funds or so.

403(b) Plan. A retirement plan offered to employees of many government and nonprofit organizations. A 403(b) works a lot like a deductible IRA, but with higher contribution limits: $9,500 in 1997. Most of these plans offer many investment options.

Fundamental Analysis. Analysis of a company and its securities based on hard data from its balance sheet and income statements, sales, earnings, and management, as well as extrinsic economic factors that affect the company's ability to operate profitably. Such analysis can be used to predict future potential. Contrast with *technical analysis.*

Fund of Funds. A mutual fund whose portfolio consists of other mutual funds.

Futures Contract. Written agreement to buy or sell a commodity or security for a specified price at a specified future date. May be used for speculation or, on the other hand, as a *hedge* against risk.

General Obligations (GOs). Municipal securities backed by the full power and taxing ability of a municipality or state (in contrast with securities backed only by the revenues from a specific project, such as a toll bridge).

Ginnie Mae (GNMA). A security backed by a pool of residential mortgages. In case of default by a homeowner, credit is further guaranteed by the Government National Mortgage Association, which has the "implicit" backing of the federal government. However, while credit quality is very high, these securities still have significant interest-rate risk.

Global Fund. A mutual fund that invests in U.S. and foreign securities.

Gross Domestic Product (GDP). The total value of all goods and services provided by U.S. companies within U.S. borders. Since December 1991, this has been the Commerce Department's primary measure of the U.S. economy's size and growth or contraction. An inflation-adjusted measure of GDP is called the "real GDP."

Growth and Income Fund (G&I Fund). A mutual fund that typically combines the objective of capital appreciation with the generation of some income. Note: Some G&I funds are very close to *growth funds*, offering virtually no income; others look almost like *bond funds*, with little room for capital appreciation. Match your objective with a G&I fund's actual portfolio.

Growth Fund. A mutual fund that invests in stocks, especially one investing in more growth-oriented stocks paying little or no income dividend. This type of fund seeks to deliver capital appreciation to its shareholders, rather than income.

Growth Stock. Stock in a company characterized by above-average growth in earnings or sales. Growth stocks tend to have a high price relative to earnings and provide little if any dividend. Growth stocks also tend to have a high beta (or risk) but can offer long-term investors the potential for solid capital appreciation. Contrast with *cyclical stock* and *value stock*.

Hedge. Not a rhododendron. A hedge, or hedging, is a strategy used to neutralize the risk inherent in an investment. The phrase "hedge one's bets," accurately reflects the objective: to break even whether the hedged assets move up or down. But hedging, which is often accomplished with the use of derivatives, sometimes fails to protect against risks.

High. The highest level at which the market or some investment has ever been, or, sometimes, the highest level it's been at in the past year (more exactly known as the 52-week high). See also *low*.

Income. Regular payment of fixed sums in return for possession of a relatively larger principal investment. Income may be paid on a bond or another loan, or on a dividend-paying stock. Income investments tend to be more stable than investments seeking *capital appreciation*.

Income Fund. A mutual fund that strives for income rather than growth. Usually, such funds invest in high-yielding stocks and/ or bonds.

Index. A standard or benchmark against which the performance of a market, industry, company, or security (stock, bond, real estate, mutual fund, and so on) is measured.

Index Fund. A fund whose objective is to match a specific market index (most commonly the S&P 500 stock index). Since most funds fail to beat their relevant index benchmark, an index fund is likely to perform slightly better than most funds in the long term.

Individual Retirement Account (IRA). A personal investment account into which individuals can invest up to $2,000 annually, and which grows sheltered from taxes. For some investors, deposits into IRAs qualify as deductions against income. Used primarily for retirement savings, since you are heavily penalized for withdrawals made before age 59½.

Inefficient Market Theory. This theory holds that a smart, informed investor stands a better-than-even chance of outperforming a chimp and a dart board—or a stupid, ill-informed investor. In contrast to the *efficient market theory,* this one encourages research and analysis in an attempt to beat fellow investors to the punch.

Inflation. A rise in the general price level of goods and services. There are two common measures of inflation: the *Consumer Price Index (CPI)* tracks prices of consumer goods, and the *Producer Price Index (PPI)* focuses on industrial goods and materials. Inflation decreases the purchasing power of your dollar in the long run. The cause is usually an increase in the money supply.

Initial Public Offering (IPO). The first offering of a company's stock to the public.

International Fund. A mutual fund that invests in securities traded in markets outside of the U.S. International funds offer long-term growth and capital.

Investment Company. An arrangement whereby investors pool their assets into a corporation or trust, which then employs professional management to invest the assets according to a stated objective. Mutual funds are one form of investment company. See *mutual fund* and *closed-end fund.*

Investment Objective. A fund's aim, as stated in its prospectus. Investors should choose a fund whose objectives match their own—although they need to go beyond the stated objective and examine the fund's history of actually hitting what it's aiming at.

Joint Account. Two or more adult shareholders who are registered to the same account. They need to have an equal interest in the account so that in the event of one shareholder's death, the other or others will inherit the property automatically.

Junk Bond Fund. A fund made up of higher-yield and high-risk bonds. These are either bonds issued by solid companies that have fallen on hard times and lost their investment quality ratings, or bonds originally issued with higher-than-average interest rates by financially troubled companies. Junk bonds are rated BB or lower by Standard & Poor's or Ba or lower by Moody's.

Keogh Plan. A retirement plan similar to an IRA, but aimed at self-employed workers only. Investors have a Keogh Plan may contribute much more than the $2,000 per annum IRA limit.

Large Capitalization Stocks (Large-Caps). Stock of a company that has a market value of more than $5 billion. These companies are well-established corporations with a long-term record of stable earnings, growth, and dividend payments.

Liability. A debt or another position with negative value. Contrast with *asset*.

Liquidity. A measure of how easily an investment can be converted into its present value for cash or cash equivalents. Mutual fund shares are very liquid because you can sell them and receive their net asset value in cash or cash equivalents on any day the stock market is open. On the other hand, real estate is not liquid.

Load. A mutual fund's sales charge. See *fees*.

Load Fund. A mutual fund that charges both front-end and back-end loads. See *fees*.

Long-Term Capital Gain. Profit you gain from selling a mutual fund or a security after you have held it for at least 1 year. Contrast *short-term capital gain*.

Low. This could mean the lowest level at which the market or some investment has ever been but is more typically the lowest level it's been at in the past year (more exactly known as the 52-week low), since the all-time low for market indices and most stocks in long-extant companies approaches zero (especially after accounting for any stock splits). See also *high*.

Management Fee. The fee that goes to pay for the analysis and selection of securities. See *expense ratio*.

Margin Account. A brokerage account in which a customer borrows money from the broker to pay for a percentage of the cost of securities. The money borrowed is the margin. The amount borrowed is restricted by the Federal Reserve, and there is a charge for borrowing this money.

Marginal Tax Rate. The highest percentage at which your income is taxed. This rate is utilized to figure out taxes on your investment income.

Market Timing. An investment technique based on a forecast about the direction of the stock market or interest rates. Market-timers will put all their money into stocks if they think the market will rise, or into long-term bonds if they think the market will fall. They will quickly turn their investment into cash if they think that this trend is changing direction. Market timing is very risky. It generates excessive taxes and trading costs and, more often than not, underperforms the simple buy-and-hold investment program.

Maturity. The date which the face value of a bond's, or some other source of debt, becomes due and payable.

Median Market Capitalization. In terms of market capitalization, the middle stock in a portfolio.

Minimum Investment. The minimum amount required to make additional investments in a portfolio or to open an account.

Money Market. A fund (or bank account) that invests in very high-quality, short-term income securities. See *cash* and *commercial paper*.

Mortgage-Backed Securities. Bond-like securities that are backed by mortgages, usually on single-family houses. Some are backed by GNMA (see *Ginnie Mae*).

Municipal Bond Fund. A mutual fund that invests in tax-exempt bonds issued by states, cities, or local governments whose interest payments are free from federal taxes and are passed to shareholders. Often referred to as tax-free bonds.

Mutual Fund. A professionally managed portfolio of securities (stocks, bonds, cash, etc.), which enables investors to pool their money and reap the potential rewards (or suffer the possible consequences). An excellent investment vehicle for getting you to your investment destination. The problem is that there are many cars on the lot, and only a few of them have a full tank of gas. Mutual fund companies buy and sell shares to the public for their underlying *net asset value* (plus any *fees*).

National Association of Securities Dealers (NASD). An organization established to provide protection for investors against fraudulent acts by executing rules of fair practice. The NASD is usually made up of brokers and dealers.

National Association of Securities Dealers Automated Quotations

(NASDAQ). Provides price quotes for securities traded over the New York Stock Exchange and over the counter.

Net Asset Value (NAB). The market price of a fund (its NAV per share) is derived at the close of market every day by determining the value of the fund's total assets (the value of each security as well as cash and cash equivalents) less its liabilities, divided by the total number of its outstanding shares. See *asset* and *liability*.

New York Stock Exchange (NYSE). The largest and oldest stock exchange in the United States. Located in New York City, it has been around since 1792.

Nikkei Index. The most widely quoted Tokyo index of Japanese stocks.

No-Load Fund. A mutual fund whose shares can be bought and sold at *net asset value (NAV)* without any sales charge—but be warned that there may be a redemption fee (a fee charged for selling the fund, generally within a specified time of purchase). See *fees*.

Offering Price. *Net asset value (NAV)* per share, plus the sales charge. Offering price is also called the "asked price." For no-load funds, NAV and offering price are the same.

Open-End Investment Company Open-End Fund. *See mutual fund.*

Option. The right to buy or sell at a designated price at a certain point in time.

Over-the-Counter (OTC). The *NASDAQ* is the leading over-the-counter market in the United States. OTC stocks aren't listed on any exchange. Instead, they are bought and sold through a computerized network of traders.

Par. The face value of a bond, and the principal amount that should be paid when the bond matures.

Part B Prospectus. Another name for a fund's *statement of additional information*.

Passive Management. A management approach that has the goal of matching risk and return characteristics of a single market segment by holding all the securities that make up the particular market segment you are looking at.

Portfolio. An investor's or fund manager's investment holdings.

Preferred Stock. This actually acts more like a bond. A preferred stock, like a bond, generally pays a fixed income. But unlike bondholders, preferred holders cannot force a company into bankruptcy for failure to make a dividend payment. (The leverage the preferred holders have is that a company cannot pay a dividend to its common stock holders until it has paid the preferred dividends.)

Premium. The opposite of a *discount*.

Prepayment Risk. The possibility that if interest rates fall far enough, a bond issuer will pay off the bond's principal early, forcing the investor to reinvest in bonds with lower yields.

Price/Book Ratio. The price of a security per share divided by its book value per share. In terms of a portfolio, it is the weighted-average price/book ratio of the securities held in the portfolio.

Price/Earnings Ratio. The current price of a security divided by the per-share earnings over the past year. In terms of a portfolio, it is the weighted-average price/earnings ratio of the securities held in the portfolio. The higher the price/earnings ratio, the higher the prospect for earnings growth in years to come.

Prime Rate. Officially known as the Federal Reserve Bank rate, this is the rate big money-center banks charge their best customers. Generally, when one big institution adjusts its prime, the others follow suit, so it is possible to speak of there being *one* prime rate rather than a variety of prime rates. Changes in the prime rate affect everyone with access to credit—not just preferred borrowers—because most other lending rates are somehow pegged to the prime. The direction of the prime rate has important implications for the overall economy: when times are good, corporations and individuals alike borrow more, driving rates up; when the economy heads down, the opposite occurs.

Principal. How much of your own money you originally contributed to an investment.

Proceeds. After sales commissions are subtracted, the amount that the seller actually acquires.

Producer Price Index (PPI). A monthly measure of the cost of a fixed bundle of industrial goods and materials. Not as well-known as the Consumer Price Index (CPI), PPI is still a useful statistic; PPI should warn of inflation before CPI, since it should generally take some time for increased producer prices to work their way into increased consumer prices.

Profit-Sharing Plan. A defined contribution plan in which contributions are based on the employee's earnings and can vary. It is still possible for an employer to contribute to the plan even if no profits are generated. Also, no minimum contribution is necessary.

Prospectus. The Securities and Exchange Commission (SEC) requires every fund to provide each shareholder with a prospectus wherein the fund describes its investment objectives, investments, past performance, fees, and services. Get it. Read it. Know it—before you invest in the fund.

Proxy. Instrument whereby someone gives another person the right to represent him or her. The two parties authorize this in writing.

QUOTRON. A stock symbol consisting of 1 to 3 letters for NYSE stocks, 4 letters for NASDAQ stocks, or 5 letters for mutual funds. For example, IBM is IBM, Amazon is AMZN, and Fidelity Magellan is FMAGX.

R^2. Simply put, for any two funds, there is a number, R^2, that shows what percentage of one fund's performance can be explained by the other fund. (A fund's R^2 when compared with itself is 100 percent.) I also use R^2 to show each fund's correlation with the S&P 500 Index—the best overall benchmark for U.S. stock investors (although it does have its limitations as a benchmark for small-cap funds). Spartan Market Index, for example, has a 100 percent correlation with the S&P 500 Index. Why is understanding your funds' correlation important? It will help you ensure that your own portfolio is well diversified. How? If you hold only two growth funds like Blue Chip and Growth Company, your overall portfolio isn't as diversified as it should be. That's because these two funds have a high correlation (88 percent), meaning that they have performed similarly and are likely to continue to do so. On the other hand, if you own two growth funds with a very low correlation, like Dividend Growth and Small Cap Selector, you've achieved added diversification (since their correlation is a low 57 percent)—not surprising, given these funds' different capitalization and industry emphasis.

Real Return. The return gained from an investment after inflation has been taken out. For example, if the return on a security was a positive 7 percent and the inflation rate was 4 percent, the real return would be 3 percent.

Redemption Fee. See *fees.*

Relative Volatility. See *risk.*

Required Minimum Distribution. The minimum annual distribution from an IRA that the holder is required to take once he or she reaches the age of 70½.

Risk. The best measure of risk is relative volatility. Volatility is the *standard deviation,* or uncertainty, of a fund's return. A fund that goes up about the same each month (e.g., a money market) has very low risk, while a fund whose performance is more erratic is said to be more risky. To calculate a fund's volatility, I take its monthly performances (for the last 36 months) and calculate the standard deviation for this series of numbers. Relative volatility is a fund's volatility divided by the volatility of the S&P 500 Index for the same period. All funds riskier than the market have risk levels above 1, and all funds with less risk than the market have risk levels below 1.

Risk-Adjusted Return (RAR). This is a figure that permits comparisons between the total return of funds (and/or investment models or the S&P 500 Index) of varying levels of risk, by factoring out differences in volatility. A fund's RAR is the return one would obtain with a portfolio holding the fund and enough cash reserves (or, for low-risk funds, enough margin) to maintain the risk level of the S&P 500. For a growth fund with a relative volatility of 1.25, a portfolio would consist of 80 percent of that growth fund and 20 percent of cash reserves, giving the hypothetical portfolio a volatility of 1. The returns for this hypothetical portfolio are that growth fund's RAR. Algebraically, to calculate a fund's RAR, you subtract the return of cash reserves from the return of the fund, divide this number by the fund's relative volatility, and then add back the return of cash reserves. See also *cash, margin account,* and *risk.*

Rollover. A movement of *cash* or other *assets* from one retirement plan to another. This transfer is tax-free.

Rollover IRA. An individual retirement account set up only for acquiring a distribution from a qualified plan so that the assets can be thereafter rolled over into another qualified plan.

Roth IRA. An IRA from which withdrawals are tax-free and which is funded by nondeductible contributions. It was formulated for people who don't qualify for tax deductions for contributions to an IRA up-front, usually because of their income level or their participation in an employer-sponsored retirement plan.

Sector. A fancy name for an industry, especially a narrowly defined industry (e.g., biotech, pharmaceuticals, and HMOs are sectors in the health care industry).

Sector Fund. A fund that invests in companies in one defined sector or a related group of sectors. Fidelity's Select funds are the best-known and widest-ranging of this speculative genre.

Securities. Stocks, bonds, and other investments.

Settlement Date. The date when a completed order must be settled. For regular-way delivery of stocks and bonds, the settlement date is 3 days after the trade was completed.

Short-Term Capital Gain. The profit you make on the sale of a security or fund after holding it for a year or less. Contrast *long-term capital gain.*

Signature Guarantee. Validating a signature by stamping or sealing, performed by a member of a bank or stock exchange. In order to change the ownership of an account, a signature guarantee would have to be provided.

Simplified Employee Pension (SEP-IRA). A retirement plan that resembles an IRA and is available to all qualified employees.

Small-Cap Stock (Small-Caps). Stock in a company whose market value is less than $500 million. Small-cap companies tend to have faster growth and more risk than large-cap stocks. They use their profits to finance development rather than pay their shareholders dividends.

Split, Stock Split. A split occurs when the board of directors of a company decides to increase the number of outstanding shares, pending approval by the shareholders. What happens is that the number of shares increases and the price of an individual share decreases. For example, if a company announces a 4-for-1 stock split and you have 200 shares of stock at $100 a share, you end up with 800 shares of stock at $25 a share. The value stays the same for the shareholder.

Standard & Poor's 500 (S&P 500). The most common index used by money managers to assess the performance of the U.S. stock market. The S&P measures the market capitalization of 500 stocks. It is a price index and does not include the value of reinvested dividends.

Standard Deviation. A statistical measure expressing how much a group of numbers deviates from its average or mean. In a normal "bell-shaped" distribution, about two-thirds of the numbers should fall within 1 standard deviation of their mean, and 95 percent should fall within 2 standard deviations of their mean. For a fund or other investment, the standard deviation of its past monthly total returns (usually 36 months) is a common measure of fund risk, or the uncertainty of return.

Statement of Additional Information. A document, prepared as an addendum to a mutual fund's prospectus, which contains more information about policies, operations, and risks of the fund. Also, it is a record of the compensations of all the fund's officers and directors.

Stock. See *common stock.*

Stock Fund. A *mutual fund* that is made up mostly of stocks.

Systematic Withdrawal Plan. A withdrawal plan whereby a specified amount is taken from another account, for example your checking account, either monthly, quarterly, semiannually, or annually so that you can add it to your investment account automatically.

Tax-Deferred Retirement Plan. A retirement plan in which earnings are not taxable.

Tax-Exempt Bond. A bond whose interest payments are not taxed. Examples of issuers are states, counties, and municipal governments and agencies.

Tax-Exempt Income Fund. A *mutual fund* that is looking to provide the highest amount of federal tax–exempt income while being consistent with capital preservation and risk characteristics.

Technical Analysis. Use of charts of a security's past price performance by technical analysts, who look for trends (and other, more abstract symbols) to indicate an investment's future prospects.

Tenure. A fund manager's time at the helm. Since managers are responsible for the performance of the portfolios they run, tenure is an excellent way to determine the relevance of any performance history. Note that even though a manager may not have a lengthy tenure at the fund you're thinking of buying (the average tenure is under 4 years), this doesn't mean he or she didn't have solid and relevant experience elsewhere.

Ticker Symbol. A group of letters used to represent a security.

Total Return. How much an investment has gone up (or down), taking into account all relevant factors: share price, income, and *capital gains distributions.*

Treasury Bills and Notes. Income securities backed by the full faith and credit of the United States government. Treasury securities have essentially no credit risk, since the federal government has the power to print money. (Printing a lot of money to pay off treasury bonds would of course be inflationary, bring on higher interest rates, and cut the value of all longer-term bonds, so let's hope it never comes to that.)

Trust. A legal arrangement whereby a person or corporation holds assets for the benefit of others.

Turnover Rate. A rate calculated by taking the value of all the fund's trades (buys and sells) and dividing it by twice the net assets of the portfolio. This figure indicates how aggressive a manager has been in trading in and out of (or within) the market. A turnover rate in excess of 100 percent generally means a pretty aggressive manager. If the manager is good, that's not a problem, but excessive turnover can drive up a fund's expenses and hurt returns.

12b-1 Fee. The part of a fund's expense ratio that pays for marketing, distribution, or both. Unlike a sales load, a 12b-1 fee is ongoing and recurrent. While some funds do not charge 12b-1 fees, others do. And even some funds that don't list 12b-1 fees could, under different legal interpretations, fall into this category. At any rate, a fund's total expense ratio is more relevant than its breakdown into 12b-1, management, and administrative and other expenses.

Uniform Gifts to Minors Act (UGMA), Uniform Transfers to Minors Act (UTMA). An account registration in which a custodian (e.g., a parent or grandparent) acts on behalf of a minor who is the beneficial owner of the account. All income and capital gains or losses in the account are reported under the social security number of the minor. For children under 14, unearned investment income up to $1,000 is taxed at the child's tax rate. If that income is over $1,000, it is taxed at the custodian's tax rate. For children over 14, the child's tax rate is the only one that applies.

Value Stock. A stock that is considered cheap relative to earnings or assets. Value stocks tend to be stodgier players in slower-growing, defensive, or cyclical areas. Contrast with *growth stock.* (Note that almost all fund managers at least pay lip service to the concept of value; even some aggressive growth players claim to be seeking "value-growth" issues!)

Vesting. A participant's interest in his or her account balance or accumulated benefit.

Volatility. See *risk.*

Wall Street. Another name for the investment community; also, the name of the financial district in New York City where the NYSE and AMEX reside.

Wash Sale Rule. An investor cannot claim a loss on a sale of an investment if that investment is bought within 30 days before or after the sale. The wash sale rule is an IRS regulation.

Yield. The level of interest payments on a bond or stock. The current yield on a bond is the amount of annual interest divided by the current value of the bond. A more complete measure, *yield to maturity*, takes into account the fact that bonds selling at a discount or premium to their *par* value will get closer to par value as they near maturity. Funds (and this book) report this yield to maturity. See also *maturity*.

Yield Curve. A graph displaying the relationship between bond maturity and yield. The longer-maturity bonds yield more than short-maturity bonds; therefore, the curve slopes up as maturity lengthens. The spread of long- and short-term rates is shown by the steepness of the yield curve. See also *maturity*.

Yield Spread. The difference between the yield on one kind of income investment and the yield on a standard investment, usually U.S. treasury bonds. The yield spread between a bond and the benchmark U.S. treasury would tend to indicate the degree of credit risk expected for the bond. Not surprisingly, yield spreads are much higher for junk bonds than for high-quality corporate bonds.

Yield to Maturity. If a long-term, interest-bearing investment is held until its maturity date, the yield to maturity is the estimated rate of return the investor will gain.

Zero Coupon Bond. A form of debt which is sold at a steep discount to its face value and which pays no annual interest. The discount from face value and the bond's maturity reflect an implied interest rate. The price of these bonds is extremely sensitive to changes in interest rates.

APPENDIX B

Mutual Fund Networks

Fund Family	Phone	State	Website
AAL Mutual Funds:	800-553-6319	WI	www.aal.org
Acorn Funds:	800-922-6769	IL	www.wanger.com
AETNA Funds:	800-238-6263	CT	www.aetna.com
AIM Funds	800-347-4246	TX	www.aimfunds.com
Alger Fund:	800-992-3863	NY	www.algerfund.com
Alleghany Funds:	800-992-8151	IL	www.alleghanyfunds.com
Alliance Capital:	800-221-5672	NJ	www.alliancecapital.com
American Century Family	800-345-2021	MO	www.americancentury.com/index.jsp
Amerindo Technology:	888-TECHFUND	NY	www.amerindo.com
AmeristockFund:	800-394-5064	OH	www.ameristock.com
Aquila Funds:	800-228-4227	NY	www.aquilafunds.com
Artisan	800-344-1770	MN	none
Babson Fund Group	800-422-2766	MO	www.jbfunds.com
Baron Funds:	800-992-2766	NY	www.baronfunds.com
Barr Rosenberg Funds:	800-447-3332	NY	www.riem.com/mf.htm
Bartlett Mutual Funds	800-800-4612	OH	none
Berger Group	800-551-5849	CO	www.bergerfunds.com
Berwyn Group	800-992-6757	PA	www.thekillengroup.com
Boston 1784 Funds:	800-252-1784	MA	www.1784funds.com
Bramwell	800-272-6227	NY	www.bramwell.com
Brandywine Funds	800-656-3017	DE	www.brandywinefunds.com
Calamos:	800-823-7836	IL	www.calamos.com
Caldwell:	800-237-7073	GA	www.ctrust.com
California Investment Trust	800-225-8778	CA	www.caltrust.com
Calvert Group:	800-368-2745	MD	www.calvertgroup.com
Cappiello-Rushmore	800-343-3355	MD	www.rushmorefunds.com

Citizens Trust:	800-223-7010	NH	www.efund.com
Clipper Fund:	800-776-5033	CA	www.clipperfund.com
Cohen & Steers	800-437-9912	NY	www.cohenandsteers.com
Columbia Funds	800-547-1707	OR	www.columbiafunds.com
Crabbe Huson Funds	800-541-9732	OR	www.contrarian.com
Davis Funds:	800-279-0279	NM	www.davisfunds.com
Delaware Funds:	800-523-4640	PA	www.delawarefunds.com
Deutsche Funds:	888-433-8872	NY	www.deutsche-funds.com
Dodge & Cox Group	800-621-3979	CA	www.dodgeandcox.com
Domini Funds:	800-762-6814	NY	www.domini.com
Dreman	800-533-1608	NJ	www.kemper.com
Dreyfus Group	800-645-6561	NY	www.dreyfus.com
Dupree Funds:	800-866-0614	KY	www.dupree-funds.com
Eclipse Funds:	800-872-2710	NY	www.eclipsefund.com
Evergreen Funds:	800-343-2898	MA	www.evergreenfunds.com
Excelsior Funds:	800-446-1012	NY	www.excelsiorfunds.com
Fairmount Fund:	800-636-5633	KY	www.fairmountfund.com
Fairport Funds:	800-332-6459	OH	www.fairport.com
FBR Funds:	888-888-8025	VA	www.fbrfunds.com
Federated Funds	800-245-2423	PA	www.federatedinvestors.com
Fidelity Funds Network	800-544-9697	MA	www.fidelity.com
Fidelity	800-544-8888	MA	www.fidelity.com
First Funds:	800-442-1941	CO	www.firstfunds.com
Firstar Funds:	800-982-8909	WI	www.firstarfunds.com
Firsthand Funds:	888-884-2675	CA	www.techfunds.com
Flex Funds:	800-325-3539	OH	www.flexfunds.com
Fortis:	800-800-2638	MN	www.us.fortis.com
Founders Funds	800-525-2440	CO	www.founders.com
Franklin Funds	800-342-5236	CA	www.franklin-templeton.com
Gabelli Funds	800-422-3554	NY	www.gabelli.com
Galaxy Funds:	800-628-0414	MA	www.fleet.com/inppgx.html
GAM Funds:	800-426-4685	NY	www.usinfo.gam.com
Goldman Sachs:	800-292-4726	NY	www.gs.com/funds
Guardian Funds:	800-221-3253	NY	www.theguardian.com
Guinness Flight Funds:	800-915-6565	CA	www.gffunds.com
Harbor Funds	800-422-1050	OH	www.harbor.fund (shareholders only)
Harris Insight Funds:	800-982-8782	MA	www.harrisinsight.com
Haven Funds:	800-844-4836	NY	www.havencapital.com
Heartland Funds	800-432-7856	WI	www.heartlandfunds.com
IAI Funds	800-945-3863	MN	www.iaifunds.com
ICM Funds:	800-472-6114	MA	www.icmfunds.com
Integrity Funds:	800-345-2363	ND	www.integrityfunds.com
Invesco Family of Funds	800-525-8085	CO	www.invesco.com

Jack White Network	800-323-3263	CA	www.jackwhiteco.com
Janus Group	800-525-3713	CO	www.janusfunds.com
John Hancock:	800-225-5291	MA	www.jhancock.com
Jurika & Voyles Funds:	800-584-6878	CA	www.jurika.com
Kaminski Poland Fund:	888-229-2105	MN	www.polfund.com
Kaufmann Fund	800-261-0555	PA	www.kaufmann.com
Kemper Funds:	800-621-1048	IL	www.kemper.com
Lazard Funds:	800-823-6300	NY	www.lazardfunds.com
Legg Mason Funds:	800-822-5544	MD	www.leggmason.com
Lexington Group:	800-526-0056	NJ	www.lexingtonfunds.com
Lighthouse Growth:	800-282-2340	TX	www.lightkeepers.com
Lindner	800-995-7777	MO	www.lindnerfunds.com
Loomis Sayles	800-633-3330	MA	www.loomissayles.com
Lord, Abbett & Co.:	888-522-2388	NY	www.lordabbett.com
Lutheran Brotherhood:	800-328-4552	MN	www.luthbro.com
Mainstay Funds:	800-624-6782	NJ	www.mainstayfunds.com
Markman MultiFunds:	800-707-2771	OH	www.markman.com
Marshall Funds:	800-236-8560	PA	www.marshallfunds.com
Marsico Funds:	888-860-8686	WI	www.marsicofunds.com
MAS Funds	800-354-8185	PA	www.msdw.com/ institutional/
Matthews:	800-789-2742	CA	www.micfunds.com
Meridian Fund	800-446-6662	CA	none
Merrill Lynch:	800-637-3863	FL	www.ml.com
Merriman Funds	800-423-4893	WA	www.merrimanfunds.com
Monetta:	800-666-3882	IL	www.monetta.com
Montgomery Funds	800-572-3863	CA	www.montgomeryfunds.com
Morg Stan Dean Witter:	800-869-6397	NY	www.deanwitter.com
Mosaic/GIT:	888-670-3600	VA	www.mosaicfunds.com
Mutual Series Fund	800-448-3863	NJ	www.franklin-templeton.com
Nations Group:	800-321-7854	NC	www.nationsbank.com/ nationsfunds
Navellier Funds:	800-887-8671	NY	www.navellier.com
Neuberger & Berman Grp	800-877-9700	NY	www.nbfunds.com
New England Group:	800-225-5478	MA	www.mutualfunds.com
Nicholas Applegate Group	800-551-8045	CA	www.nacm.com
North American Fund:	800-872-8037	MA	www.northamericanfunds.com
Northern Funds:	800-595-9111	IL	www.northernfunds.com
Oakmark Funds	800-625-6275	IL	www.oakmark.com
Oberweis Funds	800-323-6166	IL	www.oberweisfunds.com
One Group:	800-480-4111	OH	www.onegroup.com
Oppenheimer Funds:	800-525-7048	NY	www.oppenheimer.com

Paine Webber:	800-647-1568	NY	www.painewebber.com
Papp Group:	800-421-4004	AZ	www.roypapp.com
PBHG Growth Fund	800-932-7781	PA	www.pbhgfunds.com
Permanent Portfolio Funds	800-531-5142	CA	none
PIMCo Funds	800-800-0952	CA	www.pimcofunds.com
Pioneer Funds:	800-225-6292	MA	www.pioneerfunds.com
Price T. Rowe Funds	800-638-5660	MD	www.troweprice.com
Quaker Funds:	800-220-8888	PA	www.quakerfunds.com
Reserve Funds:	800-637-1700	NY	www.reservefunds.com
Robertson Stephens	800-766-3863	CA	www.rsim.com
Royce Funds	800-221-4268	NY	www.roycefunds.com
Rydex Funds:	800-820-0888	MD	www.rydexfunds.com
Safeco Mutual Funds	800-835-4391	WA	www.safecofunds.com
Schafer Value Fund	212-403-2900	NY	none
Schwab Network	800-266-5623	NY	www.schwab.com
Scudder Funds	800-225-2470	MA	www.funds.scudder.com
Seligman Group:	800-221-1864	NY	www.seligman.com
Seven Seas Series Fund	800 647-7327	MA	www.ssgafunds.com
Sit Group	800-332-5580	MN	www.sitfunds.com
Smith Barney:	800-451-2010	NY	www.smithbarney.com
Southeastern Asset Mgt	800-445-9469	TN	none
Stein Roe Mutual Funds	800-338-2550	IL	www.steinroe.com
Stratton Funds:	800-578-8261	PA	www.strattonmgt.com
Strong Funds	800-368-1030	WI	www.strongfunds.com
SunAmerica:	800-858-8850	NY	www.sunamerica.com
Third Avenue Fund:	800-443-1021	NY	www.mjwhitman.com
Thornburg Funds:	800-847-0200	NM	www.thornburg.com
Touchstone:	800-699-2796	OH	www.touchstonefunds.com
Transamerica Funds:	800-892-7587	TX	www.funds.transamerica.com
Turner Funds:	800-224-6312	MO	www.turner-invest.com
Tweedy Browne	800-432-4789	NY	www.tweedy.com
United Funds:	800-366-5465	KS	www.waddell.com/ ugmf.htm
Van Kampen:	800-421-5666	IL	www.vkac.com
Vanguard Group	800-662-7447	PA	www.vanguard.com
Vontobel Funds:	800-527-9500	VA	www.vusa.com
Waddell & Reed:	800-366-5465	KS	www.waddell.com/wrf.htm
Warburg Pincus Funds	800-257-5614	NY	www.warburg.com
Wasatch	800-345-7460	UT	www.wasatchfunds.com
Yacktman Fund	800-525-8258	IL	www.yacktman.com

APPENDIX C

Sources

Burton, Harry, and D. C. Corner. *Investment and Unit Trusts in Britain and America*. London: Elek Books, 1968.

Henriques, Diana B. *Fidelity's World: The Secret Life and Public Power of a Mutual Fund Giant*. New York: Scribner, 1995.

Horowitz, Ira. "Popularity Versus Performances: The Mutual Funds." *Quarterly Review of Economics and Business* 6:1 (1966): 45–58.

Kemp, Tom. *The Climax of Capitalism: The U.S. Economy in the 20th Century*. London and New York: Longman, 1990.

Seventy-Five Years: A History of Scudder, Stevens, and Clark. Boston, privately printed, 1994.

Slater, Robert. *John Bogle and the Vanguard Experiment: One Man's Quest to Transform the Mutual Fund Industry*. Chicago: Irwin, 1997.

Index